▼ A Parents' Guide to the Internet

... and how to protect your children in cyberspace

▼ A Parents' Guide to the Internet

...and how to protect your children in cyberspace

Parry Aftab, Esq.

SC PRESS, INC.   *New York*

SC PRESS, INC.
New York

Copyright © 1997 by Parry Aftab
All rights reserved

Library of Congress Catalog Card Number: 97-61817

ISBN 0-9660491-0-1

SC Press, Inc. books are printed on acid free paper.

Book design by Audrey Smith

Manufactured in the United States of America
10 9 8 7 6 5 4 3 2 1

To my children, Michael and Taylor Caprio, who have always surpassed my furthest hopes and dreams . . . and who love and believe in me as much as I love and believe in them

and

To the memories of my father, Mansur T. Aftab, my brother, Richard Aftab, and my grandfather, Raymond H. Hathaway . . . I think about them every day, and wish they were here to share this with me

▼ Contents

▼ Acknowledgments

I want to thank Lanell Sauer for being my best friend all these years, and for taking my phone calls all hours of the day and night, believing in me and my hair-brained schemes, and teaching me about life and loyalty. (Also for her cover photo idea.)

I would also like to thank my mother, Shirley Hathaway Hammond, for giving me the courage to write a book (after all, she's been writing one for a couple of years, too), my sister Deanna Aftab Guy for being so terrific and endorsing my book, and Deanna's husband, Dr. Jeff Guy, who got my modem to work five years ago and helped me get started online.

There are many others who have made this book possible:

I would like to thank:

Rosalie O'Hara (Sophia's "mother"), my neighbor and dear friend, who nurtured me during the long days and nights I was writing and researching this book, as only Rosalie can do;

Rich Dunn, Neil Squillante and Susan Kligerman who collectively helped carry my weight (a substantial task, I can tell you) in AOL's Legal Information Network during the researching and writing of this book;

Alyssa Aftab, my cover model and cousin, who is both bright and gorgeous (and her parents, Jay and Wendy, for letting her pose for me (for free) and for helping me with all those computer graphics);

All the families and friends who helped me by sharing their stories with me, and all the friends I met online who helped me get through this;

Jean Armour Polly (Net-mom) for her patience, guidance and help. (I think that a quote from Wayne's World is in order here. "I'm not worthy . . . I'm not worthy . . . ");

Chris Allerman, our backroom tech expert, and the one charged with cracking the parental control software programs. Chris also worked with me behind the scenes on adding the bells and whistles to the www.familyguidebook.com website;

George Dale for his ideas and support and for his gift of laughter;

Audrey Smith, my publisher, friend and confidante, without whose talents this book would have never seen the light of day;

Eileen Scanlon, my friend and legal assistant, for keeping my life organized and on track during all of this; and

All the people who by simple acts of encouragement and caring made a difference.

I would like to thank a man I love very much, who inspired me and coached me through this. He knows who he is.

And, finally, I thank God, without whom none of this would matter.

▼ Research Team

Michael Caprio Michael is a senior at Ramapo College, hoping some day to be a sports agent or sports lawyer. He is also my son. Michael was largely responsible for locating sites of interest to families. He was also in charge of the reviewing online service kids areas, and the online services features. Ever since he was a little boy, Michael has had a special writing talent. He was the first one I let edit my draft and the one we turned to when we had a dispute over a particular edit. Michael is a very special young man. He has always made me very proud of him, and I know that he will always make me very proud of him.

Michael has always been one of my biggest fans, and, until he saw Christie Brinkley for the first time thought I was the most beautiful woman in the world. (I then became, with much apology, the *second* most beautiful woman in the world. I wonder how much I've slipped since then?) I know that Michael has something special to offer the world. Someday no one will remember anything about me other than the fact that I'm Michael and Taylor Caprio's mother. His quote? "The best thing about working on *A Parents' Guide to the Internet* was being able to read it before anyone else. The second best thing was being able to work with my Mom and help her accomplish something important."

Taylor Caprio Taylor started college this Fall studying technology education. (I intend to audit her courses as often as they'll let me.) She is also my daughter. Taylor was placed in charge of finding kid reviewers, and filling in when the kids didn't come through as anticipated. She reviewed Nickelodeon's new site, Disney's sites, the Children's Television Workshop's site and several others too. Although she will protest that she only read these sites for me, I can tell you that she really enjoyed them. She brings a certain childlike joy to the project.

She also was self-charged with taking care of me. She accompanied me into New York to drop off edited drafts at *1:00* a.m., and brought me hot tea when I hadn't slept. Taylor is the one member of the group who wasn't allowed to read the proofs, so we could have a clean read by at least one of us when it was done. Since I know Taylor thinks everything I do is wonderful, she can be my critic any day. An extraordinary young woman, with everything in front of her . . . I can't wait to see what she decides to do with her life. I suspect that she will do something that will truly make a difference in this world. But, whatever she decides to do, I can assure you that she will bring joy with her wherever she goes. Her quote? "The best part of working on this book was all the times we laughed together."

Sagar S. Mungekar Sagar was Valedictorian of his high school class this year. He had been working with me for a few years, during every school break, helping us code our website and understand new technology. Sagar was my guide into the depths of the Internet where I had never ventured before. His quote? "I never thought that I could spend the whole summer surfing the Internet and get paid for it, too!"

Vinnie O'Hara Vinnie is a businessman, neighbor and friend. A novice to computing, we used Vinnie as our guinea pig to test how understandable our tech stuff was. He was also the one to find the seat-belt from the junk yard for the cover shot, chased down the color copies and everything else we needed for the project. Most importantly, he and Rosalie O'Hara (see my acknowledgement section) are parents to Sophia, our five-year old Macaw mascot you'll see silhouetted in each chapter heading. His quote? "I never knew how much is available on the Internet. The first thing I'm going to do is take Parry's chart, and go computer shopping."

Chrissy (Patricia) Peters Chrissy is our law firm administrator. She is also our mother-reviewer/reader in charge of making sure we cover the topic without boring our readers. (If you're bored, don't blame me . . . blame Chrissy.) After long hours of managing our firm, she would take home sections of the book to read through what

I had written. Then she was faced with the thankless task of telling me what I should change. (After all I still sign the paychecks.) Her quote? "Working with Parry in a different capacity than as her law firm administrator was fun . . . I'm looking forward to the next book!"

Nancy L. Savitt Nancy is the "Savitt" in Aftab & Savitt, P.C., our international business law firm. Tirelessly she would search for special sites and review laws I needed to check for the book. Painstakingly, she organized all the free speech and censorship material, only to have me shorten the section to leave most of it on the proverbial cutting room floor. Yet, when I asked for more help, she was there without a complaint.

Most importantly, she kept the law firm running during my literal and figurative absence over the last few months. She filled in for me in court, handed me the research I needed for CNN appearances as I arrived at the set and tried to placate our clients while I was involved with this project.

She is one of the best lawyers I have ever known and a dear friend ever since we met on our first day of law school. Her quote? "At least when Parry's words are reduced to paper, I have a chance of getting a word (or comma) in edgewise. Since we became friends in law school, I always knew it would be fun practicing law with Parry; helping on the researching and editing of this book has helped me remember that we have fun even when we're not practicing law [like being able finally to sneak a semi-colon or two into this book; after all, this is *my* quote]."

Melissa Shafner Melissa is a lawyer who thought she was signing up to learn about cyberspace law. Instead she became the leader of the research team, and my right hand woman on the project. For the first month she was the designated pornography, hate and violence snoop, charged with finding the worst on the Web. Then, pouring over the pornography, hate and violence she had found, she became the designated software tester. Thankfully, after awhile both of us were numb to this stuff. Ever patient with my being unavailable, hard to get along with and dense, Melissa was key to getting this book out in my lifetime. Her quote? "I knew I would become an expert on all the child-friendly sites on the Web, but never thought I would have become the world's foremost expert on the wonderful world of Internet pornography!"

Natalie Shahinian Natalie started law school this Fall. Hoping to pick up some law firm experience before she started law school, she instead found herself designated as the point contact person on the book project. She was the one who kept track of all the website operators we spoke with, and all the contacts we made during the researching of the book. Her quote? "I didn't mind having to find people who may have been located anywhere in the world, on not much more guidance than "I need to talk to that person who . . . " But doing it on thirty seconds' notice wasn't easy."

Heather C. Wilde Heather is a law student I met while speaking at a conference at Fordham Law School sharing a panel with the chief lawyers on the CDA Supreme Court contest for both the ACLU and for the Department of Justice. She was there from the beginning, since that conference started my quest to help parents find an answer to the online censorship/access dilemma. Always cheerful and easy to get along with, she patiently listened to my instructions and then went to Nancy to figure out what I was talking about. Heather was also our chart designer. Whenever we wanted a chart, she was the first person we called. When she started her classes again this Fall, we had to cut plans for some of the charts, since only Heather could figure out how to do them the way I wanted. Her quote? "Is this what practicing law is really like?"

▼ Introduction

This book was designed to level the playing field between computer-savvy kids and their technophobic parents. The real challenge is keeping you awake, though, while you learn what you need to know. When the discussion turns to computers, most people yawn and their eyes glaze over. The Information Superhighway . . . Cyberspace, the Net, the Web, Websurfing, downloading, uploading, FTPs, Gopher, browsers, search engines, local access numbers . . . have I lost you yet? Anyone . . .? Anyone . . .?

Armed with this book, you'll be able to bluff with the best of them. You'll be able, every once in a while, to drop a buzzword I've taught you, just to keep your kids on their toes. You'll have to slip it into casual conversation, though, so they won't notice. Be subtle . . . "So Tiffany, what do you think about the promise of Java interactivity in comparison to CGI script?"

(Now, if they give you an answer, immediately excuse yourself, claiming that you just remembered an important telephone call you need to return. Then read the Frequently Asked Questions section ("FAQs") at the back of the book before returning to your child and the question you should have known better than to ask before you had read the FAQs.) If your kids look at you with a stunned expression, you've made your point and I've earned the purchase price of this book. (Whether you decide to buy a pocket protector is up to you.)

This book was also designed to teach you enough about the Internet, both good and bad, to help you guide your children safely through cyberspace. Hopefully, it will teach you how to choose what your children should be exposed to online. Then, education, software and other tools can assist you in enforcing your decisions. You, not the government or special interest groups, should be setting the rules for what your children should and should not see in cyberspace or anywhere else.

Knowledge is power. And I have written this book to empower you.

▼ Culture Shock . . . understanding the spirit of the Internet

One of the good things about having gotten online several years ago is that I am considered an Internet veteran. That means I can talk about the "good old days," before high speed modems, Java and Windows 95, when we all walked to school, uphill both ways, through a blizzard just to get online.

In cyberspace, the pecking order is clear. The earlier you got online, the more senior you are. I was one of the privileged few, in those days, to have used a 9600 baud modem, when others were still using a 2400 baud modem. I know others who used to communicate with even less. I look up to them as the true pioneers—the ones who began over five years ago!

Five years is several lifetimes in cyberspace. Time in cyberspace is measured in cyberyears. Rather like dog years, time is accelerated. The Web itself has only been used since 1993. (It was invented a few years earlier, but not used by the general public until 1993, when the first software program capable of reading it was developed.)

In the olden days, the Internet was still run by its early citizens, known as "netizens." Typically scientists and academics, they laid out their own rules for correct Internet conduct, known as "netiquette." (I've included a section on netiquette later on, to help guide you on proper behavior in cyberspace.) They also enforced it strenuously. Commercialism was frowned upon and a sense of community grew. (Actually, according to Jean Armour Polly, everyone at the time had to access the Net through NSFNet (National Science Foundation's Internet access service), and commercialism violated its accepted use policy).

People who violated netiquette were quickly corrected online and those who violated the more serious rules about commercialism found their Internet connections blocked by netizens self-charged with enforcing the rules. Those were the good old days when the Net governed itself, and the community held common values.

The real netizens believed that everything, other than commercialism, could co-exist. Pornography, violence and the outrageous weren't a problem, since the original Internet users didn't include children or the squeamish. This was before the growth of services like America Online and the mass rush to get every man, woman, child and family pet online before the turn of the century.

Now, what was fine in this older and largely *laissez-faire* environment, where pornographers and scientists could coexist, is no longer fine when large numbers of children are getting online. That's the challenge.

▼ YOU DON'T NEED TO BE AN EXPERT

Since I first got online five years ago, I have rarely given my modem a rest. I spent so much time online that eventually I was asked to moderate and host the legal discussion boards where I spent most of my time educating small businesses and consumers on the law. I also found myself smack in the center of the emerging law of cyberspace, expected to become an expert in the field.

You should know, though, that this "expert" stuff is substantially overrated. Running a discussion forum or two (or more) and understanding cyberspace law, without more, doesn't make you an expert on technology any more than owning a car makes you an expert on car mechanics. Although you may know how to drive the car, most of us don't know how to build or service one.

Since I have a low "technology intelligence quotient" (TIQ), I have had to dig deeper and do it more slowly than those with high TIQs. Because of my lack of computer skill, I understand how to explain technology to others who know even less than I do. But since you are what others think you are . . . I am an "expert." (I made up the terms low and high technology intelligence quotients, but since I'm supposed to be an expert, you didn't even know the difference, did you? See . . . this is getting to be fun!)

Bottom line . . . if I can do it, so can you.

▼ H O W T O R E A D T H I S B O O K

The book is written in four parts: Part One, *Outfitting Yourself for Cyberspace*, tells you everything you need to know about the Internet, how to buy a computer, and how to get online; Part Two, *The Darkside . . . Keeping Things in Perspective*, alerts you to the dangers in the online world; Part Three *Making and Enforcing Your Choices as Parents*, helps you make the right choices about what your children should and shouldn't see. It also gives you tips on how to implement those choices, along with reviews of the most popular parental control software products; and Part Four, *The Good Stuff . . . 99.44 Percent Pure*, introduces you to the joys of the Internet and shows you how your whole family can surf the Web together. I also include a few favorites, and recommendations, for those of you who want to get online before you've had a chance to finish the book, in *Parry's Picks*.

Finally, at the back of the book are our frequently asked questions (FAQs), a glossary of frequently used tech terms, a model Internet use policy and directories of the companies and websites we've mentioned in the book.

In order to make the subject as painless as possible, at the beginning of each chapter I've included a special feature, called "A Bird's Eye View." Sophia, our blue and gold macaw mascot, introduces each topic, with a list of the subjects that are addressed in that chapter. It's an easy outline of each chapter and lets you skip the ones you already know.

You can read this book in several different ways. The preferred method is to start at the beginning, paying particular attention to the dedications and acknowledgments, and then read it without putting it down until you reach the end. (As a first time book author, I thought I'd try to get at least *one* person to do this.)

You can also skip to the ending, but since this isn't a murder mystery, it won't help to know how it ends. Or you can read whatever interests you, in any order you want. The chapters and parts are independent.

Chapters that will put some of you to sleep are there as a resource for those of you who need to know all the details. So you can skip around, and still understand the subject. If you're curious about technology and facts about the Internet, as I mentioned, I've also included a FAQs section. (That's Internet talk for "frequently asked questions.") The rest is up to you.

PART 1

Outfitting Yourself for Cyberspace

(everything you need to know to get online)

CHAPTER 1

Clueless? . . . You'll Feel Right at Home!

A Bird's Eye View—

▼ There's Nothing to Be Afraid of

▼ There's Nothing to Be Afraid of

Don't let a fear of technology or computers stop you—it's really easier than you think.

First, remember that you are not alone. Most of us are scared to death. Computers can be intimidating. And the people who understand them speak in Net and tech jargon none of us can decipher (or want to). Our computers rarely do what we ask them to, and the tried and true remedy for most finicky home appliances (a good swift kick!) generally doesn't work. (Although, trust me, I've tried!)

Parenting is tough enough, without having to worry about protecting and guiding our children in cyberspace. How can we warn them about the dangers if we don't know what they are? How can we help them or answer their questions when we don't even know how to turn on the computer?

Technology is king (and queen). It's the new media and cure for everything, including the common cold. And we're all expected to be computer geniuses when we can't even program our VCRs. When your eight-year-old knows more than you do about computers, it's hard to keep an upper hand. (And don't think they don't know it!)

But with some simple coaching, you can learn all you need to know to get online and keep your kids out of trouble. Most of it is a bluff. You just need to know a few acronyms (those three-letter words that computer geeks like to throw around to confuse you) and some basics. (This really isn't any different from trying to help your kids with their algebra homework when you are clearly math-challenged. Remember that.)

Too many of us are scared off, thinking that we have to understand computer technology to get online. We don't. All of us can use VCRs, although few of us understand how they work. If we can plop in a video tape and push the power key and play button, even we can watch the best and the worst movies.

Using computers is no different. If you can click on the power button, double-click your mouse and type in your name and password, you're surfing. Everything you need to know is in this book.

In this first part of the book, I explain how the Internet operates. Once you understand the different parts of the Internet, you'll learn the basics of how to buy computer equipment and what other options are available to you if you can't buy a computer. Finally, I'll give you some pointers on "getting connected," and what you need to know when you get there.

If you're already online, you can skip this whole section. (What a relief! You've barely started reading, and you're already a third of the way through the book!)

For those of you who want even more information than I have given you in this section, go to FAQs (Frequently Asked Questions section) at the back of the book. For everyone else: read what you like. There's no pop quiz at the end.

And remember what Representative Zoe Luftgen, a lawyer, mother, and Internet-savvy Congresswoman from California told me: "The best thing about the Internet is that no matter what you do wrong you can't break it."

CHAPTER 2

Cyberspace . . . A Map for Non-Geeks

A Bird's Eye View—

▼ What is the Internet?

▼ What is the World Wide Web?

▼ How Do You Access the Internet? . . . Online Services and ISPs

▼ What Else Do You Need to Know? . . . Gopher, FTPs, Usenet and Newsgroups, List Servs and IRCs

▼ What is the Internet?

The Internet is a worldwide network of smaller computer networks and individual computers, all linked together by coaxial cable, telephone lines or satellite links. (The Integrated network of networks . . . the Inter-network . . . the Internet!)

The Internet isn't owned by anyone. It isn't controlled by anyone and has no geographical boundaries. It isn't located anywhere. It is timeless and spaceless. It's currently made up of roughly 60,000 individual computers and computer networks (called peers). Once you have an Internet account, either through an Internet service provider (an ISP) or through an online provider, like America Online or CompuServe, you can connect to this network through your provider's "gateway" (their entrance ramp to the Internet).

Everything on the Internet is global. When you access something on the Net, people everywhere in the world can access it too. When you publish something on the Net (that means putting it on a computer connected to the Net, which is called a "server"), others can read it, immediately, all around the world. The global aspect of the Net is one of the best things about it. It offers worldwide communication, instantaneously, at negligible cost. People are able to talk to other people without regard to geographical borders. It makes you stop and think, doesn't it?

What an exciting future for our children! (And for us . . .)

▼ HOW DOES IT WORK?

Different parts of the Internet work differently, but they all use the same network of computers and transmit information in the same way. All information travels around the Internet in small units, called "packets." When you send anything on the Internet bigger than the proverbial cyber "breadbox," it's broken into several packets which are reassembled at their destination. As they work their way to their destination, the packets bounce separately like pinballs from peer to peer around the Internet. They are directed around the Internet by computer routers, which determine the best and fastest route for each packet.

Our air traffic controllers can learn from the routers. They are the real beauty of the Internet. Routers reroute information around any system problems or shutdowns. If the traffic is too heavy in New York City, your information may arrive via Philadelphia with some packets arriving via Denver. It's simply a matter of finding the most efficient route. Physical distance means nothing in cyberspace.

▼ WHERE DID THE INTERNET COME FROM?

The Internet was developed in 1969 by ARPAnet, the Advanced Research Projects Agency of the U.S. Department of Defense. It was designed to allow the Department of Defense and universities to do defense-related research on different computers around the country. It was also specifically designed to survive a nuclear attack that would have cut off normal communications, like telephones. It is self-healing. That means if one part is shut down, the routers reroute traffic around the shut down. It fixes itself. (Now, if I could only figure out how to do that with my plumbing, I'd really be happy!)

▼ HOW MANY PEOPLE ARE ON THE INTERNET?

No one really knows for sure. Estimating how many people use the Internet has become as popular a pastime among Internet statisticians as predicting the weather, and just about as accurate. Anyway, there are an estimated 40 million people on the Internet—30 million from the U.S. and 10 million internationally. And, it's growing exponentially.

Families are getting online in greater numbers than ever before. According to the 1996 *Family PC* survey published in the December 1996 issue of *Family PC* magazine, the number of homes with modem-equipped computers increased by almost 70 percent from 1995 to 1996, and one-third of all household computers in use were purchased within the last two years.

The number of children online is growing at an even faster rate. Jupiter Communications, an Internet research group, has reported that there were 4 million children between the ages of two and seventeen online in 1996, and project that more than 20 million children will be online by the year 2002.

Nothing in the history of mankind has ever caught on this fast or, perhaps, with greater potential impact.

▼ How do people around the world speak to each other on the Internet?

The computers and networks comprising the Internet all speak the same language, TCP/IP (transmission control protocol/Internet protocol). People on the Internet, though, speak different languages. But since the Internet originated in the United States, English is considered its official language (except in France and parts of Canada, where all websites must be maintained in French as a primary language if the server that hosts the website is located there).

Although other languages are being used more often on the Internet (and I've included some recommended places on the Web which let you converse in several languages), English still predominates, and is likely to continue to do so. (Although my friends in the UK, Canada and elsewhere in the English-speaking world still protest that what we speak, in the USA, ain't English at all . . .)

▼ What is the World Wide Web?

"WWW" stands for the World Wide Web. When people talk about surfing the Net, they are really talking about surfing the Web. The Web is a section of the Internet where information is linked to other related information, allowing you to jump from one place to another. (Actually, you don't go anywhere, the information comes to you. It just feels like you're jumping around.) It is also rich with graphics and sound. With the introduction of new applications, like Java (you can learn more about Java in the FAQs), the Web has become more interactive and more loaded with multimedia fun.

The Web is the most popular area of the Internet. It now accounts for more than 90 percent of all Internet usage. It's also the fastest growing segment of the Internet. From only 130 websites in 1993, there are now 1.1 million separate websites, with millions more sub-pages within those websites. (You should note that different people use the term "website" to mean different things. When we use it, we mean a distinctive webpage, which may have hundreds of separate sub-pages and URLs. (I'll teach you what a URL is shortly.))

The Web is still in its infancy, though. Less than eight years old, it was conceived when Tim Berners-Lee, while at CERN (the European Particle—atomic research—Physics Laboratory), in Geneva, Switzerland, developed HyperText Transfer Protocol (HTTP). HTTP is the language that web browsers (the software program that lets you read text, graphics and other multimedia, and navigate the Web) use to move around the Web, by hyperlinks. (Don't worry, I'll explain hyperlinks and more about web browsers shortly.)

Although HTTP was released in 1992, the Web didn't become popular until Mosaic, the first web browser, was developed in 1993.

Before then, it took an advanced degree from MIT to find anything on the Internet. Prior to the Web, the Internet was merely text and programs; it contained no graphics or sound, no animation or videos. It was a place for academics, scientists and programmers. Loaded with a lot of hard-to-find information, it was BORING.

▼   WHAT DOES "SURFING THE WEB" MEAN?

"Surfing the Internet" is a phrase coined by Jean Armour Polly, Net-Mom (mom@netmom.com), and generally considered the "mother" of the Internet. Jean first used the phrase in an article titled "Surfing the Internet," in 1992. (A copy of that article can be found at her site, www.netmom.com).

The term "Web surfing" explains what it feels like to ride the wave from one website to another. Using HTTP, the Web works through hyperlinks, which are interconnected documents and multimedia applications (such as audio and video). Your web browser is the software program that makes this all work. (There's more on Web browsers throughout this section, so keep an eye out.) Like a spiderweb, where one thread is connected to many others, which are in turn connected to many more, you can click on one hyperlinked topic, and be whisked away to another connected place on the Web, anywhere in the world. (They work like footnotes which allow you to view the source or reference when you click on the linked text.)

Hyperlinks are included in a Web document as a computer code called "HTML" (HyperText Markup Language). HTML uses Berners-Lee's protocol and allows the website operator to include cross-references to other documents within the site, and from there to other sites or documents within those sites.

When you view the page with your web browser, the hyperlinks appear as text highlighted in another color (often underlined, too) or as a graphic. One way to spot a hyperlink is when you run your cursor over any text or graphics that are hyperlinked, the arrow converts to a hand, to "grab" the link.

When you click on the highlighted text or the graphic with your mouse, you are transported to that site (in reality, the data from the site is transported to you, not vice versa). You never see the code. It merely acts as an instruction to your web browser to go to another location on the Web. (Netscape Navigator and Microsoft Internet Explorer are the two most popular web browsers. We'll talk about them more in the *How Do You Get Connected?* chapter.)

An Internet address is called a "URL" (universal resource locator, and pronounced either like "earl" or "U-R-L"). They are also commonly called "domain names." URLs are typically case-sensitive, which means lowercase and uppercase letters should be typed exactly the way they are written in the URL. Each part of the URL means something different, and is separated by dots from the other parts of the URL. (I know they look like periods to you, but the techies who develop this stuff need to make sure that you can't figure anything out on your own. So call them "dots." It'll impress your kids.)

The first part of an URL is the "scheme." It tells you where on the Internet (really, which "protocol") the information you are seeking is located. (Remember that there's more to the Internet than the Web.) The most common scheme since the development of the Web is "http." The letters "http" in the URL tell you that it's a Web address (because it uses HTTP, Berner-Lee's protocol). (Gopher sites use "gopher:" and FTP sites use "ftp:" instead of the "http:" in the URL.) The URL may also contain the directory and the file name for a particular file. That looks like this—http://www.domain.com/directory/file. When you are accessing a particular file in a large site, knowing the directory and file name will save you a lot of time.

All domain names have to use a three-letter suffix (or zone), which indicates the type of organization or entity involved. The ".com" (read "dot com") indicates a commercial organization site, rather than an Internet network (.net), international organization (.int), higher educational institution (.edu), not-for-profit organization (.org), military (.mil) or government (.gov) site. ".Com" is clearly the most popular zone, followed in popularity by ".edu." (Only a few years ago, ".edu" sites predominated.)

Given the high demand for domain names, additional zones are expected to be added to identify the type of commercial site, such as ".law," ".med," and ".biz." Websites from countries other than the United States may also use a two letter country code, rather than one of the three letter zones. Sites without a country designation are assumed to be U.S. sites.

▼ How Do You Access the Internet? . . . Online Services and ISPs

You will either need an online service (such as America Online, CompuServe, Prodigy, or Microsoft Network) or an internet service provider (an ISP) in order to access anything on the Internet. An ISP provides you access to the Internet so that you can surf the Web and use e-mail. Online services have their own proprietary content that is available to their subscribers, in addition to providing access to the Internet and e-mail. (I discuss ISPs and online services in detail in *How Do You Get Connected?*, so be patient.)

▼ What Else Do You Need to Know? . . . Gopher, FTPs, Usenet and Newsgroups, List Servs and IRCs

▼ GOPHER

Gopher was the first tool that made the Internet understandable and searchable to non-geeks. It was designed in 1991 at the University of Minnesota to index the Internet databases. Predating the unveiling of HTTP in 1992 and Mosaic in 1993, Gopher was the best (and only) way to find information on the Internet.

Gopher displays several menu selections. When you select one of the menu items, it scours the Internet and indexes the results of your search. But it's not the Web, remember. It's a great source of certain technical information, but whatever it displays is shown in dry, unformatted textual format—no graphics, sound or animation.

There are conflicting stories about where the name "Gopher" came from. Some people credit the University of Minnesota's furry mascot, while others credit the fact that the application "goes for" information. But everyone agrees that, however it got its name, its introduction was an important event in the evolution of the Internet. Next to the Web, it remains one of the most popular tools for finding information on the Internet.

▼ FTP

FTP (File Transfer Protocol), allows users to transfer (download and upload) files and programs to their computers from special FTP servers. Most people use FTP to get software and lengthy documentation from public sites. Public sites (or "anonymous" sites) are computers which store data and are accessible to everyone. You log in as "anonymous" and use your e-mail address as your password for access to the site.

Even if you're not asked to do that, it's FTP netiquette to use your e-mail address as your password, so the FTP host knows who is accessing the site. It's also correct FTP netiquette to access the FTP site only after business hours, if possible (but you need to know what time zone they're in to figure out what their business hours are), to put less strain on the server which may be used for other business purposes during regular business hours. See the *Ms. Parry's Guide to Netiquette* chapter for more tips on correct Internet behavior.

Since FTP is typically used to transfer large computer files, many of these files have been compressed (or "zipped") to make them transmit faster. You'll have to use a special software application to decompress (or "unzip") them. Decompression applications are available at FTP sites, and America Online and other online services automatically unzip all compressed files when you log off. (If you use an ISP, it will usually supply you with an unzipping utility.)

Kids often access FTP sites to download games and upgrades to programs they use. Aside from accessing computer programs and games, however, it's unlikely that you'll be using FTP often. I only use it, actually, to maintain my websites.

▼   USENET AND NEWSGROUPS

Usenet is a worldwide collection of newsgroups. A newsgroup is a discussion group devoted to a particular topic. The newsgroups collect articles, discussions and other messages on a particular subject, and then broadcast them or make them available to users over the Internet. Some newsgroups are moderated, which means the material is screened by a moderator before being posted. Many are not.

Participants in many newsgroups are known for their opinionated discussions, and flaming often abounds. (Flaming is when someone insults, annoys or attacks someone else online.) Although there are many wonderful newsgroups, especially for special parenting needs (try "misc.kids"), there are some where chaos and outrageous behavior rule.

As the Web develops, Usenet and newsgroups are becoming less prominent. But with many diehard Usenet fans out there, they're unlikely to disappear anytime soon. They are still a great way to reach people who are interested in the same things that you are. Finding a newsgroup is as simple as searching www.dejanews.com, the main newsgroup index. And posting is as simple as following the Dejanews instructions. Just remember that given the "wild west" atmosphere of many, your children should be carefully supervised when using any of them, or kept off them entirely until they're old enough to look out for themselves.

▼ LIST SERVS. . . .GETTING ON E-MAILING LISTS

A list serv is an e-mail mailing list you subscribe to. It's essentially a discussion group where all messages and responses are e-mailed instead of being posted on a bulletin board. For example, if you want to know more about people who own or are interested in Hummers (those huge off-road army-style vehicles my daughter adores), you can subscribe to "HML" at the server majordomo@lists.4x4.org. You will soon be receiving lots of messages from other people who like Hummers too.

Subscribing and unsubscribing to a list serv can be confusing, though, because there are two e-mail addresses for each mailing list—one for list serv discussions and the other for list serv administration. Sending e-mail to one of the addresses relays your messages to all of the other subscribers and theirs to you. Sending e-mail to the other address, the administrative address (which usually starts with "listserv," "listproc," or "majordomo"), allows you to subscribe and unsubscribe to the list.

When you enroll in any list serv, a computer-generated message telling you how to unsubscribe will arrive. Save it! Trust me, you'll be thankful you did. I've been stuck on many list servs, begging other members (very bad netiquette) to help me get off the list.

Another problem with list servs is that the popular ones send out forty or more e-mails a day. Rather like King Midas, who wanted everything he touched to turn to gold, only to find himself surrounded by gold without food, water or his beloved daughter, a popular list serv can prove to you too that there can be too much of a good thing.

One solution is to set your subscription to "Digest," if available (read the message sent to you when you first subscribe—it may tell you how to do it). "Digest" means you get one huge e-mail per day, containing a "digest" of all the other messages combined.

▼ IRCs: INTERNET RELAY CHATS

IRC is one of the most "lively" areas of the Internet. It's comprised of thousands of chatrooms on the Internet designed around any subject, or no topic at all. Users have conversations (by typing in what they want to say) in real-time. They can read what others say and reply to them as if they were all in the same room talking. Many parenting sites use IRCs to hold their chats.

Internet Relay Chat is run by IRC servers, and you need IRC-client software to use it. Most ISPs provide this software. The online service providers generally don't.

Unlike many chat rooms of online service providers, the IRC discussions are typically not monitored. Unmonitored IRCs are probably the worst Internet offenders in terms of inappropriate discussions for children (and for many adults, too).

While the initial concept of Internet Relay Chats was good—to form a type of virtual chat room where any number of users could talk about a particular topic—IRCs now are often overrun by topics such as hardcore sex, drugs, software piracy, etc. Many parental control software programs block IRCs completely for these reasons. While you might enjoy many IRC topical discussions, your kids should be kept off IRCs unless you're online with them and familiar with the IRC group.

CHAPTER 3

Hardware Technology ... Don't Worry, I'll Go Really Slow and Draw Lots of Pictures

A Bird's Eye View—

▼ What Do You Need to Know to Buy a Computer?

▼ What if You Can't Afford a Computer?

▼ Alternatives to a Computer ... WebTV and Internet Box Technology

▼ What Do You Need to Know to Buy a Computer?

If you already have everything you need, or don't plan to buy a computer, skip this section. Otherwise, you're stuck. As I've already told you (I really sound like a mother, don't I?), you don't have to be a car mechanic to drive a car . . . you don't have to know how to program a VCR to play a tape. All you need to know, really, are the basics.

Computers are major investments, though, and you should know what you actually need before you waste money on bells and whistles you'll never use. You will need a computer, a monitor (preferably color), a modem, a phone line (preferably a separate one from your main phone line), a mouse, a keyboard and, if you can afford it, a printer and a CD-ROM drive. (As an alternative to a computer, you could use an Internet appliance, like WebTV, which allows you to get online, but it can't process data the way a computer can.)

I suggest that first you ask your friends what they like. That way, if you buy the same kind of computer that they buy, you can both get confused together. (It's always better getting confused in groups of two or more.)

Often my friends give me better advice when they tell me what *not* to buy. If they tell you they bought a lemon, or the tech support and customer service of one company or another is impossible to reach, listen carefully.

You might also want to ask the librarians at your children's school. (Librarians are the secret weapon of anyone smart enough to consult them. They know everything there is to know, although they are often too modest to tell you so.) They know what systems your kids are using, what works and, more importantly, what doesn't.

Then armed with my explanation of computer specifications, start trying out different computers wherever you can. Take your time. You'll be living with this purchase for a long time. Take a tip from Goldilocks on this one. Not too big, not too small . . . you want one that's "just right."

Ready? Armed with this book and lots of antacid, you're ready to take the big leap. You've put it off as long as possible. You even went out and bought one of those cool ergonomic chairs so you'd be comfortable surfing. Anything to delay the inevitable: computer shopping!

This is a good time to apologize to my Mac-user friends (actually, if I didn't, it's unlikely this book would ever have seen the light of day . . . research team members, our book designer and our graphics designers are *all* Mac users . . .). We're only talking about PCs (that's computer talk for an IBM or IBM-compatible personal computer), not Macs, in this chapter. I've tried to include Mac tips whenever I can elsewhere in the book, though.

So, no more delays. You're ready, trust me. Repeat after me . . . "computers are my friends . . . computers are my friends . . ."

▼ Where do you shop for Hardware? . . .you won't find this stuff at Home Depot

There are many places that you can go to buy your PC. Usually, electronics stores (like ones that sell TVs, VCRs, stereos etc.) and large department stores sell computers. There are also specialty computer stores, which don't sell anything but computers and computer accessories. Many of them will let you test drive a PC in the showroom to see what it's really like before you purchase it.

Then, there are mail-order companies. You order your computer through a catalogue, online or from an advertisement, and it is delivered to you. You can only judge the computer by the name brand (if it has one) and the specs and technical data advertised. It's usually less expensive to buy a system from a mail-order company than from a computer retail store.

A third place to buy computers is a computer fair or show. At computer fairs, run periodically around the country, computer vendors from all over gather at a large site (often a college or convention center) to display their wares. These fairs are analogous to car auctions: while there is a chance you will get a very good deal on a brand new computer, there is also a chance that you will get a lemon and not be able to return it. (The prices are usually much lower at computer shows than at retailers, though.) These fairs are okay for buying software or peripherals (that's computer talk for computer accessories, such as printers, scanners and keyboards), but I would be careful about buying an entire system unless you're a computer geek. (In which case, why are you reading this chapter?)

The best place for non-geeks to shop is the specialty computer retailer or a brand name mail-order company like Gateway or Dell. They usually have knowledgeable computer salespeople who can answer your questions.

If you insist on buying a clone (a non-name brand) at a computer show or fair, or through mail-order, put it on your credit card. If anything goes wrong, you may be able to get some help from your credit card company in enforcing the warranties or getting a credit if things don't work as promised. As enticing as the "cash price" may be at the computer show, pay the extra 3% to get the added protection of being able to assert whatever consumer rights may be available to credit card purchasers if things go wrong.

▼   HOW DO YOU KNOW WHAT TO BUY?

Wherever you buy one, though, the computer system will probably be labeled or advertised roughly like this:

Brand name and model. 200 MHZ MMX® Pentium® processor. 32 MB RAM. 3.0 GB HD. 12X CD-ROM. 28.8 voice/fax/data modem. SoundBlaster 32 AWE. 3-1/2" drive. 15" monitor. Mouse. Keyboard. Windows 95 and software package.

I've got to be kidding, right? I promised you easy reading . . . nothing too tech-y. Sorry, I lied. (After all, I *am* a lawyer.). But I did it for your own good, remember that. (Now I really sound like your mother, don't I?) Computer specs are the real revenge of the nerds—trust me. Computer specifications are filled with numbers and acronyms designed to intimidate the non-geeks among us. But bear with me just a little longer. I'll teach you what you need to know to bluff with the best of them.

If you look at the chart below, you'll see a simple breakout of the terms and specifications and what they mean. After the chart, I explain each in more detail. I've compared the components to parts of a car. Since a computer costs as much as a small car (well, maybe a very small, old car), I thought it would be easier to understand this way. (Frankly, I didn't think it would be easier, but one member of our research team did and I wanted to humor him . . .)

Brand and model	the make and model (make sure it's a name you trust, but since I bought an AMC Pacer once, what do I know?)
200 MHz	the speed (like horsepower)—the higher the faster
Pentium®	the power (like the number of cylinders)—Pentium® is the equivalent of a "586"
MMX™, etc.	a multimedia turbocharger (the jury's still out about whether it's worth the extra money, but if speed's your thing. . . you should consider it)
32 MB RAM	the amount of space available while the computer is on (like head and legroom in a car)—the more memory, the more comfortably programs run (buy at least 16 RAM if you're using Windows 95). If you use games often, I'd even suggest getting 32 RAM. You'll see the difference immediately.
3.0 GB HD	the amount of permanent space available on the computer (like the size of the car's trunk)—the higher the number, the bigger the space. The extra size doesn't usually cost much more. Buy at least 2 gigs or you'll run out of space fast. Kids' games take lots of space.
28.8 modem	the computer's telephone—in theory, the higher the number, the faster it is. Don't buy anything slower than a 28.8 modem . . . you'll regret it.

▼ THE CPU (CENTRAL PROCESSING UNIT). . . THE CORE OF
   YOUR COMPUTER

Brand name is important, especially to a first time computer buyer. I've bought many no-name clones, and have been burned almost as often. You want a company you can call when things break down, or when you have questions. Customer service and tech support are key factors in choosing your brand name.

A lot of the big companies manufacture different models and lines of computers for different needs. They often come in no frills, standard and premium models. Depending on the type and amount of usage, you have to decide what model you need. For a family computer—one that will sit in the den or family room and be used by parents and kids alike—a desktop model is better and cheaper than a laptop. (A notebook is merely a smaller laptop.)

The "200 MHz MMX™ Pentium processor" tells you about the engine of the computer. Horsepower is to a car as MHz (megahertz) is to a computer. The higher the number, the faster it goes. For surfing the Internet or word processing, a blazingly fast computer isn't really necessary. (You don't really need 250 horsepower to commute to and from work.) But you may want to get the fastest one you can afford for those days when you feel like passing everyone on the highway, and so that you can brag to your friends about how much power your computer has.

Pentium is actually Intel's trademark for the 586 processor chip. The number, (386, 486, 586, etc.) is like the number of cylinders your car has. A V-8 has more power than a V-6; a Pentium (586) has more power than a 486. (The new generation of Pentium is called Pentium II.)

Although newer technologies constantly replace older ones, the best advice is to get the fastest computer that you can afford. Sometimes, along with the chip number the specs will say MMX™ (as above) or something else. The MMX™ is a multimedia booster, which increases your computer's speed in certain applications, like a turbocharger on a car. MMX™ speeds up all pictures, sounds, movies and animation on your computer. And since multimedia is the core of the Web, it is a good option if you can afford it.

What we just covered is the most important part of the computer, so you can breathe again. Congratulations! You've made it through the hardest part.

▼ MEMORY. . . . RAM AND HARD DRIVE SIZE

Now, just a few more numbers. Both 32 MB RAM (read "thirty-two megabytes of ram" or just plain "32 ram") and 3.0 GB HD (read "a three-point-O gigabyte hard drive" or "a 3 gig drive") refer to the computer's memory.

RAM actually stands for "random-access-memory," but is just called "memory." This is how much headroom or legroom you have in the car. The more you have, the more comfortable you'll be. The more RAM (remember, memory . . .) your computer has, the more applications you can run comfortably. For normal everyday surfing and typing, 32 MB RAM is plenty. (I wouldn't use Windows 95 unless I had *at least* 16 MB RAM, even though Microsoft tells you 8 MB RAM is okay.) It's always a good idea to have a little extra memory rather than getting caught short when you need it.

The hard drive is the equivalent of the luggage compartment. The bigger your hard drive, the more programs and files you can store. This particular computer has a "trunk" that holds 3 gigabytes. To help you gauge what that means, a word processing program typically will take up about 30–50 MB (only about 1–2 percent of the entire space). For normal usage, a 3 gig drive is more than enough. By the time your family manages to fill it up, you'll be ready for a new computer.

▼ THE CD-ROM

The CD-ROM drive is like a hard drive but it reads CD-ROMs (they look like music CDs). (The "ROM" stands for "read-only-memory," in case you're dying to know.) That means that the drive can read from the CD but not save to it. (Just like your music CDs, you can play them, but not record on them.) Once the manufacturer puts the data on the CD, it's etched in stone (. . . or polyurethane as the case may be).

CDs can hold a lot more information than floppy disks and are often used to store large programs or movies. (Your CD-ROM can play music CDs too, assuming you have a sound card.) The 12× ("12 times" or "12-speed") refers to its speed. In the olden days, CD-ROMs were single-speed (like music CD players) and took a long time to get from one "track" to another. Then double-speed CD-ROMs boasted they were twice as fast. After that, triple- and quad-speeds quickly followed, only to be replaced by 6×, 8×, 10×, etc. There seems to be no end to this escalation. Once again, the faster the better.

Don't try to save money by not buying a CD-ROM drive. Buy a slower one if you want, but make sure you get one. Too many kids' programs are only available on CD-ROM to be without one. You'll probably use your CD-ROM more than any other component of your computer.

▼ THE MODEM

The modem (the *modulator-demo*dulator) is what usually connects your computer to the Internet. Modems are designed to be either installed inside your computer (an internal modem) or plugged into the back of your computer (an external modem). They come in different speeds, measured in "baud rate."

When you see a reference to a modem baud rate or speed, it means that the modem can transmit a thousand times that many bits per second. A 28.8 modem is really shorthand for 28,800 bits per second and is twice as fast as a 14.4 modem. For a few years, modem speeds were doubling every few months like the CD-ROM speeds are now. But with current technology reaching the speed limits of most of our POTs, plain old telephone lines (see how simple these acronyms are?), the modem speed race has slowed.

Check with your ISP or online provider to see what modem speeds they can accommodate. Then, buy the fastest modem you can afford that your provider can handle. (When you get to our chart on ISP services, you'll see that a few offer premium high speed ISDN (56.6 baud and higher) access for an additional charge.)

As you start using the Web, speed makes a big difference, especially when you're viewing sites with a lot of graphics. (A popular derogative of the World Wide Web is the "World Wide Wait." It's a reputation well-earned, even with high speed modems.)

The most promising of all the new speed and access technologies is cable Internet access. Cable companies throughout the United States are jumping on the Internet access bandwagon, although they won't be available everywhere for a few years. Their cable access technology permits access at several hundred times faster than a 28.8 modem. (I've included more information on cable modems in *How Do You Get Connected?*)

▼ THE SOUND CARD

"SoundBlaster 32 AWE" refers to the computer's sound system. Ask any teenager and you'll know that "a car's gotta have a good sound system!" The same is true with computers. A 32 AWE is a great sound system. (A SoundBlaster 16 is okay for us old fogies, but expect to hear complaints from your kids.)

The number used to identify the version of a sound card can be confusing though, because it means something different, depending on which brand of sound card you're talking about. For SoundBlaster, the numbers stand for voices—the maximum number of sounds that can be played simultaneously. For other sound card manufacturers, this number stands for bits—the quality of the sound instead of the number of voices. The best way to decide on the sound, however, is listen to the sound and let your ears do the judging. Just be sure that the sound card is a SoundBlaster or is SoundBlaster-compatible—that's the standard these days.

With the standard PC speaker, you'll only hear beeps and chirps. Who wants to be stuck in a car where the only sound you hear comes from that annoying chime that rings when the door is left open or you forget to put on your seat-belt? Not my kids!

▼ FLOPPY DRIVES AND OTHER STUFF YOU NEED

The 3-1/2 inch drive is the regular floppy drive that reads from floppy disks. (They're actually not floppy, since they're made from hard plastic, but never mind . . .) This drive is usually standard and many companies don't even mention it in their advertisements. The same is true for the keyboard and mouse. They should come with the computer, but it's a good idea to make sure anyway. Sometimes the manufacturer will list these components as well as things like "1 parallel port, 1 game port, 2 serial ports" to make the computer sound like it has more than it really does. (A port is a socket that lets you plug extra equipment into your computer.) These are standard devices that should come with the computer anyway. It's like a car manufacturer passing off "high-beam headlights" and "a glove compartment" as options.

▼   THE MONITOR

The monitor is very important, much more so than most people realize. It's like a television screen but is often designed to be clearer and brighter because it is meant to be seen from a closer distance. Because you will probably be staring at it for hours on end, you want it to be comfortable. Just imagine driving a car where all of the gauges and meters are tiny, badly lit and impossible to read.

The monitor's ability to show detail is called "resolution" and is often expressed as a combination of numbers ("dimensions" actually). The dimensions you'll see most frequently are 640×480, 800×600, or 1024×768. The higher the number, the more detail is visible, but the smaller the image. Many monitors allow you to switch between modes as necessary.

The other dimension usually mentioned is the physical size of the monitor—here, 15 inches—and is measured on a diagonal the same as television screens. For home use, a 15- to 17-inch will do. (I prefer a 17-inch, if you can afford it, especially if you'll be looking over your kid's shoulder.) Many find anything smaller uncomfortable, and anything bigger a waste of money.

There are many other things that determine the quality of a monitor (dot pitch, white point, refresh rate), the description of which would cause your eyes to glaze over and your head to spin, even before you look at the screen. The best thing to do is look at the monitor at the store. Look at pictures, fine text, and movies. Stand or sit as close to it as you would in your home.

If you feel that the monitor causes too much eye strain or is difficult to see, don't buy it. Remember, you and your family will be sitting in front of that screen—buy what you think feels best.

▼ "Included" software

The last item on the list, "Windows 95 and software package" is what the company puts on the computer's hard drive at the factory. (They should also give you the disks, even if they are preinstalled.) Windows 95 is the operating system (or OS) in our example. It is what you first see when you turn on the computer, and is what makes the computer work.

Windows 95 is the standard nowadays for all new PCs. The software package consists of other programs that the company feels you should have. Often it includes a word processing program and some Internet software. It's best to ask exactly what programs the package contains. If you don't know what a particular program does, ask to see how it works. If you think you have a use for it, get it. If you think it's something that you'll never use, ask if you can switch it for another program. Sometimes, the salesman will be flexible in letting you choose your own programs.

▼ Price

The final factor, and probably most important, is price. It is almost impossible to give an exact price for any type of computer, because in less than a week it will be cheaper, as this week's technology replaces last week's. The best course of action to follow is call around.

Buy a copy of *Computer Shopper* at your local magazine or book store. It will help you get a rough idea of how much a computer with the features you want costs. (I'll warn you in advance, *Computer Shopper* can be intimidating, and is not written for non-geeks. But the prices are the best you can get, outside of a computer show, so it's worth the intimidation. Besides, if you leave it out on your coffee table you can impress your friends and family who'll think you actually read it.) Then find a local retailer and ask the salesperson to beat that price.

While the speeds of computers are surpassed everyday, the price for a "good" family computer has held relatively constant at about $2000–$2500. What you will have to keep in mind is that you are almost guaranteed that the day after you buy your brand new computer, you will see another one advertised that's cheaper, more powerful, and faster.

Don't be discouraged and think that you were cheated out of a good deal. It's not necessary to buy the biggest, fastest computer that's out there. Just buy the biggest, fastest one that meets your needs and that you can afford. (None of us really need the power we have in our computers . . . it's just an "ego" thing most of the time.)

▼   PRINTERS

Printers have come a long way from the modified typewriters they once were. There are three major types of printers used by homes these days: dot-matrix, ink-jet or bubble-jet and laser.

Dot-matrix printers are slowly being phased out in homes. While they are versatile in printing text, their low print quality and inability to print discernable graphics have kept them from being an ideal printer for the home. They work by moving a head across the paper. Little pins in the head hit a ribbon, which makes dots on the paper. These dots then form letters. Dot-matrix printers are usually very inexpensive—$100–$200—but shouldn't be used for anything other than plain text.

The next step up is ink-jet or bubble jet printers. These are the most popular for home use. They function like a dot-matrix printer, but shoot little drops of ink (ink jet) or boil a drop of ink to form a bubble (bubble jet) to make very tiny dots on the paper. Their advantage is that they allow you to print in good-quality color. While their color output won't be mistaken for photographs, it can be quite impressive. These printers usually cost from $250 to $550 and are a good buy.

But expect to go through your color ink cartridges quickly printing out copies of Elmo and Arthur for your toddlers. This can be an expensive hidden cost. Many generic ink-refills are available, though, and may save you money over the name brand refills. But be careful, since cheaper-quality ink may run and/or bleed if the image is very colorful.

The final type of printer is a laser printer. Laser printers work very much like a copy machine and use lasers to mark off the areas to shade. They use toner (laser ink) which is fused with intense heat onto the paper. The toner won't smear like an ink jet printer's ink may.

Laser printers provide exceptional quality (and may rival the text found in magazines). If you are looking to print primarily text and some grayscale (black-and white) graphics, these printers will work wonders. Be prepared to spend some money, though. Even black-and-white laser printers run about $400–$1000. (Color lasers run several thousand dollars.)

Okay, let's do a quick review:

Printer type	Good	Bad
dot-matrix	• cheap • fast for plain text	• text only • slow on formatted text • noisy
ink-jet or bubble-jet	• fairly inexpensive • good quality on text and graphics • can do color • quiet	• slow in comparison to laser • ink may run • ink used up quickly on full-color images (but you can buy compatible nonbrand refills)
laser	• exceptional quality • very fast • quiet	• expensive, even in black-and-white • color is so costly it's not practical for a home printer

▼   SCANNERS. . . . COMPUTER PHOTOGRAPHY

A scanner is like a camera for your computer. It can take "snapshots" of a document, a photograph, a graphic, etc. and display it on the monitor. Once there, you can edit, print out, and save the graphic, as your programs allow. It's a good way to put your children's artwork, family photos and other memorabilia online.

There are many different types of scanners. Most come in two types, color and black-and-white. If you are going to be scanning text only, black-and-white will do. Photographs will require a color scanner.

The cheapest are hand-held models. These look like a mouse and scan as you run them over the image. The quality isn't the greatest because your hand may shake as you are rolling the scanner across the image. And though they only cost between $100 and $200 they are slowly being phased out.

The next type is a roller-type desktop scanner. These look like little fax machines and are great for scanning forms, letters or sheets of graphics. You simply put the paper on the feeder and it's fed through automatically, just like a fax. Often these can scan color photographs as well. The only disadvantage is that, since the paper must be fed through, you can't scan a page from a book without ripping it out. Still, these scanners are versatile and often provide good image and color quality. They also take up very little space (often taking up only as much space as a box of aluminum foil), and cost from $200 to $300.

If you plan to scan photos and drawings to share them online, this is the best kind of scanner to buy. Don't waste your time with a black-and-white scanner, though. If you can't afford a color scanner, office support businesses like Kinkos can do the scanning for you, in full color to be used online. Your photograph developer can also save your photos to digital form which works just like a scanned image.

The best (and most expensive) type are flatbed scanners. You probably won't need a flatbed scanner for home use. These look like the top part of a copy machine—you lift the cover and place the document or image to be scanned on the glass, and it is scanned quite quickly. Many have automatic document feeders, too, allowing you to stack several sheets to be scanned. These scanners combine the best of both worlds in that they perform steady scans and can scan from virtually any source. Their only downfall is their price, although prices have been coming down lately. They run from under $300 all the way up to $1000 or more.

▼ PLUG AND PLAY

Plug and Play (often abbreviated PnP) is a new technology that lets you install new hardware easily using Windows 95. Mac technology was always known to be easier, basically because Apple made everything you used with a Mac, so all the Mac technology was compatible with each other. Because IBM-compatible machines are manufactured by many different companies, installing new hardware was always a real problem for PC users.

That's because your computer has to be instructed to "find" the new hardware electronically, so that it can be integrated with the rest of your computer setup. It is very aggravating to have a new printer properly plugged in, and then have your computer insist that there is no printer installed. (When I began using AOL, I couldn't configure my modem for over three months. Plug and Play would have fixed it immediately.)

Plug and Play identifies products that, as its name suggests, only require you to plug in the device to use it. Many new peripherals carry the Plug and Play logo and work with operating systems, especially Windows 95, to ease installation. For most products, once you install them, Windows 95 should automatically be able to find and configure them so them so that they "fit" your computer setup. Now once again, the operative word is "should." Neither Windows 95 nor the manufacturer of the computer part makes any guarantee that this will always work. If it doesn't, you're back to square one and have to configure the printer, modem, scanner, etc. the old fashioned way . . . by calling a friend who knows how.

▼ What If You Can't Afford a Computer?

There are two options for families who can't afford to buy a computer for their home—(a) use a community computer (from your children's school, the library or a local organization's computer lab) or (b) buy an Internet appliance or box, like WebTV. An "Internet box" or "Internet appliance" lets you surf the Web, access the Internet, send and receive e-mail and, with the right hardware, print. It doesn't have the "thinking" ability of a computer, can't play CD-ROMs and doesn't do word processing. But it also costs one quarter the price of a computer. (I'll explain more about them shortly, in *Alternatives to a Computer . . . WebTV and Internet Box Technology*.)

In my opinion, buying a used computer isn't an option. If you know someone very well who's upgrading to a new system, that may be a different story. But, because so many people (including *moi*) have been burned by buying systems that don't work, die right away or are missing key components, I recommend that you wait until you can afford new equipment rather than buy used equipment.

▼   FINDING A COMPUTER TO USE IN YOUR COMMUNITY

If you don't have a computer and can't afford to buy one, . . . you're in luck. More and more communities have computers available for their residents. Finding them may not always be easy, though.

Start with your local library. Many public libraries are already connected (44.6 percent of all U.S. public libraries were in 1996), and most librarians are well advanced on the cyberlearning curve. If they don't offer online access to the public, they will know who does. (Seventy percent of the libraries not already connected will be by the end of 1997.)

While some people (obviously not in the know) think that the Internet marks the end of public libraries, the public libraries have used the electronic age to their advantage. Some libraries have paired parent-child workshops with their Internet access services. Others have scheduled "family-safe nights" where families can congregate at the local library for Web surfing, family discussions and community projects. Libraries' roles are expanding, not contracting. They're a great resource for learning about the Internet, and about how to get the most out of cyberspace.

Sometimes you can make arrangements with your child's school or a local college to let your children use their computers after-hours or with a community group to use their computer lab. Many local community groups are partnering with the computer industry to supply computers and Internet access to schools and community organizations to get all children online. Local computer clubs have also been very active in getting community kids online. For example, in a town near Tampa, Florida, the Sun City Center computer club (at the local senior citizen community center) is committed to getting a public park's ancient computers up and running. And they're not alone. Computer clubs are great community resources.

If there aren't enough computers in your community, go to work to get more installed. Contact your local retailers, community groups, computer and software manufacturers, computer clubs and the local telephone company to see if they'll help. Many businesses will support your plan to build a computer lab so every child in the community can learn and have fun online. It's good public relations for them, and really makes a difference to the community.

▼ Alternatives to a Computer... WebTV and Internet Box Technology

Internet access doesn't require an expensive computer and modem. New (or "box") technology permits you to get online using Internet appliances. These appliances look like your standard cablebox and sit on top of your TV. (This is also a great way to get people who are deathly afraid of computers online ... look Ma, no computer!)

WebTV has already sold about 120,000 sets, and Jupiter Communications predicts that by the year 2002, WebTV and other Internet appliances will account for 22 percent of all consumer online usage. Although many earlier reviews of the current Internet appliances complained that the technology left much to be desired, the technology has improved rapidly. Using an Internet box, at a cost of about $600 (including a portable keyboard), is a very real and affordable option to spending $2500 or more on an entire computer. If you don't need a whole computer, why pay for equipment you don't need?

Rather than using a mouse with an Internet box, you use a remote control or fully remote keyboard (no wires!) to move around the Web. Computer-experienced surfers find it awkward, having to scroll using buttons on the remote, rather than using a mouse. But newbies don't have to make the mouse-to-cursor adjustment. To them, it's just like using any game controllers or remote controls. The remote keyboard also makes it easier for bed-ridden surfing. A child can sit in her bed and surf on her TV and there aren't any wires to get tangled.

I was very impressed with WebTV when we tested it—surprisingly so. I would strongly recommend it for grandparents who want to stay in touch by e-mail and want to get out there and surf the Web, but who don't need a whole computer.

One of the best things about Internet appliances is the fact that you can surf the Internet from your sofa or easy chair and everyone in the room can watch the surf results together from your big screen TV. That makes them especially good for family surfing, since you can all join in. Even the most diehard technophobes will eventually want to join the fun.

They're very compact, and can sit on top of your TV. Internet appliances are also easy to install. You connect them to your TV (rather like connecting a computer game player or VCR), and just plug them into the phone line. Some require that you use their designated online service provider; others allow you to choose your own. The leading brand in the Internet industry game is Sony's WebTV (www.webtv.com) but others have either introduced or are introducing similar products.

CHAPTER 4

How Do You Get Connected?

A Bird's Eye View—

▼ Getting Online . . . Choosing the Right
Service for You

▼ Comparing ISPs with Online Services

▼ What's the Difference Between the
Online Services?

▼ If You Choose an Online Service . . . How
Do You Get Signed Up?

▼ If You Decide to Go with an ISP . . . How
Do You Select the Right One for You?

▼ Confusing Matters Further . . . Using a
Cable Company as Your ISP

▼ Getting Online . . . Choosing the Right Service for You

An Internet service provider or an online service? This can be a difficult choice. An Internet service provider (ISP) simply gives you Internet access and e-mail, while an online service gives you both of those things, plus extra content available only to their own subscribers.

▼ ONLINE SERVICES

There are four major online services: America Online (AOL), CompuServe Interactive, Prodigy Internet and The Microsoft Network (MSN). Online service providers offer fun and interesting content in addition to e-mail and Internet access. The content is broken into two groups—content provided by outside sources, like ABC News and Nickelodeon (provided under contractual relationships usually combined with advertising revenue sharing), and content provided by members, volunteer hosts and paid representatives of the online service. (I volunteer my time when I host and moderate areas online.)

The online services are like small towns on the entrance ramps to the information superhighway, complete with maps for helping you get around. Each one also offers chatrooms and discussion boards. You can wander around the "town" and never venture onto the Internet proper. Without leaving the online service's own territory, you can communicate publicly with fellow subscribers in two ways: posting and chatting. You can also communicate with people who are not on your online service via e-mail and access the Internet itself. It is often the best of both worlds.

Chatting takes place in aptly named chat rooms. They are usually dedicated to a single topic or interest (for these purposes, we'll skip discussion of the . . . um . . . "romance-related" rooms). Some chat rooms operate only on a preset schedule, while others are open all hours. AOL leads all of the other services in the chat room game.

Chatting, like IRCs, is a typed live conversations. You sit at your computer and type in your message. The instant it is sent, it appears on everyone's computer screen, where anyone in the chat room can respond to it and everyone can read that response. It is a large group conversation, in real time, but instead of words being spoken and heard and responded to in kind, they are typed and read and responded to in kind. It can get confusing, though, with many conversations going on at the same time. In addition, if you want to chat, you should learn some acronyms, as conversation shorthand. Without them, you'll be lost as people converse in short-hand around you. (I've shared a few in the *Ms. Parry's Rules of Netiquette* chapter.)

The more popular chats aren't special scheduled topic chats. They're the *ad hoc*, drop-in-and-see-who's-there chats. Sometimes the chat room has a desig-nated topic, but it's usually something like "single parents" or "New Yorkers." In these unmonitored chatrooms, the conversation can quickly deteriorate, which probably accounts for both the chat rooms' extreme popularity among adults, and their corresponding risk to children.

An "event" is usually a special chat orchestrated by the online service, with a guest celebrity. Held in cyber auditoriums, they're promoted heavily by the online service. In most events members can't chat directly with the guest, but can post their questions and comments to a moderator who screens the questions, submitting some for the guest's response. Some terrific people appear as guests in cyberevents, and you might even get a chance to ask them the question you've always wanted to.

Discussion boards are bulletin boards. Just like tacking a note on a bulletin board at your local supermarket, any member can post a message on a discussion bulletin board. Then, whenever someone else wants to comment on the posting, answer the question or add a question of their own, they can post a reply or another message to the board. Instead of using thumbtacks and scribbled index cards, online service members use electronic posts. It's more high tech, but really the same thing. You can post something at a time convenient to you, and others can reply (or just lurk, which means you don't respond but just read what others have to say) when it's convenient for them.

Discussion boards are broken into topics located in separate topical forums, like Court TV Law Center (where I hosted the Legal Helpline for a year) or my Legal Discussion boards in Legal Information Network on AOL (keyword "lin"). My sis-ter, as Kid Doc, has her own child health discussion boards in Thrive on AOL, too (keyword "Thrive"). (I couldn't help the shameless plugs . . . so shoot me!).

Chatrooms and discussion boards are two of the biggest draws for online service providers. Several media companies have great forums online, like Oprah (keyword "Oprah"), CNN (keyword "CNN") and ABC News (keyword "ABC"), where they can maintain closer touch with their regular viewers. (They're all wonderful sites, and if you haven't checked them out yet, I suggest that you do.) Even if they also have websites with the same content, the online service is a much more pleasant forum in which to navigate. That's the secret to the online service's real success, especially in capturing the beginners' market.

The biggest advantage to these forums is that they're easy to use. Anyone can get online for the first time and start enjoying themselves within minutes. You don't have to worry about setting up your browser or configuring your e-mail. (I've given you a whole section just on e-mail later on in the chapter *Person-to-Person Online . . . E-mail*, so hold your horses.) It's all preset and automatic. Some people outgrow the online service eventually, but many of us still spend a large part of our online time in our favorite forums. It's often much easier than having to venture onto the Internet itself.

▼ I S P s

Internet Service Providers, or "ISPs," give you direct access to the Internet. Aside from some limited content that some services use on their initial screen—called a "home page"—the content you get is the Internet itself.

Since content isn't an issue in comparing one ISP to another, the main choices among them relate to tech support and local access telephone numbers. (I'll explain all these in detail later.) Each carrier also supplies all the tools necessary to access the Internet. Usually for a flat fee of around $19.95 per month for unlimited access, an ISP will provide the user with the requisite software, Web browser and an Internet account. The account will include the basic features of Internet communication: an e-mail account, the ability to access websites and newsgroups, the ability to transfer files to and from different networks (FTP) and the ability to chat "live" with others on the Internet, using the IRC.

You can use a large carrier, with international access numbers (to let you surf while traveling) and more tech support, or a local carrier who may give you better service . . . because after all, you know where they live! It's a matter of weighing the features that work best for you.

The ISPs may also function as landlords to the tenants of the Internet for those interested in putting up their own website, by providing space on their computer "server" for websites. Some services, like Mindspring, also include website server hosting for a small site in certain packages for a flat monthly fee.

A server is a computer attached to the Internet and set up to hold information to be accessed from the Internet. You may also read about "host" and "client" designations. These define the role the computer is playing at the time. Is it asking for information?—then it's a client. Is it supplying the information?—then it's the host. One computer may play both roles, at different times. (Sorry . . . sometimes I get carried away. . . .)

▼ Comparing ISPs with Online Services

Pepsi or Coke? Great taste or less filling? Butter or Parkay? Some things can never be resolved.

But there's no way out. In order to get online, you need an Internet account of some kind. There are two ways to get online. (Actually, there's a new third hybrid type of service that the Microsoft Network has spearheaded, but I couldn't think of any three-choice examples as good as these two-choice examples . . .) You can use an online service provider (like AOL, CompuServe, Prodigy and The Microsoft Network) or a regular Internet service provider (like Netcom, AT&T, Sprint and MCI). That means you have to choose. (If you want to use special technology, though, you may not have a choice. You might have to use the service provider connected to the technology, like with WebTV or with the new cable high-speed modem access such as Time Warner's Road Runner or Comcast Cable's @Home.)

I've set forth the strengths and weaknesses of each in a simple chart. See if it helps.

Getting Online with . . .	Strengths	Weaknesses
DIRECT INTERNET ACCESS, USING AN ISP	**SPEED** Generally, ISPs have faster Internet access than online services. It's a result of the technology. (If you get cable modem access, the speed difference becomes even more significant.)	**DIFFICULTY FOR NEWBIES** It's harder to get up and running when you use an ISP than when you use an online service provider. You have to configure a Web browser in order to get around and receive and send e-mail.
	EASIER ACCESS Most of the large ISPs have more local access phone numbers than the online services, which is useful, especially if you travel frequently and need local access numbers in a variety of locations. Large ISPs have many more international access numbers than the online service providers.	**NO SPECIAL CONTENT** Aside from the homepage itself, most ISPs do not offer any special content. You get the Internet, pure and simple.
	GADGETS AND GIZMOS FOR EXPERIENCED NETIZENS As you become more experienced online, you may want to try out new Internet gadgets and gizmos that generally aren't available on any online service.	**PARENTAL CONTROLS** Aside from being able to filter based upon Web browser configuration, most ISPs leave parents on their own when it comes to filtering content. You can use filtering technology, but you need to buy and install it yourself. A few are starting to offer a server-based blocking option, though, and I expect more to join them.

Getting Online with . . .	Strengths	Weaknesses
	EASIER TO USE You can start using the service the minute you get online. There are no setup problems and nothing to configure.	**NOT ENOUGH LOCAL ACCESS NUMBERS** Especially if you travel frequently (or internationally), you may find a problem getting a local access number in your area.
ONLINE SERVICE PROVIDERS . . . LIKE AOL, COMPUSERVE, PRODIGY AND MSN*	**LOTS OF SPECIAL CONTENT** You never even need to venture forth onto the Internet if you don't want to. The content is also easy to find.	**SPEED** When you want to surf the Net, it's generally slower than an ISP.
	KIDS' CONTENT Many online services have special forums just for kids. Some of them offer different content for different ages.	**WEB BROWSERS** If you want to take full advantage of the Internet, you may have to configure your setup to use a Web browser other than the ones provided by the online service. It can be difficult.
	PARENTAL CONTROLS The big guys offer parental control features where you can screen or limit what your children see.	**NO GIZMOS** The latest Internet tools and gizmos may not work with an online service provider. You may not be able to use IRCs, access newsgroups or use FTP. (Although AOL's FTP access is one of its most popular features.)
	PRICING For the same money that most ISPs charge for unlimited service, you get the Net, e-mail and all the extras, too.	

* MSN is neither fish nor fowl, it's part ISP and part online service, with the best of both.

▼ What's the Difference Between the Online Services?

If you decide you want to use an online service, you'll have to choose among them. There are four major online services. America Online is by far the most popular of the online service providers, with over eight million members. Until recently, CompuServe had always been known as the preferred service for professionals and businesses, and Prodigy had always been known as the family online service until AOL became more popular. The popularity of CompuServe and Prodigy has generally decreased as AOL's has increased.

MSN, Microsoft's online service network, is a hybrid. It works from a Web-based system, like a large website, rather than a special proprietary system like AOL. (It's the third type of system I mentioned: part ISP / part online service provider.) And when the dust settles we may end up with many more hybrid services, part online service provider and part ISP. Both CompuServe and Prodigy have also redesigned or are going to redesign their systems to look more like an ISP service.

▼ AMERICA ONLINE

"The Internet is too valuable a tool to be left to the techies of the world." That's how America Online begins its description of what it has to offer to members. It's the reason that AOL has grown so quickly and become so popular. AOL is not for techies . . . it's for everyone.

AOL is undisputably the most popular of the four leading online services. It also has the most discussion groups (25,000). According to industry reports, AOL has about 2 million child users, approximately half of the entire 1996 worldwide Internet children's population. One of the main reasons for its popularity with kids is the wealth of its child content. Outside child content providers like Nickelodeon, ABC Kidzine (from the ABC network), Disney.com, Highlights for Children, and DC Comics keep the content fresh and varied. (Some of these content providers are now also offering websites, so anyone with Internet access can enjoy them.)

AOL charges the same as most ISPs, $19.95 per month for unlimited usage. But for the same $19.95 you get much more.

The real power of AOL for its members of all ages is its chatrooms and its "channels." Each channel covers a different subject, represented by a different graphic which you can click on to get to the area of AOL that you want. One of the most popular channels on AOL is their "Kids Only" channel—recommended by more children I spoke with than any other children's online site.

Parents like "Kids Only" for more than its content. It's a childsafe environment, especially for the younger children. Parents can configure their AOL account so that when their child logs on with her username and password, she can only access "Kids Only" and can't get into any other area of AOL. The parental controls can block instant messages too (a smart thing to do for younger kids), which is a vehicle many adults use when trying to lure kids into private communications. You can also block their receipt of e-mail, a precaution you may want to take if your kids are young and you're not prescreening their mail.

"Kids Only" even has a homework helpline (so that you don't have to tell your child that you forgot how to calculate the square root of a number over twenty years ago). There are also additional parental control features, where parents can use Cyber Patrol's technology to filter what their children can access outside of the "Kids Only" boards. (We'll review Cyber Patrol later on in the *Using Technology to Implement and Enforce Your Choices* chapter . . . don't worry.)

For older children and teenagers, there are other channels with information on topics that they'll find interesting, like "Computers & Software," "Entertainment," "Games," "Sports," "Style Channel," "Life Styles and Interests" and "Music Space." There are also sections that they'll find helpful, even if not as interesting, such as "Learning & Culture" and "Reference Desk."

Older kids and teens also appreciate a couple of features unique to AOL, such as its Buddy List and Instant Messages. With the buddy list, a member can be alerted if any designated friends or family (who also use AOL) are online at the same time she is. She then can send an Instant Message to her buddy with a message that pops up on her buddy's screen. (This feature can be turned off if she is trying to get homework done and her friends' messages keep popping up; let's face it, they are probably more interesting than her research on the major export of Tunisia).

And here's another shameless plug of my sister's forum, Thrive. Deanna Aftab Guy, M.D. (my mother always makes me use the "M.D." part whenever I talk about DiDi) as "KidDoc" on Thrive, answers parents' questions in live chats and discussion boards. She's a terrific pediatrician and a very popular cyberceleb on AOL. (She must be great, since she gets paid to run her forums and I'm still an unpaid Host running my legal discussion boards . . . oh, well.)

Unfortunately, though, AOL's popularity has been its biggest problem since late last year. Until the end of 1996, AOL charged for hourly usage. Recently, with its new unlimited usage plan, the amount of time its users spend online has increased and many new people have signed on, putting an impossible strain on the service. Unable to handle the increased demand, it became known as "America Offline" by disgruntled users. Now, after AOL invested approximately $350 million to expand their capabilities, it's becoming easier to get online again.

I guess it's like having your favorite restaurant get a four-star review and then not being able to get a table without waiting an hour and a half. If the food is good enough you'll wait, and keep coming back. Even with the difficulties in getting connected to AOL, the variety and quality of content kept their user base intact. They'll complain, but they stay (or have come back). Our family reviewers tell us AOL is worth the wait.

▼ CompuServe Interactive

CompuServe Interactive is free for the first month for up to ten hours, then there are two pricing options of $24.95 per month for unlimited usage, or $9.95 per month with five free hours included, and each additional hour charged at $2.95. According to the numbers provided by CompuServe, approximately five million home and business users subscribe to their service.

CompuServe currently has many areas of interest to children and teenagers. With "KidsNet," "eDisney," and "Tell Me a Story," CompuServe provides content to appeal to children from ages six to sixteen. It provides chat rooms where children, teens, and adults can converse in real time in a forum chosen for a particular content. There is a "Research and Reference" section that includes an online encyclopedia and a "Study Guide Forum" to help kids with study topics including literature, social science, and history, just to name a few.

CompuServe has a Parental Control Center which allows parents to limit what their children can access online. In addition, as a member of CompuServe, you can download and use Cyber Patrol for free for one year. Although CompuServe's own parental controls cover a wide range of topics (a list of all the blocked topics are available online), they suggest using it in conjunction with Cyber Patrol for maximum protection. To turn on or shut off protection, your password is required. Then, you can choose to block sites and places on CompuServe, on the Internet, or both, as well as choose whether you want to block these areas permanently or only for one session. The program simply returns "Access Denied" if someone tries to go to a blocked area.

CompuServe also has many kids' sites. By simply searching for "kids" in the find menu, a range of links comes up. One such area is "Kids Central." It has a link to "Kool Kids Websites," which offers names of safe and kid-oriented pages. "Kids Central" also offers "Friends & Pets," a page of links to animal areas online; "Fun & Games," links to sites related to cartoons and kid-TV shows; and "Study Hall," with access to encyclopedias and educational sites. The online sites offered by the first two links seem thorough. Just about every hobby and/or activity is covered. "Study Hall" provides a lot of information as the search engines peruse CompuServe's own databases as well as information from the Web.

Another advantage to choosing CompuServe is that their technical support is very helpful, resourceful, and patient with any technical questions. This can be a big plus for any newbie struggling to get online. (They didn't know who we were when we called for tech support, and we called them repeatedly with lots of inane questions. They were always helpful and patient.)

▼   PRODIGY INTERNET

Prodigy Internet is available for $19.95 per month with unlimited usage, and together with Prodigy Classic has approximately 1.5 million users. New members join Prodigy Internet, which is an ISP/online service provider hybrid service. Prodigy Classic is being phased out totally over the next year.

Prodigy doesn't have much in the way of its own kids' content, and mostly uses general Web content. Prodigy has "communities," approximately fifty different websites with hundreds of links on specific subjects. It also has multiplayer games, sports, music, and an education area. The education section includes Compton's Encyclopedia, which has over 37,000 articles plus images and sounds. So if your child is doing a report on Mozart, she can not only read about him, but also hear nine sound files of his great works.

Prodigy Internet also provides a compilation of educational reference websites including "Study Web," "WWWebster Dictionary," "Roget's Thesaurus," "Digital Library for School Kids," "Magellan Geographix," "Library of Congress," and the "Smithsonian Institute." But remember, these are websites, available to anyone on the Web. They are not proprietary or exclusive Prodigy content.

For your children's safety, there is also an "Access Control" area where parents can use Cyber Patrol software, without charge, to block chat areas or newsgroups completely, as well as blocking access to certain sites.

▼   MSN

The Microsoft Network, which has over 2 million users, offers a number of different pricing plans to suit your needs. The Premier Plan is $6.95 per month and offers five hours of access monthly. Each additional hour costs $2.50. This same plan can be bought on a yearly basis for $69.95. With this, you get 12 months for the price of 10. The Premier Flat Rate Plan is $19.95 a month and offers unlimited access. The Premier

Destination Plan is $6.95 a month and is meant for those who already have Internet access. With the $6.95 plan, you get full access to MSN's programming (including Disney's Daily Blast).

MSN's areas are broken into channels. Channel 1 is the news channel, 2 offers entertainment, 3 is education, 4 is lifestyle, 5 is for young adults, and 6 is for kids.

MSN has perfected the hybrid model. I consider MSN more of an ISP than an online service provider. It is Web-based (which means it's harder for newbies to navigate), but also provides its own content. Once you've perfected the use of a web browser, it becomes easier.

One of the best things about MSN is Disney's Daily Blast, a family site filled with lots of . . . (surprise!) Disney content. (It's available to anyone with Internet access for $4.95 per month at www.disneyblast.com.) Although I don't recommend paying for kids' content generally, given the amount of free kids' content available, Disney's Daily Blast is a great site. Since it's included in MSN, you get an ISP and Disney's Daily Blast for the price of an ISP alone.

Even though there isn't a lot of MSN kids' content, what they have is first rate. "Scrawl," an interactive participant computer game, works like the game Pictionary. You play it "live" with other people online. Microsoft seems to have found a special niche in game sites. "The Zone," according to our teenage (and adults who wished they were) reviewers, is one of the hottest sites on the Internet.

Another popular feature is their "Computing on MSN." Diehard Microsoft fans join with newbies in exploring every conceivable computer topic. Even Microsoft-bashers have to agree that computing is what Microsoft does best. (I used to get an immediate argument from my Mac-user friends. But since Bill Gates and Apple have decided to cooperate recently, their arguments have turned to mere grumbles.)

▼ COMPARATIVE ONLINE SERVICE INFORMATION

I've compared certain online service information in another chart. It makes it easier to compare the key information of each. (Note that this information is current as of Fall 1997, but may change.)

Comparative Online Service Information

Online Service	Default Web Browser	Available for OS	System Requirements*	No. of Users	Pricing	Parental Control Features
America Online (AOL)	Internet Explorer (can download Netscape Navigator)	Windows 3.1 or higher Mac	Windows 3.1 4 MB RAM 5 MB HD Windows 95 8MB RAM 5 MB HD	8 million	$19.95 / mo. unlimited usage; or $4.95 / mo. 3 hrs. free (each add. hr.$2.50)	Can restrict to "Kids Only" and use other "Parental Control" features and although it doesn't offer Cyber Patrol it uses their technology.
CompuServe Interactive (CSi)	Internet Explorer	Windows 3.1 or higher Mac	Windows 3.1 or higher 8 MB RAM (16 MB recom-- mended)	5 million	1st mo. free up to 10 hrs. then: $24.95 / mo. unlimited usage or $9.95 / mo. 5 hrs. free (each add'l hr. $2.95)	"Parental Control Center" allows parents to use Cyber Patrol

*Minimum MB RAM; Available Hard Disk space.
Although each online service offers e-mail and Internet access, the other features of each are different.

Comparative Online Service Information

Online Service	Default Web Browser	Available for OS	System Require- ments*	No. of Users	Pricing	Parental Control Features
Prodigy Internet	Internet Explorer (can download Netscape Navigator)	Windows 3.1 or higher Mac	Windows 95: 16 MB RAM 45 MB HD (includes adding Internet Explorer) Windows 3.1: 16 MB RAM 30 MB HD (includes adding Internet explorer)	1.5 million	$19.95 / mo. unlimited usage; or $9.95 / mo. 10 hrs. free (each add'l hr. $2.50)	"Access Control" area, block chat or newsgroups and Cyber Patrol included
The Microsoft Network (MSN)	Program Viewer (based on Internet Explorer)	Windows 95	Windows 95: 8 MB RAM 50 MB HD	2.3 million	$19.95 / mo. unlimited usage; or, $6.95 /mo. 5 hrs. free (each add'l hr. $2.95)	If activated, can use the PICS standard with default set to RSACi ratings**

*Minimum MB RAM; Available Hard Disk space
**These are described later in the book in the *Rating the Web . . . PICS, the Platform for Internet Content Selection* chapter.
Although each online service offers e-mail and Internet access, the other features of each are different.

▼ If You Choose an Online Service . . . How Do You Get Signed Up?

Getting the software you need to connect to an online service isn't an issue if you have a computer manufactured in the last few years. Most computers already have the online services software preinstalled. If they don't, you probably receive ten copies of the installation software each day. Stop tossing them, and install the one you want to try. (Remember that you can change your mind, and many services will give you a free trial period to try them out.) If you can't find a copy on your hard drive or in your mail (or from your friends) the telephone numbers for the online services are listed in the directory in our Appendix. You can call the companies and they'll be thrilled to send you free software. (And you should note that the MSN software preinstalled on your computer may be out of date. Mine was. Just call for an updated copy.)

The software walks you through installation. You can get online right away, but need to give a credit card number to charge service to. (Once your membership has been confirmed, if anyone sends you an online message asking you to give them your credit card information again, for any reason, don't! It's a scam hackers use to get your credit card information.)

The hardest part about getting started is finding a screen name you like. On AOL, after they tell you that the screen name you want is taken (with eight million members, you run out of choices fast), they'll offer you some gibberish of name and numbers. Don't take it. Hold out for a better offer.

A hard-to-remember e-mail address is as bad as a hard-to-remember telephone number. You can use spaces to break up parts of a name, and that sometimes makes it easier to get a real name. But be prepared to get lots of e-mail that belongs to the person who uses the same name but without the space. If you forward it to the right person, they might even forward some of your mail that they get back to you.

Remember not to let your kids use their real names as a screen name . . . it's not a safe thing to do.

▼ If You Decide to Go with an ISP . . . How Do You Select the Right One for You?

You'll want to find the best combination of price, easy setup, good tech support, local access numbers and Web browser selection. While you're at it, you should also check to see if they offer newsgroups, FTP and compression software. (The hybrid online service providers, like the Microsoft Network and Prodigy Internet, are something to consider as well. MSN is by far the larger of the two, and when its credentials are compared to many of the ISPs, it looks even better.)

When you choose an ISP, remember that you'll probably need a lot of tech support in the beginning. That means you want an ISP with a lot of patient people to answer all your questions. If they're not patient with your questions now, it's unlikely that they'll be patient with them later. So courtesy should play a large part in your decision.

I've included the telephone numbers for each of the big five ISPs, as well as MSN, in the directory in the Appendix. There may be others you want to call as well. Ask around. There's even a great list you can access online at www.cnet.com/Content/Reviews/Compare/ISP/sample.html. (The C|Net site is a great resource for most Internet-related information. This is only one of their very helpful lists.)

When you call an ISP, ask the following questions:

1. *What are your local access numbers in my area?*

Check to make sure with your local telephone company that these are truly toll-free numbers. If they're not, you may be able to make special arrangements with your local telephone company to add another number to your local access for a flat additional monthly charge. Depending on how often you use the Internet access, you could save a lot of money.

2. *How many modems do you have per user? When are your peak times? Can you handle high-speed modems?*

Make sure that they have enough access available during the times you are most likely to be surfing. And the recommended user-to-modem ratio is ten to one.

3. *What programs do you have other than unlimited access?*

How much do you expect to use the Internet service? You might be surprised to see how much fun it is to surf the Web. But if you just want to test the water, try an hourly rate plan. Nothing's etched in stone. You can always upgrade to an unlimited time plan later. Just make sure there's no set-up fee that you would have to pay to change plans.

4. *What hours are your customer tech support numbers staffed? How many people answer your tech support lines?*

Make sure that there are enough people working when you're likely to be using the service and needing support. The traffic gets heavier, typically, once the West coast gets home from work, around 8:30 p.m. EST. Take that into consideration when you set your surfing schedule.

5. *Will you walk me through installation?*

It's comforting to know that you'll have this available even if you don't need it.

6. *Do you provide compression, Usenet, FTP and Gopher software?*

Even if you won't use it often, get it . . . (what the heck).

7. *What browser do you offer? Which version? Do you have support if I need help installing another browser?*

I prefer when they use both Microsoft's Internet Explorer and Netscape's Navigator, so you can have an option available when you want it. Both are available on the Web, though, and you can use either Internet Explorer or Netscape Navigator with any ISP.

8. *For Mac users: Do you have Mac service? Do you have Mac tech support people? How many?*

Bad enough that everyone except graphic designers makes you feel like a second-class citizen—you should be able to get knowledgeable tech support when you need it.

Head-to-head, here are the basics on AT&T, MCI, Sprint, Mindspring, Netcom and MSN.

ISP	Approx. no. of subscribers	Maximum modem speeds	Rates for for unlimited usage*	No. of local access numbers (POPs)**	Web Browsers Offered	FTP, news-groups and Gopher	Tech support
AT&T	1 million	28.8	$19.95 (hourly plan available)	200+	Explorer 3.0	all	24 hrs. 7 days a week
MCI	250,000	33.6 (56.6 by 10/97)	$19.95 (plus $4.95 shipping and handling)	300	Explorer 3.02	No FTP	24 hrs. 7 days a week
Sprint	150,000	28.8	$19.95 (hourly plan available)	220	Netscape Navigator 3.0 (default) Explorer 3.0	all	24 hrs. 7 days a week
Mindspring	185,000	56.6	$19.95 (plus $25 startup fee)	235-240	Explorer 3.1 Netscape Navigator 3.0	all	24 hrs. 7 days a week
Netcom	580,000	28.8 ———— 56.6 premium plan access	$19.95 ———— $24.95 for premium plan	330	All users: Netscape 3.0 Windows 95 only: Explorer 3.01	all	5 a.m.-9 p.m. free, 24 hrs, and 7 days a week for pay-per call support ------- Premium gets free calls
MSN	2.5 million	28.8 ———— 56.6 premier plan available	$19.95 ———— $49.95 for premier plan	460	Explorer 3.0	Need third-party client for Gopher	7a.m.-2a.m. weekdays; 10a.m.–8p.m. weekends

Head to Head Comparing Internet Service Providers

*Some providers may offer special introductory rates and/or prepaid plan discounts, as well as other plans. You should call around to find out.
**"Points of presence."

▼ Confusing Matters Further ... Using a Cable Company as Your ISP

The most promising of all the new high speed and access technologies is cable Internet access. Cable companies throughout the United States are jumping on the Internet access bandwagon. Their cable access technology permits access at 2–5 million bps, several hundred times faster than a 28.8 modem.

Although cable modems hold tremendous promise, they aren't available everywhere yet. Before they can reach their full potential, cable connections everywhere will have to be upgraded to permit two-way communication by hybrid fiber coaxial systems. Until then, the cable companies are offering cable ISP service only in limited markets.

Time Warner currently leads the cable modem pack with its Road Runner cable Internet service, although the total number of households accessing the Internet with cable modems may be less than 100,000. (Just to contrast, about 120,000 households access the Internet using WebTV.) According to one estimate, though, there will be at least 3 million households connected to the Internet through cable modems by the year 2002. (But that may be a gross under estimate since Time Warner tells me they expect to have 2 million households connected by year-end 1997, and that doesn't include all the households connected by Comcast, TCI and Cox cable services through @Home, which I've discussed below.)

Cable companies are in the content business. And they're using their content to supplement their Internet services. Time Warner is tapping into the extraordinary content resources of its "Pathfinder" search engine / content collection, to provide special content to Time Warner Internet Cable subscribers. (Pathfinder is my favorite popular information search engine.)

In addition to providing faster access and their regular content available in all markets, the cable companies are providing special local content, like local news and weather too. Comcast (the fourth largest cable TV provider in the U.S.), has joined forces with its cable partners Cox and TCI in introducing @Home (pronounced "at home"). @Home is a good example of how a provider can blend material from its content provider partners and from its local cable companies. @Home uses its www.InYourTown.com website for local content, providing local events, news and weather.

It will be interesting to see how the cable content changes the Internet industry's content model.

A cable modem costs about $400, roughly two to three times its standard analog modem equivalent. One major benefit, in addition to speed, is that for about $150, the cable company will install and setup your modem. This is a big advantage for those of you who are technology-challenged.

However, the increased convenience and speed cost more. Most ISPs offer unlimited Internet access for a flat fee of $19.95 per month. @Home, as an example, costs $39.95 per month for unlimited Internet access and e-mail service, although they reduce the monthly charge to $29.95 per month if you purchase the modem from them.

But for the $10–$20 per month additional cost over a standard ISP, you are surfing at hundreds of times the speed of your old 28.8 baud modem. A file which takes over six minutes to load using a 28.8 modem takes only one second on a cable modem. Having been kept waiting forever trying to download long documents and fancy graphics one time too often, I think $10 is a small price to pay for instant access.

CHAPTER 5

Once You Get There . . . How Do You Find Anything?

A Bird's Eye View—

▼ Search Engines

▼ Bookmarking—Leaving a Trail of Breadcrumbs

▼ Hello Information? . . . I'd Like the E-Mail Address for . . .

I've promised you a world of fascinating information never before accessible to non-geeks. Millions of sites covering every topic imaginable . . . Wait a minute. You should know by now when a lawyer offers you something that terrific for free, there's a catch.

What's the catch? . . . You've got to find the stuff yourself!

By now, we are all familiar with the domain names registered by major corporations, such as www.disney.com and www.sony.com and www.nbc.com. (None of us ever had any idea what "dot com" meant, but it's now become a common part of our vocabulary.) But what if you're looking for someone and don't know if they have a website? And even if you know they have one, if you don't already know the domain name, how do you find them?

In the early days of the Web, yellow-pages books with domain names were published in hard copy, listing categories of sites, the same way a phone book would list types of businesses. These went out of fashion as people learned how to find their way around on their own. But a new edition of a popular yellow pages is the exception to the rule. *The Internet Kids & Family Yellow Pages,* written by Jean Armour Polly (the original "Net-Mom") and published by Osborne/McGraw Hill has sold over a million copies. (I intend to take lessons in book marketing from Jean.) Recently revised and released, it's a quick way to find lots of family-friendly sites. Jean has reviewed them all to make sure they're "childsafe." As Net-Mom, Jean was one of the early Web pioneers and knows everything there is to know about kid resources online. You can find Jean at www.netmom.com and can e-mail her at mom@netmom.com.) Tell her I sent you.

Almost all the yellow pages other than Jean's were replaced by search engines (indices of websites) where you can search for websites registered with the search engine. Any site could be registered with the search engine. Until then, Internet users would not be able to find your website unless they knew your domain name.

(It's like having an unlisted phone number.) As the search engines matured, they added robot software (called bots, spiders and crawlers), which search the Web to find the websites and index them based on the words used in their site.

Now there are many search engines on the Web. The most popular ones are: AltaVista, Excite, Infoseek, Lycos, and Yahoo!

There are two ways to use a search engine—searching by typing a specific word or words joined by a connector, or by using directories, which are divided into different topics (except for AltaVista, which only uses the specific word or phrase search).

Web search indices can index pages based on the information contained at hundreds of thousands of sites, and each of those sites have many subsites, documents and graphics (each qualifies as a separate URL file). (AltaVista has over 31 million web pages indexed.) Their robot spiders are software programs (AltaVista's is called "Scooter") that scour the Web searching for websites. The spiders search every word at the website, and in some cases, all pages linked to from those sites. It then indexes all those sites, based upon the number of search words used and how often they're used.

When you want to search for something specific, you should do a "keyword" search, listing all the words that are necessary to your search. When the search results are displayed for you, the pages with the most matches are listed first. The rest are listed in declining order.

The best thing about using this search method is that you can access many more sites and can customize your search. The worst thing is that your search may turn up umpteen zillion sites if you don't frame it properly. (Trust me . . . I've been there.) You should read the help files at the particular engine to learn how to improve your search results, so you'll get an answer, not a research project.

When you want to do a broader search, or aren't exactly sure of what you're looking for, you should use a directory search. When websites are registered with a directory-type search engine, people who work for the search engine review the sites and classify them under topics (just like encyclopedias classify information under topics). Directory-type search engines have far fewer websites categorized than the index sites do, just because it takes much longer to classify them than to just index them electronically by keywords. But when you don't know where to start on a search, the directories can be very helpful.

The directory topics range from very general to very specific, depending on how far down the topic list you go. Once you've found the right topic, a list of websites that cover the topic will be listed. You can get to those sites by clicking on their titles. Your Web browser will then whisk you away to check out the site. When you want to try another site from the search result list, you just click on the "Back" button of your browser and you're back where you started.

After you've been online for awhile, you'll find that some search engines work better for you than others. You may also find that you'll use one for certain kinds of searches, and others for a different kind of search. Before you start your search, decide what kind of information you need. Indices have many more sites, but you may find that many of them are totally irrelevant. (Bots aren't, after all, as smart as humans, even though they work faster and take shorter lunch breaks.) But since humans need to classify the sites for the directory search engines, there are far fewer sites listed in those directories. Overkill or undershooting . . . pick your poison.

If you just can't make up your mind, there are some sites that let you type in one search which goes out to more than one search engine at the same time. All4one.com is one of the most popular group search engines. (www.all4one.com)

Whether you prefer one search engine over another, you should get used to playing with all of them, because each search engine has different strengths and weaknesses. (For example, I use Time Warner's Pathfinder for all media searches. If I want to see which magazines have done an article on something, I look there first. However, I use AltaVista first on all broader topics and to find more specific information. If I have no idea where to begin, or am just surfing, I'll use Yahoo!)

Try to find a combination that works for you.

▼ KIDS' SEARCH ENGINES . . . SAFE SEARCHING AND SURFING

Some search engines, concerned about adult content being accessible to children, have set up a special search engine site just for kids.

▼ YAHOOLIGANS!

Yahooligans! is Yahoo!'s search engine designed specially for kids seven to twelve years old. It has a limited list of sites that it links to, each designed to be kid-friendly. Yahooligans! only lists sites that pass certain screening. The links are divided into eight categories, ranging from "Around the World" (politics and history) and "Science and Oddities" to "Entertainment" and "The Scoop" (comics, newspapers and weather).

There are also features such as links to "new" sites and those rated "cool." Some of the "cool" sites were dressed-up advertisements, like the link to Disney Books. Yahooligans! makes it easy to request that a site be added or deleted from their roster. Real people (not bots) review all sites to make sure that they are appropriate for kids.

Note that this search engine is not intended to function as a substitute for parental control software. For example, a search for an R-rated movie may show no matches, but the link to movie-related sites such as www.777film.com will give your child information about such movies.

Surf Watch's new search function allows parents to limit their children's searches to Yahooligans! It is a safer search environment than the general search engines, especially for younger kids.

▼ NET SHEPHERD / ALTAVISTA COOPERATION

Net Shepherd, the parental control software that uses a database of over 300,000 prescreened sites, has announced its intention to cooperate with AltaVista to prepare special search databases, prescreened for special interest groups.

Don Sandford, Net Shepherd's president, explained that he expected to set up a prescreened family friendly search engine within the next year. I'll be keeping an eye out for it.

▼ Bookmarking—Leaving a Trail of Breadcrumbs

You've read the section on finding your way around. You've found a site. Even better, it's the site you meant to find! Congratulations! This site is everything you ever hoped it would be . . . and has all the information you need or has links to "related" sites you want to read. But you don't want to read everything now. Now what? (Hmmm . . . it's sort of a "computerbook cliffhanger" isn't it?)

Bookmarking is the easiest way to return to a site over and over again. Just as you would slip a bookmark into a book to find your way back to the page you marked, you can do this online too. Each web browser and online service has its own way to mark a site. (Come on, you didn't expect them to make this easy, did you?) They also call it different things. Netscape uses the term "bookmarking," but with Explorer it is called "favorites." Whatever they call it, it works the same way.

Using Netscape Navigator as the example, you just click on the "Bookmarks" button on the toolbar at the top of your screen. Then place your mouse cursor on "Add bookmark" and click. That's it. The software saves the name and address of whatever page you are currently on to a list of bookmarks. Anytime you want to visit the sight again, just open your bookmark menu, scroll down to the site you want . . . and *voila!* No need to type in the address each time, and no need to remember what letters are upper case and which are lower!

Remember, though, that if you have a site on your bookmark list that you don't want your child to see (and you don't have software to block that site), you might want to use this option sparingly or rename it something far less enticing than "Bouncy Babes in Bikinis." Something like "Accounting aspects of short form mergers" is likely to guarantee that no one will ever try to use that bookmark.

▼ Hello Information? . . . I'd Like the E-mail Address for . . .

I saw a piece on television where someone claimed they could find anyone's e-mail address easily. I obviously need lessons from her, because I don't think it's easy at all. Maybe in the future there will be a central e-mail registry, but for now, you have to search several different places and hope you get lucky.

There are several directory websites that contain e-mail addresses and sometimes home addresses and phone numbers. These are called "white pages." They get their information from public telephone directories, voluntary listings (when people register this information directly with the site) and spiders.

If you want to be found, register your e-mail or your business address with them. (Never include home addresses.) On the other hand, if you "vant to be alone . . .," make sure you're not listed.

Finding People, Places, and Things . . . a few website search locations

Business Yellow Pages	www.bigbook.com
Dun and Bradstreet's Companies online	www.companiesonline.com
Directory assistance	www.555–1212.com
Directory of 800 numbers	att.net/dir800
Directory Organization— companies, e-mail, etc.	www.dir.org
411—Internet white pages	www.four11.com
E-mail addresses, phone and address, communities, home pages, internet phones, U.S. government pages (Who Where)	www.whowhere.com
E-mail directory search	www.bigfoot.com
Finding people	www.1800ussearch.com
Finding people and addresses	www.switchboard.com
Finding telephone area or country codes	www.inconnect.com/~americom/ aclookup.html
Looking up people and businesses	www.databaseamerica.com
National Telephone Book—White Page	www.yahoo.com/search/people
NYNEX nationwide yellow pages	www.niyp.com/newvisit.html
Yellow Pages	www.yellownet.com
Yellow pages on-line	www.ypo.com
Zip code look-up (U.S. Postal Service)	www.usps.gov/ncsc

▼ Cybersleuthing . . . a tip to finding an unlisted e-mail address

If people aren't listed in any of the white pages I mentioned above, you may be able to find them if you know some things about them. Do you know their online service provider? You can e-mail the postmaster@whatever Internet service provider they use .com, asking them to forward a message to the person you're trying to reach. They won't always do it, but it's worth a shot.

CHAPTER 6

Person-to-Person Online . . . E-mail

A Bird's Eye View—

▼ Getting an E-mail Account

▼ Your E-mail Box

▼ Spamming and Junk E-mail

▼ How Secure Is Your E-mail?

▼ "Daemon" . . . Does that Mean My
E-mail Is Possessed?

▼ Getting an E-mail Account

Join the club. Send an e-mail message to someone on the Internet. It's one of the easiest things you can do online. It's also one of the most popular.

Everyone's using it at home, at school and at work. It's used 150 percent more often than the Web is. Want to send a note to your sister? E-mail it. Want to send a copy of your daughter's report to your husband? E-mail it. Got a photo of the new baby you want to share with everyone in the family? You've got it . . . e-mail it.

And the best part is when they write back. It's instant gratification. You'll soon learn that there are few sounds sweeter than the sound of "You've got mail!" when you sign onto America Online. (My three-year-old niece chants that line whenever my sister or brother-in-law logs-on.)

You can get an e-mail-only account, although most ISP accounts and online service accounts include at least e-mail and Internet access. One company, Juno Online, offers free e-mail accounts. It sells advertising space to defray the cost of the e-mail service. If you're willing to put up with the advertisements, you can get free e-mail. You can reach Juno Online by phone at 800–654–JUNO, or reach them online at www.juno.com. They'll send you the software at no charge.

Your ISP or online service will supply you with their e-mail software. There's no additional charge for this software. Online service providers, such as America Online and CompuServe, automatically configure your e-mail, so you can send it and receive it as soon as you get online. It's a lot harder to configure your mail program when you're using an ISP, since it requires configuring your browser. This is one of the reasons I suggest getting online with America Online, CompuServe, Prodigy or MSN before you venture forth into the uncharted wilderness of ISPs and web browsers.

(Hang in there . . . I promise that this stuff will be over before you know it . . .) There are several popular e-mail programs used with ISP accounts, including Netscape Navigator's and Microsoft's Internet Explorer's e-mail programs. These are browser mail programs. They're a pain in the neck to set up, but worth the trouble. Once they're set up, they're easy to use.

If you know someone who can configure the browser for you . . . this is a good time to call and plead . . . bribes are usually in order. (I understand that Twinkies, Yo-Hoo and Cheese Doodles are the bribes of choice among computer geeks "in the know.")

▼ Your E-mail Box

Each e-mail address has two parts, your mailbox user name and the domain name of your e-mail server, separated by an "@." But many people using online services, such as AOL and CompuServe, have gotten used to using just their screen name and those of their friends on the same service to address mail and leaving out the "@" and domain name part.

These are short form e-mail addresses that only members of the same e-mail system can use. If you're both members of AOL, you can give them your screen name, and don't need to add the "@aol.com" part. (It's assumed.) It's like giving your address to someone you know lives in the same town. You give them your street address, but leave out the town part of your address.

It won't work, though, when you try to send an e-mail to someone who uses a different service than yours. Try sending a letter to someone using the U.S. Postal Service with just a name and street address—leaving out the town, state and zip code. What are the chances of it getting there? (Now I know it's tempting at this point to speculate about how likely it is that any letter, even those properly addressed, will get delivered by the Post Office, but since many of the postal workers are my friends . . . I have refrained from commenting here.)

E-mail is sent to your ISP's mail server. It's like having all your mail sent to a post office box at your local post office. Instead of having to retrieve your mail yourself from your mail box, though, you can send your mail program. (Now if I could only train it to pick up my snail mail too (regular old fashioned postal service mail) . . . I'd never need to leave home again.)

▼ Spamming and Junk E-mail

One of the worst things about e-mail is the ease with which people and businesses can send you junk e-mail. And lots of junk e-mail! Junk e-mail is often referred to as "spamming" to the chagrin of Hormel which feels that comparing their "well-loved luncheon meat" to junk e-mail denigrates their product. (I "won't even go there," as my kids say . . .)

Some lawmakers are considering adopting laws that will regulate unsolicited e-mail. Until then, though, you're on your own. Many ISPs and online services give you controls to help keep junk e-mail from clogging up your e-mail boxes. When choosing your service provider, ask them what they have to help you with this problem.

Be careful when allowing your children to read spammed mail, since many hardcore sexual sites are linking to their sites directly from spammed e-mail messages and including sexually explicit graphics. When you open the mail, clicking on the text will whisk your children away to the site or give them a first hand view of what you're trying to filter. (Some online services give you a parental control option that limits your children's e-mail to text only, to avoid the problem with spammed sexual images.) Let your service provider know if you receive these e-mails. Hopefully, they'll help.

▼ How Secure Is Your E-mail?

I advise clients never to send anything over the Internet that they wouldn't want others to read. Think of e-mails as postcards. If you don't want your mailman to read it, send it another way. That's just plain smart computing.

You should know, though, that it's not very easy to intercept e-mail messages (employers monitoring and intercepting e-mails excluded). Remember when we talked about how messages on the Internet are broken into smaller units called "packets" that travel separately around the Internet? That makes it harder to intercept any message on the Internet unless you do it at the sending or receiving points.

But if you want to use e-mail to send your message and still want some guaranty of security, you can use an encryption program. My favorite is PGP (Pretty Good Privacy). If you're ready for encryption, however, you've already outgrown this book. I suggest that you contact Phil Zimmerman at www.pgp.com. Tell him Parry sent you.

▼ "Daemon" . . . Does that Mean My E-mail Is Possessed?

Sometimes you may receive a message from "Mail Delivery Subsystem" or "Mailer-Daemon" that says the e-mail address you were sending mail to could not be found, or that the message you sent "bounced." This means that there may be a problem with the e-mail address or the recipient's mail server. Check the address to make sure you sent the message to the right place. Sometimes, if the address is right, the recipient's e-mail server may have been down, and couldn't accept it. Try sending it again.

If none of those things work . . . call an exorcist. It can't hurt.

Hooray!! The Hard Part is Over!!!

PART 2

The Dark Side
...Keeping
Things in
Perspective

(everything you
need to know about
online risks)

CHAPTER 7

What's Really Out There . . . and What Can We Do About It?

A Bird's Eye View—

▼ Keeping It in Perspective

▼ Adult Site Self-Regulation . . . A Partial Practical Solution

▼ Global Access . . . Means Finding a Global Solution

▼ Keeping It in Perspective

As much as I wish I could, I can't write this book without focusing on some of the dangers in cyberspace. It is my goal to make you careful about surfing the Web, not to scare you away from it entirely.

Although no one can dispute that there are some really nasty things on the Internet, the amount is vastly exaggerated. Unfortunately, the bad things receive a lot more press than the good things, even though the good far outnumber the bad.

In large part, the Internet's bad reputation is attributable to an unreliable survey, which was picked up by the press and used by proponents of Internet censorship as a scare tactic. This information, faulty as it was, was the catalyst for laws attempting to regulate sexual content on the Internet. It is also the root of many parents' fears.

In addition to being criticized for hardcore sexual content, the Internet gets blamed for anything and everything negative that happens online. Whenever something hits the news that is in any way related to the Internet, the talk shows are filled with people blaming the Net. Parents are frightened by all the hype, and vow that their children will never be allowed online.

And that is the real tragedy. It's rather like never taking your children to a Broadway show, the Empire State Building, the Statue of Liberty or the Museum of Natural History in New York City, because some areas of the City might be more dangerous than others. (This was just an example. One that I suspect I will regret. In fact, I'm regretting it already . . . I know that New York City was recently found to have the lowest crime rate of all major cities in the U.S . . . no calls or letters, please . . . .) Or never taking them to Rome because of the pickpockets at the Spanish Steps. (I wish I had thought of this example earlier, since I suspect that it's less likely the Mayor of Rome will write me to complain . . .)

A woman (and cyber-celebrity) I admire, Robin Raskin, the editor-in-chief of *Family PC* magazine and perhaps best known as "Internet Mom," put it best. She wrote an article for the *Family PC* website following the Heaven's Gate mass suicide, titled *Blaming the Net, A parent laments: Why did it have to be the Internet?* Her article still echoes in my ears, and I'd like to share part of it with you.

> When I first heard that the mass suicides in San Diego were tied to the Internet (the cult members built Web sites to raise funds and recruited on the Internet), an exhausted sensation overtook me. I'd just come off months of television and newspaper interviews about kids' safety on the Internet, and while I'd been realistic in my responses to those queries, the Web can be an equal opportunity offender in that there's something to offend just about any parent.
>
> As a result, when I heard that the Heaven's Gate cult used the Internet to espouse its beliefs and recruit members it was as troubling to me as if they'd used a home in my own neighborhood. After all, I'd been advocating Internet use for families and I knew now that the medium would take lots of the blame for the tragedy. I wondered: "Why blame the Internet?" If it had been a TV cult that used late night infomercials to recruit new members, no one would be questioning the value of television.

I agree. It's become a kneejerk reaction . . . to blame the Internet. (Although I'm not a big fan of infomercials either.)

▼ YOU READ IT SOMEWHERE . . . THEREFORE IT MUST BE TRUE

Whenever I speak on the subject of the Internet and children, I hear the same things from concerned parents: they're afraid of the perceived online dangers and are starting to overreact. Parents, every day, bad mouth the Internet. Most of these parents have never been online, though, and are only repeating what they've heard and read in the media.

And, the stories which appear in the media are usually the online horror stories: cyberpredators, pornography, people stalking others online, online scams . . . There's on overwhelming amount of negative press, and parents are, understandably, confused about what to believe. I want to put these things in perspective.

What they say: There's hardcore and perverted sexual content that our kids are accessing every time they get online.

Keeping it in perspective: Most of the time when kids use the Internet to access inappropriate sexual content, the information they access is often only this generation's version of the contraband issue of *Playboy* magazine, tattered and dog-eared, passed from friend to friend and stored under the mattress. It's undesirable, many agree, but not likely to pose a serious danger to your child's physical well being and safety.

In addition, although there's still too much hardcore sexual content available to everyone, more and more of these sites are requiring proof that the viewer is over eighteen. Unless they're really looking for it, it's not likely that your children will stumble on hardcore sexual content. (Read on for the NASA site story where I contradict myself by discussing inadvertent exposure, but that's far more rare than people think.)

Education and building a solid and trusting relationship with your children is the first line of defense against these dangers.

What they say: The Internet is loaded with criminals who try to lure your children into sexual encounters and steal your credit card information.

Keeping it in perspective: The Internet is a community, and like all communities it has its good and bad actors, its safe and dangerous places. Predators exist everywhere, online and off. The proportion of bad actors in cyberspace is no different from that in the real world.

As long as we have criminals in this world, though, we will have ingenious people who abuse the system through the use of new technology and media. They are often the first to learn how to manipulate the new medium. The trick is knowing how to avoid trouble and taking whatever steps are necessary to protect yourself and your family and prevent problems.

What they say: The only way to keep your children safe is to keep them offline.

Keeping it in perspective: The only thing you are guaranteeing if you keep your children offline is that they will fall behind in knowing how to use and enjoy the most powerful educational and communication medium in the history of the world.

There are many things you can do to protect your children in cyberspace. It's just like protecting them anywhere else. You don't let six-year-olds wander into a big city all by themselves. You know what dangers exist "out there" and you teach your children how to avoid those dangers. You set rules and enforce them.

Protecting your children in cyberspace isn't any different. The only problem is that you don't know what the dangers are. Once you do, you can set the rules and enforce them, just like you do in the real world. It's really that simple.

▼ Adult Site Self-Regulation . . . A Partial Practical Solution

Although some of us may debate whether certain information should be censored on the Net or anywhere else, there are a lot of sites that can be labeled as "over-the-line," to which no children should be exposed. (An argument can also be made that no adults should be exposed to these sites either, but that's another story.)

These are sites which contain hard core sexual content. They are, by and large, commercial sites which charge for access or charge for viewing special graphics or photos.

Fortunately, many of these sites now require that visitors use adult identification services or a credit card to gain entrance to the site, in order to screen out children. After all, in commercial sex sites, the website operators are marketing to adults, not children. So, in many ways, parents have an "unholy alliance" with the operators of sexual sites that have voluntarily adopted the screening systems previously mandated in the now defunct sections of The Communications Decency Act. They're doing what they can to keep your children out.

▼ Global Access . . . Means Finding a Global Solution

The Internet is global. Whatever you put up in New Jersey is immediately available everywhere else in the world. (No New Jersey jokes please . . . I live there, thank you.) That means in order to control what is accessible on the Internet, we have to regulate it globally. That involves setting global standards and being able to enforce the laws on a worldwide basis.

Unfortunately, U.S. constitutional standards don't cut it everywhere else in the world. What's acceptable and legal in the U.S. may be criminal elsewhere. Some countries, to protect their citizens from political information and opinions, censor everything. Everything that their residents can access from the Internet has to run through their central government servers for prescreening and filtering.

As we seek to find ways of controlling access to certain Internet content, we need to remember that we are only a small segment of the world. Even the most extensive U.S. legislation cannot reach international sites, unless we too are willing to censor the Net through government servers, as Singapore, China and Saudi Arabia do. But since giving the government control over what information we can access is inherently offensive to most Americans, we need to find other ways of protecting ourselves and our children. And whatever we come up with will have to work world wide. (Internet site ratings, using a standard known as PICS (the Platform for Internet Content Selection) probably has the most promise. I'll discuss that in the chapter *Rating the Web . . . PICS, Platform for Internet Content Selection.*)

That's what this book is all about: alternatives to censorship on a worldwide basis.

CHAPTER 8

The Law . . . Is the Bad Stuff Legal?

A Bird's Eye View—

▼ What is the Communications Decency Act and Why Was It Ruled Unconstitutional?

▼ You Say "Obscenity" . . . I Say "Serious Literary Value"

▼ Your Community or Mine? . . . The Thomas Case

▼ Child Pornography . . . It's Still Illegal

▼ The Anatomy of a Cyber Predator . . . Protecting Your Children from Pedophiles

▼ What is the Communications Decency Act and Why Was It Ruled Unconstitutional?

(This is really boring stuff . . . but since you asked, your wish is my command.) In February 1996, as part of a larger bill deregulating the telecommunications industry, Congress enacted the controversial Communications Decency Act of 1996 (usually referred to as the "CDA"). The CDA was an attempt to regulate what was being transmitted over the Internet to children. In June 1997, the United States Supreme Court ruled that most of the CDA was unconstitutional.

First, a little legal background about free speech in the United States is in order. The First Amendment to the U.S. Constitution gives everyone in this country the right to free speech, unrestricted by government interference.

Now this doesn't mean that government is powerless to act when speech is concerned. For example, governments can set rules about when, where, and how a group can stage a protest march and forbid marches to take place at, say, three a.m. with noise levels loud enough to puncture eardrums. These "time, place, and manner" restrictions are fine, as long as they apply to everyone and are reasonable.

Generally, the government can't set rules about the content of communications. But certain exceptions to that rule exist, including one for obscenity. This is called "unprotected speech." If something is obscene, the government can regulate it, and criminalize its use.

However, the CDA tried to regulate "indecent" material, not "obscene speech." And that was its biggest problem. There's a big difference between "obscenity" and "indecency" legally, although to many of you they may seem the same. (Lawyers never speak the same language as normal people . . . you should know that by now. If we did, you wouldn't need us, and we'd all have to write books to make a living . . .) Unfortunately, Congress confused them as well. (Most members of Congress are also lawyers, so what does that say about us?)

Indecency, unlike obscenity, *is* protected by the First Amendment, and is most easily described as what makes a movie "PG"-rated rather than "G"-rated. Because it attempted to regulate indecency, the CDA, if fully enforced, could have sent parents to jail just for sending an e-mail to their teenager about responsible birth control (since information necessary to that discussion could fall under the definition of "indecency"). That's why the CDA ruling is good news for free speech advocates, but makes things more confusing for parents.

Does the CDA decision mean that parents don't have any laws to protect their children from pornography and obscenity? Of course not!

Long before the CDA was dreamed up, there were already laws on the books that outlawed pornography. Parents have a lot of laws in their arsenal. And laws that protect people on the ground almost always apply equally in cyberspace.

▼ You Say "Obscenity" . . . I Say "Serious Literary Value"

Whenever people discuss Internet hardcore sexual content and the need for regulation, they don't seem to realize how much of this content is already regulated.

As we discussed, obscenity is already illegal. Unfortunately, there is no clear definition of "obscenity." U.S. Supreme Court Justice Stewart defined "obscenity" over thirty years ago when he said, "I know it when I see it." Although that makes sense, given the difficulty in defining obscenity, it is an impossible standard to follow. We can both look at the same thing, and I'll "know" it's obscene, and you'll "know" it isn't. That's why the Supreme Court has tried to develop some tests to help other courts and communities determine what is obscene.

Right now, something is obscene if:

[1] the average person, applying contemporary community standards, would find that the work, taken as a whole, appeals to the prurient interest [the "community standards" test]; *and*

[2] the work depicts or describes, in a patently offensive way, sexual conduct specifically defined by the applicable state law [the "violation of state law" test]; *and*

[3] the work, taken as a whole, lacks serious literary, artistic, political or scientific value [the "lacks serious value" test].

In order to be obscene, the communication or work at issue must meet *all* three tests. Even if a book contains so much sex performed in such a manner that your community would find that the whole book appeals to prurient interests, and it described sexual acts that violated state law, the book would not be obscene if, "taken as a whole," the book had some serious literary or scientific value.

Also, because the test is based on community standards and local state laws, what is "obscene" under Tennessee standards may not be considered "obscene" under California standards. That makes enforcement more difficult and things a lot more confusing.

It also makes it an impossible standard when something is published on the Internet from a server in California, and is immediately available everywhere, including Tennessee. Which community standard should apply?

▼ Your Community or Mine? . . . The Thomas Case

Robert and Carleen Thomas were unlikely pornographers. Married for more than 20 years, with two teenage sons, they maintained a members-only bulletin board system (a BBS) in 1993, which predated the Web-type discussion boards. The Thomases' Amateur Action BBS was an electronic pornography "retailer" located in Milpitas, California. It sold videos and hard core sexual graphics to members of the BBS. Amateur Action had already been investigated by a local California police department a year earlier. The investigation disclosed no criminal activity (since they didn't find any child pornography and what remained didn't violate California's community standards), and the BBS posted a disclosure of the results of that investigation.

The Thomases were adamant about keeping their adult BBS free of child pornography, and would not allow any uploading of any photos to the BBS to avoid the risk of uploading any illegal material, such as child pornography. They also were very careful to make sure that any photos they used were of women over the age of eighteen. (They displayed nudist colony photos, which included children, but nothing involving sexual activity. Therefore, the photos were completely legal.)

They were also very careful to keep minors out of the membership. A text-only description of the photos was available to non-members to entice membership. Prospective members then had to fill out a form and snail mail it to the Thomases in California, who used various methods to prescreen members based on age.

In order to address the fetishes of their members, the Thomases used suggestive labels for the photos and video graphics. These labels suggested that some of the participants in these sexual activities were underage. A Postal Inspector from Memphis, Tennessee, David Dirmeyer, was searching for child pornographers and was tipped off about the BBS by someone who had discovered the site. There was an investigation, which smacked of the old Keystone Cops films, but the Thomases were tried in Tennessee using Tennessee local community standards, and found guilty on obscenity charges.

Although many of you may not be terribly sympathetic where the Thomases are concerned, you need to remember that we live in a free society where adults can do many things that children cannot. Adults can be licensed to drive cars, and can legally buy and consume alcohol and cigarettes. The U.S. Constitution prohibits any regulation which attempts to require adults to live by standards appropriate for six-year olds.

In 1957, U.S. Supreme Court Justice Frankfurter (generally thought of as one of the most brilliant of all the Supreme Court jurists) wrote the decision which overturned a Michigan state statute that made it a crime (actually a misdemeanor) to publish or sell publications tending to corrupt the morals of minors.

The Supreme Court found that states may not impose a standard which restricts adults to reading only that material which is suitable for young children. Justice Frankfurter compared the restrictive state statute to "burn[ing] the house to roast the pig." The lowest common denominator test for sexual content was thus firmly rejected by the Supreme Court. Yet, with the advent of technology and worldwide access to everything published on the Internet, that issue needs to be clarified, especially in light of the Thomases' conviction.

So, where is the community standards test now, with a worldwide community of viewers of all website material? I suspect that we'll be addressing this issue again, before long, in the courts.

▼ Child Pornography . . . It's Still Illegal

Transmission of obscenity and child pornography is already illegal, whether it's transmitted online or by any other means. There are many laws (both federal and state laws), and many ways in which those laws can be enforced to prosecute pedophile sexual offenders, child solicitation and child pornography.

In the United States it's already illegal to:

* entice or coerce a minor to engage in sexually explicit conduct
* import or transport obscenity
* knowingly receive child pornography
* advertise child pornography
* depict minors engaged in sexually explicit conduct (even virtually)
* depict someone engaged in sexually explicit conduct who appears to be a child
* advertise or promote sexually explicit conduct by giving the impression that minors are engaged in sexually explicit conduct

In order to avoid the community standards problem, and recognizing that child pornography has a serious adverse impact on the welfare of children, Congress enacted special laws outlawing child pornography. The U.S. Supreme Court supported this view when it determined that child pornography didn't have to be "obscene" to be subject to regulation. Child pornography was deemed to be a separate unprotected speech category under the First Amendment. The Supreme Court set out a new standard, just for child pornography, which differs from the three-prong standard for obscenity I already described in the subchapter *You Say "Obscenity" . . . I Say "Serious Literary Value."*

Under this special child pornography standard, it is no longer necessary to find that the materials appealed to prurient interests of an average person, that the sexual conduct portrayed be done so in an offensive manner, or that the material be considered as a whole.

The courts now focus on:

(1) whether the depiction focuses on the child's genitals or pubic area; and

(2) whether the setting is sexually suggestive; and

(3) whether, taking into consideration the age of the child, she or he is depicted in an unnatural pose and inappropriate attire; and

(4) whether the child is only partially clothed or nude; and

(5) whether the depiction suggests sexual "coyness" or is designed to elicit a sexual response.

The federal laws are very comprehensive in outlawing child pornography. (Most states have very comprehensive child pornography laws, as well.) The federal Protection of Children Against Sexual Exploitation Act of 1977 (the "PCASEA") makes it a federal crime for anyone to employ, use, persuade, induce, entice, or coerce any minor to engage in, or assist another person in engaging a minor in, any sexually explicit conduct for the purpose of producing a visual depiction of such conduct. It also criminalizes activities of parents, legal guardians, and custodians of minors who knowingly permitted the minors to engage or assist in such conduct.

The provisions of the PCASEA have been amended several times to expand its protection. The most recent of these amendments, the Child Pornography Prevention Act of 1996 (the "CPPA"), was enacted specifically to combat the use of computer technology to distort visual depictions of pornography to convey the *impression* that children are involved in sexual activities, even if no children were actually used in the creation of the images. The law is based on the premise that depictions of children engaged in sexually explicit conduct is inherently dangerous. (It's already under challenge as being unconstitutional, although a recent decision found that it did not violate the constitution.)

Specifically, the CPPA outlaws:

any visual depiction, including any photograph, film, video, picture, or computer or computer-generated image or picture . . . of sexually explicit conduct, where

(A) the production involves the use of a minor engaging in sexually explicit conduct;

(B) such visual depiction is, *or appears to be*, of a minor engaging in sexually explicit conduct;

(C) such visual depiction has been created, adapted, or modified to *appear* that such an identifiable minor is engaging in sexually explicit conduct; or

(D) such visual depiction is advertised, promoted, presented, described, or distributed in such a manner that *conveys the impression* that the material is or contains a visual depiction of a minor engaging in sexually explicit conduct. . . .

18 U.S.C. § 2256(8).

Many parenting groups have been active in getting new laws passed on the federal and state levels. Enough is Enough (www.enough.org) stands out as being very active in this area. Donna Rice Hughes (of former Gary Hart fame), a spokeswoman for Enough is Enough, appeared with me on Comcast's Family Talk Show, hosted by Mary Ambrose, to discuss protecting children in cyberspace. She has been lobbying for stronger laws to protect children. Although Ms. Hughes and I may disagree on certain matters, including the coverage of the CDA, there are many matters upon which we agree and the group has been very effective.

I warned you that the legal discussion can be very boring, but so many of you have asked me to include this information that I have broken my rule about trying not to sound like a lawyer. These laws, remember, are currently in effect, and only a small sampling of laws regulating child pornography and child welfare. In addition, these laws may change, and may have changed since we published this book. Finally, you should not rely on this discussion or any legal discussion as legal advice.

As I mentioned, there are many state laws, which supplement federal protection, as well. But since cyberspace crosses state lines, and uses other interstate devices, such as telephone lines, federal laws typically apply to these matters. And, as I have said repeatedly, the Clinton-Gore administration has been very sympathetic to parents' concerns about protecting children in cyberspace.

▼ The Anatomy of a Cyber Predator . . . Protecting Your Children from Pedophiles

There have been many cases recently in the press where pedophiles and other adults have abducted and attempted to abduct children and teenagers they have seduced online. I debated whether I should discuss any of these cases, not wanting to sensationalize them. But if explaining the methods used might make parents more aware, and their children safer, it's worth it.

Each case differs, but the pedophiles tend to use the same general tactics. They first strike up a conversation with the child, trying to create a relationship of trust and friendship. They often masquerade as another child or teenager, typically of the opposite sex. Once they have broken down barriers of caution, they begin introducing sexual topics gradually, often with the use of child pornography to give the child the impression that other children are regularly involved in sexual activities. Then they begin to approach the child's own sexuality and curiosity, by asking questions and giving them "assignments," like wearing special underwear or performing certain sexual acts. These assignments eventually broaden to phone calls and the exchange of sexually explicit photographs or videos of the child. Finally, the pedophile attempts to arrange a face-to-face meeting. (They may also have divulged their true age at this point.)

There are many stages at which the pedophile can be thwarted by an observant parent. In addition, children with healthy friendships and a strong and trusting relationship with their parents are less likely to fall victim to pedophiles. Pedophiles typically prey on a child's loneliness. They feed the child's complaints about her homelife—creating an "us" versus "them" atmosphere. This atmosphere does two things: it creates a distance between the child and her parents while at the same time bringing the child into a special secret alliance with the pedophile.

I have followed one particular case involving a New Jersey teenager and an Ohio adult predator. Luckily, the liaison was discovered before the girl met the man face-to-face. But it had gone on for one and a half years before being discovered by the girl's mother. As you read the details, think about what could have been done to discover the situation earlier and how you can use these precautions to protect your children.

Paul Brown, Jr., an Ohio resident, was 46 years old. He was also unemployed, over 400 pounds and living in a basement. He had accounts with AOL, Prodigy and CompuServe. Mary (a hypothetical name for the young girl involved) was twelve when her mother, a school teacher, bought her a computer, reportedly because Mary was having problems making friends. When she got online, Mary posted a message on Prodigy, in Spring 1995, looking for a pen pal. In her message she described herself as a teenage girl. Paul Brown, Jr. responded to the message, using his real name but identifying himself as a fifteen year-old boy.

Brown and Mary maintained an e-mail and telephone relationship for several months. As the relationship became more involved, they began writing letters and Mary sent Brown a photograph. He told her that he was living at home with his mother, and was hoping to find a girlfriend. In early August, Brown asked Mary for a "favor."

> If I sent you a roll of film, could you get one of your friends to take pictures of you in different outfits and maybe hairstyles. Make-up if you use any, and different poses. Some sexy if possible. Please. Baby for me. Thanx. You're the best. Love Ya.

Mary complied. For the next eight months, they continued to converse and correspond and Mary sent additional photos. Brown encouraged her with juvenile antics, such as using stickers in his letters to her saying things like "Getting better all the time!" In May 1996, Brown sent Mary a special love note. "Saying I love you . . . seems to be an understatement. At the age of [14] you have captured my heart and made it sing . . . I love everything about you . . ."

Shortly thereafter, Brown confessed to being in his twenties. He also suggested that Mary videotape herself in sexually provocative poses. She did. After Brown had reviewed her videotape, he returned it to her with instructions to redo the tape and include views of her genitalia and breasts. He later admitted to being divorced and in his thirties.

He reportedly also sent her small gifts, from time to time. A few months later, in response to Brown's promise to pass copies of the tape to four members of a rock-band Mary admired, she sent additional videotapes to Brown. (Brown told Mary that he knew the band members very well.) Each tape was sent to Brown, designated for a different member of the band and containing sexually explicit conduct.

Brown apparently had also sent her his size 48 underwear. When her mother discovered the underwear, the authorities were notified. Tracing Brown through phone records, special agents of the FBI in Cleveland seized the videotapes and photos of Mary and of more than ten other teenage girls from across the country as well.

Mary was fourteen when this was all discovered. Brown recently pled guilty to enticing a minor to produce sexually explicit photos and videos and was sentenced to a little less than five years (the maximum penalty for a first offense). In a written statement to Brown, following all of this, Mary said "I trusted you. I thought you were my friend."

There are several things which stand out in this case. One, interstate phone calls were made by Mary. Parents should always be reviewing long distance bills for suspicious calls. Two, Mary was lonely. These kinds of children are often the most vulnerable. A parent should be involved in their online friendships, and monitor their online lives. And, three, as hard as it is to know what our kids are doing when we're not around, a year and a-half is a long time for a relationship to be going on and not discovered. You should spend time learning who your children's friends are.

But, Monday morning quarterbacking is always easier than playing the game in real time. We may look at the situation and say that could never happen to one of our kids. However, there but for the grace of God go all of us . . .

Knowing your child is lonely and has problems making friends is the first sign that your child may fall prey to a pedophile or cyber predator. They can spot lonely children. They can also spot kids who are new online and may not yet know all the rules. Pedophiles befriend these kids, and patiently build trust and a relationship . . . looking towards the day when they can meet face-to-face.

Encourage your children to make online friends, but keeping the computer in a central location and learning about their online friends is an important way to avoid these special secret relationships. Education is important in avoiding this danger too. (Had Mary been forewarned about how pedophiles operate online, she may have been more attentive to how old Brown sounded on the phone, and been more aware of his classic tactics.) So is control over incoming and outgoing information, using technology blockers. (You'll learn about all these options in Part Three.) These kinds of situations can be avoided, if you're very careful, educate your children and keep your eyes open.

CHAPTER 9

Cleaning Up Cyberspace . . . Helping to Enforce the Law and Get the Web Rated

A Bird's Eye View—

▼ Who Enforces the Laws in Cyberspace?

▼ How You Can Make a Difference

▼ Who Enforces the Laws in Cyberspace?

In surfing the Web for sexual and other objectionable content, I have learned far more about the dark side of the Web than I would have cared to know. Late one night, while I was clicking on mini-photos of outrageous sexual acts to see what was screened by filtering software and what got through the software, my eighteen-year-old daughter walked into my room. I found myself trying to block my monitor screen to prevent her from seeing the photos (like a child trying to conceal something from a parent, rather than *vice versa*).

Many of the sites I found contained sexual content already illegal in the United States, and most of those sites were hosted in the U.S. Each of us can bear some of the responsibility for cleaning up these sites by reporting them to law enforcement officials. The number of these sites is growing so quickly that law enforcement officials can't keep up without our help. Often they don't even know where or how to start.

Part of the problem in enforcing these laws is the lack of cybertraining and resources for law enforcement. It's hard enough for them to try to locate criminals in their own jurisdictions, without having to now track website operators and cyberpredators located anywhere in the world.

Remember that if something happens in cyberspace that would constitute a crime in real space, it's still a crime. Unfortunately, there is no law enforcement group specifically charged with enforcing the law on the Internet. Some U.S. law enforcement agencies, however, have been designated as the first line of defense when U.S. laws apply. (Actually, as I've already told you, parents and schools are the first line of defense, and law enforcement is a distant second, but who's quibbling?)

The U.S. federal government has now made protecting our children in cyberspace a priority. According to President Clinton, the number of people assigned from the Justice Department and FBI to protect children from computer-related exploitation, pornography, solicitation and obscenity was recently increased by 50 percent. It's an important start.

In addition, a special task force of the U.S. Customs Service has been set up to handle Internet child pornography complaints. 1-800-BE-ALERT (1-800-232-5378) is a 24-hour hotline that will route your complaint to the right law enforcement agency. Many states are also setting up similar task forces. You should contact your state attorney general to find out whom you should contact locally.

Several not-for-profit organizations are also devoted to child safety and helping parents protect their children in cyberspace. One of the best is the National Center for Missing and Exploited Children at 1-800-THE-LOST (1-800-843-5678). Their website is at www.missingkids.org. A few other organizations are particularly noteworthy, and have great websites devoted to this subject, as well. I'll list them at www.familyguidebook.com.

▼ How You Can Make a Difference

We're really a very powerful group, parents. If we act together, we can make a huge difference.

If you find an objectionable site, let the rating and blocking software companies know about it. Bess, the server-level blocking and filtering software that we review later on, already has a form you can submit to have a site reviewed, either to get it blocked or unblocked. We decided to borrow this idea.

To get this movement started, at www.familyguidebook.com we have set up a form where anyone can notify the major parental control software companies about a site they want to be reviewed or added to their "bad site lists." We will also have a form you can submit if you think a site has been improperly listed in the "bad site list" and should be removed. You fill out the form once, and we submit it to all the companies for you. It's a start.

If you visit a site you enjoy, ask them to make sure it's rated using a PICS-compliant standard (a Webwide rating system standard which allows sites to be rated by rating agencies like movies are rated, based on content.). We have a form you can use for that too, which notifies the webmaster that you want their site rated so you can access it using the PICS standard ratings. It also copies the biggest rating agencies with your request so they can follow up.

It's not a perfect system, but it might get things moving. And within the next year, with the help of interested parents everywhere, I suspect that much of the Web will be rated. Hopefully other child safety program companies will do the same thing, and parents, librarians and teachers can work together to help rate the Internet. If we all pitch in, the whole Web will be rated before you know it. (Even if you oppose filtering, rating the Internet is the best defense we have to attempts to regulate free speech.)

CHAPTER 10

Understanding the Other Risks . . . Hidden Dangers

A Bird's Eye View—

▼ Misinformation and Hype . . . Know Your Source

▼ Hatred and Bigotry

▼ Cyberstalkers and Predators

▼ Just Plain Rude People . . . Flaming

▼ Cookies and Other Risks to Your Privacy

▼ Targeting Cybertots . . . Marketing to Your Children Online

▼ Mom . . . How Do You Build a Bomb?

▼ Drugs, Alcohol and Tobacco . . . Oh! My!

▼ Are We Raising Future Riverboat Gamblers in Cyberspace?

Even though pornography and sexual content are receiving most of the attention, there are other dangers in cyberspace too: tobacco and alcohol advertisements, violence and gore, misinformation and hate, and sites that collect and sell private information about your kids and your family, and use interactive marketing strategies that target cybertots. These may be far more dangerous to your children than sexual content. Online "addiction" is also a growing problem.

And, since we're here to discuss risks and how to avoid them, we need to warn you about the dangers your children (and their friends) may pose to others in cyberspace, including you. They may give out credit card information, share private information about you and your family, infringe copyrights, commit computer crimes and lose or destroy your files. (Just ask my sister about her cherubic three-year-old daughter.) In some cases, they may not even know they're doing it, but the dangers are just as real.

Finally, there are risks that viruses pose to your computer files. Lots of things to think about . . . but we provide solutions and tips for all of them here and elsewhere in the book.

▼ Misinformation and Hype . . . Know Your Source

The Internet is an inexpensive and easy method of publishing information. Anyone can be a publisher, and everyone is an expert. Separating the truth from fiction in cyberspace is one of the hardest tasks we have. Con artists, scam artists, cultists and just plain nut cases thrive in this free atmosphere.

And how can you tell marketing hype from fact? What information is reliable and what is pure bunk? How do your kids separate Elvis sightings from scholarly discourse? How do we, for that matter? (I guess that's another book . . .)

Robin Raskin (Internet Mom), sees misinformation as a big problem too, one that the latest technology can't provide a quick fix for. "Most parental control software," she states, "while it does a decent job of blocking pornographic material, does not do a very good job of blocking kooks, pyramid schemes, racism, or outright lies. These are subtleties that no technology can easily block." I guess that leaves it up to us.

Whether we like it or not, the buck stops here. It's our job as parents to teach our children the difference between hype, misinformation and quality sources wherever they find them. We also need to teach them that not everyone is what he or she seems. Most of us have already started teaching them that. Unfortunately, our children have to learn these things early.

Every time I used to wheel my kids through the supermarket checkout aisle, supermarket tabloids would blast outrageous headlines at them: "Men from Mars Father Children in Indiana," "Four Hundred Year Old Woman Shares the Secrets of Long Life" . . . Once they could read, I would have to explain the truth. (Although I could rarely explain it well enough, since I'm not sure I understand how they can get away with saying these things . . . and I'm a lawyer.)

Every time a publishing company's sweepstakes envelope would arrive, addressed to them, heralding that they had won umpteen million dollars, I would have to explain the small print.

But whether we're in the supermarket or handing out the mail, we're there to answer any questions. When our kids are surfing alone, we need to teach them how to do it for themselves. That's much harder. Try to get them to share what they learn and read in cyberspace with you, so you can do a reality check. Surf with them and point out outrageous sources, which should be approached with skepticism.

HBO had done a great special teaching children about truths (and tricks) in advertising. Something like that may be in order about cyberspace sources, too.

▼ Hatred and Bigotry

Questioning the source, and understanding that hate groups abound on the Internet go hand-in-hand. Ideas repugnant to many people have found a global audience in cyberspace. We need to make sure that our children become an informed, skeptical and unwilling audience where hate and bigotry are concerned.

We have to teach them that many people on the Internet have biases and prejudices that clash with our values. It's a good time to explain what your values are, and to explain why you believe what you do. A solid grounding is your best weapon against others trying to sway your children's opinions.

When our children are exposed to outrageous bigotry and hatred online or anywhere else, we can help them understand the dangers of prejudice and the importance of tolerance. The more they have a chance to talk and share ideas with other children around the world, the more they will learn how alike we all are. (I've included some international kids sites in Part 4, just for this purpose.)

The Internet strips away everything but how well you communicate your ideas. The Internet is gender-age-physical disability-race-and religion-blind. When you meet people online, you don't know how old they are, whether they are male or female, what color their skin is or how they pray. It's the most egalitarian environment in the world. No geographical borders ... seamless global communication. That's the beauty of the Internet.

People are often surprised to learn I'm a woman, because I have an unusual name. Their tone online often changes, too, after they find out I'm a woman. Why that should be the case, I don't know. But, we all do it. We all treat people differently based on their age, or where they're from. It's part of how we're trained.

Point out faulty expectations and prejudices with your children by asking them what they think the person they're talking to online is like. Then give them alternative descriptions telling them that the person is 50, not 15, male, not female, and of a different race. Ask them how that changes things ... and why. This may be an easy way to start to teach them about prejudice and stereotypes.

Mark Twain put his finger on it when he said: "Travel is fatal to prejudice, bigotry, and narrow-mindedness, and many of our people need it sorely on these accounts. Broad, wholesome, charitable views of men and things cannot be acquired by vegetating in one little corner of the earth all one's lifetime." On the Internet, our children travel the world everyday. We need to make sure that they understand that they are truly part of the global community.

▼ Cyberstalkers and Predators

One of the biggest problems with cyberpredators is that they operate in your home. But improving your alarm system and adding better locks won't keep them out. They enter your living room through your computer. Your children feel safe in their pajamas and slippers, with you seated a few feet away watching television or reading. They are otherwise safe and secure. Therefore, people who converse with them while they are in this comfort zone are safe, too, as safe as any other invited guest in your home.

Cyberpredators count on this sense of security in lulling your children into letting down their guard. There is a sense of intimacy online that cyberpredators take advantage of to convince your children that they are not strangers at all.

It's your job to teach your children that these people **ARE** strangers, no matter how friendly they sound. If you're close at hand, and make it a point to get to know their online friends, the cyberpredator's task will be much harder. Protecting your children online is like buying an anti-theft device for your car. Although it can't completely prevent thieves from stealing your car if they really want to, hopefully you've made it hard enough that they'll go somewhere else.

Report any attempts to lure your child into a face-to-face meeting to law enforcement officials immediately! And if anyone is harassing your children online, by sending repeated unsolicited e-mails and stalking them elsewhere online, report it to the sysop.

▼ Just Plain Rude People . . . Flaming

Sometimes, largely because they feel that they are somewhat anonymous (hiding behind their computer screens) and because they have a captive audience, people say things they would never dream of saying to someone's face. Often these messages are directed at our children, in discussion rooms, chatrooms and e-mail messages. It also happens more often than most of us would like.

Many parents who have been online for awhile have worked out ways of dealing with abusive or vulgar messages (flames) that are sent to their children. One of these parents, Bill Bickel, has several personal websites where he highlights stories about his children. (His websites can be found at www.concentric.net/~Bbickel.) He posted the message below at his site to help other parents deal with flaming directed at their children. (Bill wrote it referring to messages received in connection with his children's sites, but it applies equally as well to e-mail messages or chatroom flaming.)

It is reprinted here, with his kind permission. It's good advice, and I suggest following it (whether your child is on the receiving end or on the sending end):

[Sometimes people send our children] inappropriate, vulgar, or even abusive messages. Aaron's received one of each.

Of course we all pre-screen our kids' e-mail, but it's still upsetting to think that somebody's sending our child this sort of thing. The fact that it's probably just another child doing it isn't much comfort, because it isn't a physical threat we're worried about (the abusive mail Aaron received came from Australia. We live in New Jersey).

My suggestion is: Don't ignore it, and don't wait for a second message. The next message will probably get sent to another child. This sort of thing should be stopped immediately.

Send a copy of the message to POSTMASTER@whatever.com, adding, simply, "Please do something about this." I did this twice, and one account was shut down and the other was suspended (the account holders' little darlings had done this sort of thing before). For good measure, I cc'd my messages to the account holders, leaving the subject blank (so the kids wouldn't be alerted and try intercepting them).

For the message that was merely inappropriate, I just sent a copy of the original to the account holder, again deleting the subject. We received an apology within 24 hours, and a promise that their teenage daughter would not be sitting in front of the computer for some time.

Big brother is watching you . . . Even if you don't take the action that Bickel did, you should try to screen e-mail so that you can intercept hurtful messages to your younger children.

Your older children and teens should be taught to report the flame, or ignore it. They shouldn't get involved in a flaming war, no matter how tempting it may be. These things escalate fast, and get out of control quickly.

And teach them not to flame others, either!

▼ Cookies and Other Risks to Your Privacy

There are two ways you lose anonymity online—automatically, through "cookies," and voluntarily by supplying information when you register at a site or fill out a form sharing that information. Either way, you should know who's collecting the information and what happens to the information they collect.

▼ COOKIES

Cookies are software applications (mini-programs) that a website server passes to your computer where it is installed on your hard drive and instructed to collect and store certain information. The stored information can then be transferred back to the server upon request. By using a cookie, a website operator can tell where you've been and a lot of information about you and your computer.

Cookies aren't all bad, though (especially the chocolate-covered mint Girl Scout cookies . . . sorry, I couldn't control myself). Many perform helpful functions, like making it easier to access a site that requires you to register. It remembers the information you gave the website when you first registered, and recalls it when you type in your password and screen name for your next visit. If you didn't have a cookie, you'd have to completely re-register every time you visited the site.

In addition, if you're shopping online, and want to purchase more than one item, you need a cookie. It's one of the ways you can collect all your purchases to transmit to the server at one time (in a cyber shopping cart). Otherwise you'd have to select and purchase the items one-by-one.

The cookies are added to your hard drive by your web browser. Sometimes Web advertisers add cookies when you click on their ads, to track where you go. They should be asking if it's okay to install a cookie, and as the technology improves, each of us will be able to tell our web browsers to reject all cookies, unless they're cookies we need. You can look into your hard drive directory and probably find several sitting there now. Most of them use the word "cookie" in their name. Netscape allows you to set it to ask permission before accepting a cookie.

There are websites that help you test what information is available to others from your computer through cookie technology. The Federal Trade Commission has a very good site located at "www.ftc.gov/WWW/bcp/privacy2/comments1/ junk/cookies.htm#request." When you visit the page it lets you know what information is available from your web browser about you and your computer. It also tells you what others can determine based on that information. You may be unpleasantly surprised.

There are ways to remove cookies and ways you can surf anonymously. Before you remove any, though, you should make sure you don't need the cookie to access any particular site with which you're registered. For example *The New York Times* site uses a cookie. If you remove it, you won't be able to access their site and will have to reregister.

The balancing act is between allowing websites to customize their information delivery to match your needs and allowing certain companies to invade your privacy just to collect data about you for their own purposes. The secret is to let you make the choice as to where you share the information.

▼ WHAT WE GIVE AWAY . . . GIVING UP PRIVACY

The information we give away is far more dangerous than current cookie technology. (Due to the quickly advancing technology, if you ask me again in another year, my opinion might change.) When you combine the two, though, the amount of personal information available online about us is scary. The information our children give away is the most dangerous of all, because we don't know what they're telling people, and who those people are. And . . . they're giving it away every time they log on!

According to a recent survey conducted by the Center for Media Education, a children's media watchdog group located in Washington, D.C., roughly 90 percent of the major children's sites they surveyed solicit personal information about the children. The information they seek differs site by site, but in most cases includes at least the child's full name and address, as well as age.

Rarely do the sites recommend that the children check with their parents before giving out this information, and often the children receive free gifts or chances to win prizes for completing the questionnaires.

Some sites are using this information just for their own marketing, while others are selling the data they collect to third parties and advertisers.

Most of us, who specialize in online privacy legal issues, separate the data-gathering purposes into three groups:

- data gathered by the site operator to track your activities at the site and your preferences, for internal marketing and planning purposes only.
- data gathered by the site operator and disseminated to third parties, in aggregate form, for various purposes, including demographics and preferences of site visitors as a whole.
- data gathered by the site operator or advertisers at the site, which is identifiable as to each visitor and disseminated to third parties.

In an attempt to provide guidance to members of its advertising industry group, The Better Business Bureau's Children's Advertising Review Unit (CARU) compiled voluntary guidelines to be used when gathering children's data on the Internet. I've described them below, and we should all be insisting that sites that gather information about our children adhere to these guidelines. If they don't, be sure to let the website operator know how you feel. We plan to set up a spot at our site to "blow the whistle" on the kid sites which don't adhere to the guidelines, so you can share this information with other parents.

CARU's Recommended Guidelines to Website Operators Who Collect Information From and About Children

1. Children should be reminded to ask their parent's permission before supplying the requested information and told clearly when the information is only optional.
2. The advertiser should disclose the purpose for requesting the information, in language the child can understand.
3. If cookies or other similar electronic tracking devices are used by the site, they should be disclosed to the child and her parent. They should also disclose what information is being collected.
4. If advertisers collect identifiable information from children online, they should take reasonable efforts to make sure parents consent, and if possible, use a secure site for transmission of the children's e-mail addresses.
5. Children should be encouraged to use a screen name or alias when posting publicly at the site, even if the child has to register using her entire name.
6. They should also let the child know if the information will be shared with third parties, and take reasonable measures to give the parents an opportunity to object.
7. Finally, if e-mail is sent to the child from the site for promotional purposes, the advertiser should provide a mechanism for the parents to remove their child from the mailing list.

▼ KidsCom and the FTC

KidsCom was one of the earliest kids-only sites on the Internet, having been online since February 1995. It doesn't use cookies or similar devices to gather electronic information, but collects data through its registration forms, contests and in connection with finding pen pals.

KidsCom has a terrific children's site for children from ages 4–15 (www.kidscom.com), but ran into trouble recently for insufficient disclosure about data collection from children at their site. Last year the Center for Media Education filed a petition with the Federal Trade Commission asserting that the

KidsCom site's data collection violated the consumer protection laws because they failed to disclose the purpose for collecting the data.

In July 1997, the FTC agreed, but declined to take any punitive action since KidsCom had already changed their data collection practices and cooperated in the FTC investigation.

In all fairness, KidsCom wasn't any worse, and in many ways was substantially better than many other children's sites. (They didn't share specific data for third party commercial use, only aggregate anonymous data. In addition they always suggested that children consult with their parents before supplying information.)

In making this ruling, the FTC for the first time issued guidelines for data collection from children on the Internet. It is now clear that companies cannot gather "personally identifiable information" from children unless parents are notified. In addition, these companies have to obtain parents' consent before sharing such information with third parties.

KidsCom now sends a confirmatory e-mail to parents when kids register at the site, disclosing their data collection practices. Then parents can object to releasing aggregate data, containing their child's information, to third parties.

Prior to the investigation, KidsCom used to make certain information available to prospective pen pals when the children signed up for their "Key Pal" pen pal program. Now KidsCom requires parents to authorize the release of this information by facsimile or snail mail (a regular letter) before the pen pal information can be released to prospective pen pals.

▼ KIDSCOM AND KIDBE SAFE

KidsCom has used the adverse press and media attention to its advantage. It is now attempting to lead other child content sites in the "safe site" initiative, and is introducing a new cartoon character to identify preapproved safe sites. If a site satisfies strict guidelines for protecting children's privacy and encouraging parental involvement, it will be eligible to display KidsCom's Kidbe Safe character. Finding a brand to approve site content is a good idea, but perhaps another less involved testing agency should be leading the movement.

▼ Targeting Cybertots . . . Marketing to Your Children Online

As more and more kids are getting online, more and more advertisers are marketing to kids online and seeking private information about them and about you in order to better define that marketing. Online advertising, unfortunately, when compared to television advertising, is still the Wild West when it comes to marketing to kids—the Wild West during the early Gold Rush days.

Although advertising on the Net hasn't panned out as advertisers originally hoped, it's the next frontier. And the statistics are very appealing to marketers.

Children Purchasing and Advertising: Quick Facts

- Children control over $150 billion in purchasing power.
- Children's television advertisers spend $700 million annually.
- Sales of children's computer products exceed $5 billion each year ($1.6 billion in hardware and $3.5 billion in software).
- Jupiter Communications estimates that pay-game sites will be a $2.5 billion industry by 2002 (at least $745 million of this will be attributed to children) and $350 million of all services online will be purchased by children.

To understand the impact advertising can have on children, we only need to think about how many commercial jingles our kids know, and remember how young they were when they could first identify the Toys "R" Us sign and McDonalds' golden arches. (My kids were under a year old.)

And our kids aren't much different from us when we were young. Remember Soupy Sales? In his most famous (infamous?) TV show segment, he asked his viewers to go into their Mommy's and Daddy's wallets, take out all those little green pieces of paper and send them to him. A lot of kids did. It created a scandal for Soupy and proved how susceptible children are to media influence.

You should be teaching your children to be smart consumers . . . "buyer beware" should be the motto. Teaching them to be smart consumers online is the same as it is offline, with one exception. Online, the ads are customized to your kids. They're designed to reach one kid only, yours, and can use his name, your pet's name and the town you live in to help customize the sales pitch. They are also interactive and mesmerizing. It's our job as parents to help our children separate advertising fact from fiction and limit the amount of hype delivered to our children online.

▼ HELPING YOUR KIDS UNDERSTAND WHERE THE ADS START
AND THE CONTENT ENDS

One of the biggest issues relating to children's advertising is helping them understand when the show ends and the ads begin. Ever wonder why we only hear "Now, a word from our sponsor . . ." during children's programming? Television advertising directed at children has been specially regulated by the Federal Communications Commission since 1974. During children's shows, commercials can only be aired after a five-second gap, called a "bumper," from the program itself. It marks the end of the show and the beginning of the ad. (That's the reason for the announcement.)

In addition, the amount of time, in aggregate, devoted to commercials during a children's program is limited. Finally, in order to keep their favorite cartoon character from turning the entire program into a commercial, other restrictions also exist that are aimed at separating the show's content from the advertising. Products cannot be promoted as part of the television show's content, and characters from the show cannot be used in commercials aired during their show.

But these restrictions have not yet been adopted in cyberspace. At this time, other than FTC and state regulation of deceptive advertising, there are no laws specifically applicable to online children's advertising.

▼ WHAT'S BEING DONE TO ADDRESS PARENTS' PRIVACY AND
ADVERTISING CONCERNS?

The Children's Advertising Review Unit (CARU) of the Council of Better Business Bureaus was created twenty-three years ago by the National Advertising Review Council (NARC) as part of an effort by the advertising industry and the Council of Better Business Bureaus to be responsive to the concerns of parents and to provide an advertising industry standard for children's advertising. They recently added new guidelines relating to online advertising to children, in addition to the privacy and data collection guidelines discussed previously.

CARU's first rule is that "children should always be told when they are being targeted for a sale." The guidelines (found at www.bbb.org/advertising/caruguid. html#making) also call for advertisers to make a reasonable effort to make sure that any purchase made by a child is made with the parents' knowledge. Otherwise, parents should be able to cancel the purchase and receive a full credit. They also warn advertisers that under existing state laws, parents may not be held responsible for sales contracts entered into by their children.

Advertising industry groups have recommended voluntary compliance, hoping to hold off government regulatory action, and certain children's sites have implemented programs to address parent's concerns.

KidsCom (the same site that was cited by the FTC for deceptive practices in gathering children's data at the site) is way ahead of the pack when it comes to helping children identify advertisements online.

 Last year, it introduced The Ad Bug, a cartoon character who identifies advertisements and promotional material at the KidsCom.com site and on other sites participating in the program, like Avery Dennison Corporation's Avery KidsSite, "www.avery.com/kids." (It's also a great way to make sure our kids notice each ad!)

These are just a few of the potential solutions being offered, but only time will tell if they'll be enough. Unless the companies promoting to your children online start addressing parents' concerns, they may have to face government regulations aimed at U.S. advertisers' marketing to children online.

In the end, though, advertisers have nothing to gain by alienating parents. The smart ones know that. Let the website operators (and me) know if you think they're doing a good job in balancing promotion and content, and make sure you let them know if you think they're marketing irresponsibly to your children. If cleaning up their act means that they'll sell more products, it'll get cleaned up faster than any of us could have imagined.

Parent power!

▼ Mom . . . How Do You Build a Bomb?

There are plenty of books available on the Internet. *The Big Book of Mischief* is just one of them, but a very special one. Don't be fooled by its innocent name, the "Mischief" it refers to is serious injury and death. It teaches violence, and gives our kids the tools they need to get the job done.

Part I is subtitled, "The Terrorist's Handbook." Of course it comes with the requisite disclaimer: that serious injury or death could result from any attempt to make the recipes it contains, and that the book is being provided merely for your reading pleasure. (Apparently, everyone has a lawyer these days . . .)

Then there's the *Anarchists' Cookbook*, which explains how you can buy whatever you need to build a bomb at your local grocery, hardware and farming supply stores.(It even includes a recipe to make nitroglycerine.)

And who are the terrorists armed with this deadly and easily accessible information? According to local newspaper reports from around the United States, these "terrorists" include our kids.

So, what can you do? You can take measures to make sure your children understand the dangers of these kinds of things and you can keep a lookout for signs that your kids may be getting into trouble. Serious trouble.

After a bombing near-miss, the police department in Jackson Township, New Jersey identified things parents should look out for if they're concerned that their children may be getting into the bomb building business: pails or buckets, soda or bleach bottles, pipes, ammonia, glycerine or paraffin. "Bomb guide found at Jackson school," by Jeffery S. Rubin, *Asbury Park Press*, Feb. 1, 1996]

Parents should also be on the alert for children collecting empty containers, or containers that appear out of the norm, and shotgun shells that may have been broken open and emptied of their powder. Parents in Jackson Township were warned to call the police if they found anything that looked suspicious rather than attempting to deal with the "bomb" or bomb ingredients themselves.

Technology may also be a big help in making sure your kids aren't accessing this information online. I've discussed filtering at length in Part 3 and how you can block incoming content which uses certain words, like "bombs."

An interesting account appeared in a *Ladies Home Journal* article in March 1997 about a mother, Cheryl, whose thirteen-year-old son, Michael, suffered burns over 25 percent of his body when he and a friend were building a smoke bomb from instructions they had found on the Internet. It turned out that while Cheryl didn't have a home computer, her son's friend had Internet access at home, and the boys would go online unsupervised. Learning how to build a bomb turned out to be as simple as typing the word "bomb" into their favorite search engine.

At first, understandably, Cheryl was furious and blamed the Internet. Her anger that this type of information was available to children online, however, softened when she realized that her son could just as easily have found the bomb-building information at their local library. Then, recognizing the importance computer literacy plays in a child's life, the family bought a home computer four months after the accident, and subscribed to an online service. But they vowed to protect themselves and their son online.

And what did they do to protect themselves and Michael while online? They put the computer in the family room, not in Michael's bedroom. They also set rules for him, such as only going online when a parent is home. They also monitor him closely. They chose not to use any parental controls or filtering software, deciding instead to trust Michael to follow the rules. This is one family's way of dealing with Internet risks, and a good one. Trust and education go a long way with the right child. ("My son built a bomb." by White, Cheryl; Johnson, Heather Moors, *Ladies Home Journal*, March 1997.)

▼ Drugs, Alcohol and Tobacco . . . Oh! My!

Everyone else seems to concentrate on Internet sites that promote the use of drugs, alcohol and tobacco. I don't think there's much more to say, other than the fact that there are many glossy commercial sites that promote drinking and smoking activities which are otherwise lawful for adults and many sites that promote drugs.

These sites are also attractive to children. (Many child protection groups believe that children are being targeted by these advertisers, and they may be right.) But whether the attraction is intentional or not, our children need to be educated about the dangers of drugs, alcohol and tobacco. (With the new tobacco company litigation settlement, tobacco advertising on the Internet will probably be wiped out soon, anyway.) Keyword blocking software can be used to make sure our children don't stumble across these sites while surfing. In addition, sites that you have found which promote these products can be placed on a "bad site" blocked list.

But education and values enforcement is the best defense against this kind of information. You may already have educated your children thoroughly on these topics. Ask them. You might be surprised how much they already know.

▼ Are We Raising Future Riverboat Gamblers in Cyberspace?

There is no doubt that the Internet is an equal-opportunity vice provider . . . gambling hasn't escaped cyberspace anymore than the other vices have. In fact, gambling is thriving in the Internet arena, while facing strict governmental controls elsewhere. (The sites are illegal if they offer gambling within the U.S. without being properly licensed.)

Most of the gambling sites are hosted offshore (which makes law enforcement more difficult). They require prepayment in the form of credit card advances, debit card advances or wired funds. A simple search on any of the search engines will result in hundreds of illegal gambling sites. And your teenager's money is as good as anyone else's.

Frankly, I was surprised that our kids are using the gambling sites as much as they reportedly are. But with more and more children having their own copy of our credit cards for emergency purposes, generous allowances and access to their savings accounts which hold birthday cash, babysitting and paper route money gathered over the years, it's apparently easier than ever. Sometimes, they'll just use our credit card and hope we don't notice when the statement arrives.

Keep an eye on your credit card statements and on your children's savings account balances. Blocking their ability to send out credit card information over the Internet might make it harder for them to gamble online. In addition, if the computer is centrally located under your watchful eyes, you may be able to keep them out of the gambling dens entirely.

Also, teach them that the only people who make money on gambling are the gambling site operators themselves. (I represented casinos for years, and know how profitable it can be for the gambling establishment.) Let them also know that many of the gambling sites are scams, and a lot of those that aren't hold onto your winnings under the guise of international currency laws. Gambling online is a no-win game.

CHAPTER 11

The Bad Stuff Goes Both Ways ... Protecting Others and Yourself From Your Kids and Their Friends

A Bird's Eye View—

▼ Hacking and Computer Crime

▼ Breaking the House Rules

▼ Hey! ... That's My Intellectual Property!

▼ Protecting Your Boss ... Don't Use Your Business Account for Family Computing

▼ Protecting Your Computer in Cyberspace ... Viruses

▼ Hacking and Computer Crime

Fortune Magazine reports that financial losses from computer crimes run about $10 billion per year. What's even scarier is that more than 95 percent of them, according to FBI estimates, go undetected. Last year a new law was passed making it easier to prosecute hackers for commercial computer crimes.

But the biggest part of the problem is that hackers are the heroes of their Internet generation. According to *Fortune*, a manager at Panasonic said that hacking is how computer experts learn. "You break into programs, commit piracy, all kinds of wild and crazy things." ("Who's reading your e-mail?" *Fortune*, February 3, 1997.)

The fact that adults who are computer experts can classify these things as "wild and crazy things" is the essential problem. Kids don't understand that hacking is a crime, and a serious one. When I was running the Court TV Law Center Legal Helpline, one day we logged on to find all of our legal discussions replaced with pornographic pictures. While we all laughed, it meant that everything had to be reconstructed at a huge cost, and the people who had asked us legal questions had to repost their questions.

In order to make kids understand how bad hacking is, they'll need to identify with the victim, since to them hacking is a victimless and faceless crime. If you try to "bring it home," showing your kids how horrible it would be if a hacker got into your computer at work and destroyed all the work you've done, or got into your home computer and destroyed their files or destroyed their favorite websites, they may be able to appreciate the seriousness of the crime.

Keeping an eye on their computing makes it a little harder for them to commit computer crimes. Look over their shoulder from time to time, and don't put the computer in their bedroom. Keeping it in a central family location is one of the best tips I can share with you.

▼ Breaking the House Rules

As much as we have focused on protecting your children from others in cyberspace, dangers exist to you and others as well. And these dangers may be caused by our children and their friends, inadvertently or intentionally.

It's not a matter of whether or not you trust them or how well they listen to you. Simply by filling out a survey or a form online they may divulge personal and private information about us and our families. They may be giving out our telephone numbers or our addresses online, without understanding the risks associated with sharing this private information.

Remember, that even if you trust your own kids not to break the rules, you need to be able to trust their friends, too. Their friends may be using your account when they visit—friends who may not know your rules, or if they do, may not follow them. I wish I had thought of this before learning the hard way myself.

Since I host several boards in an AOL legal forum, I'm expected to be online regularly, monitoring activity while policing my boards. One night, when I tried to log on, I learned that my account had been closed. I was told that someone had violated AOL's terms of service. Not able to reach anyone in AOL administration in the evening, I had to open a new account just to get online. The new account didn't have my board tools, so I couldn't police the boards. I was angry, and my forum suffered. It took days to get things sorted out, and all my e-mails were returned to their senders during that time.

Apparently, friends of my daughter had been over and had used my AOL account to get online. These kids had gotten into a flaming match in a teen chat room (remember . . . "flaming" is when you insult or act in a discourteous manner in an online discussion), and when their bad behavior was reported to AOL, my account was closed for violating the terms of service.

In addition, children armed with powerful computers have proven themselves very good at manipulating others' computer systems and cyberspace. They are breaking into other computer systems, sending e-mails and pretending that someone else sent them (remailers) and ordering goods and services with our and others' credit cards. Because they do this from their home, they think they are anonymous. They also often don't understand how serious these activities may be.

A close friend of mine, one of the first cyberspace lawyers in the United States and very tech-smart, called me recently complaining about his children. Apparently they had found his credit card information stored in a computer file for easy access. They called their friends, and together ordered a big screen TV and surround sound system from a vendor on AOL.

Luckily AOL staff—noticing that the delivery and the billing addresses were different (the kids were smart enough to have it delivered down the street to their friend's house), called to confirm. My friend was able to cancel the order before too much damage was done. Knowing a lot about computers doesn't always prepare you for what your kids, or their friends, will dream up next. Remember that.

▼ Hey! . . . That's My Intellectual Property!

Many people forget that the laws that apply on the ground apply equally in cyberspace. U.S. and international intellectual property laws and treaties protect copyrighted material. And copyrighted material doesn't have to have been filed with the Copyright Office to be protected by the copyright laws. It doesn't have to be labeled as "copyrighted" and doesn't need the © mark. Under intellectual property laws, if you write it and publish it . . . it's protected against infringement.

Given the ease with which anyone can block, cut and paste anything from any website, or download and save it as a document or graphic on your computer, people forget that anything more than "fair use" is an infringement. Our children need to learn to attribute the material (by correct bibliographies), and not use more than a simple quotation or two.

Recent changes in the U.S. copyright laws, to bring them in line with the world community, make copyright infringement a crime, even if the infringement was not for the purposes of making a profit. Many kids swap software, trading a copy they have of something for a copy someone else has of whatever they want. The new law changes make this a crime. Although it's unlikely that the U.S.

Attorney's Office or Department of Justice will start arresting our children in droves, it's an additional risk which didn't exist before.

Teach them to respect others' property, even if it looks like it's available for everyone to use freely. The Internet works because people are willing to publish proprietary information for public enjoyment and learning. It's important that the rights of those people are protected or the flow of information might slow, to everyone's detriment.

▼ Protecting Your Boss . . . Don't Use Your Business Account for Family Computing

It is estimated that half of the people on the Internet access it in connection with their work. Problems for employers from misuse of their Internet access by employees, or others using an employee's account, include defamation, copyright infringement, trade secret protection and confidentiality, harassment (including hostile work environment issues), and criminal accountability (such as for hate crimes and hacking).

As easy as it might be to use your business Internet account at home to get online with your children, don't. Just to save $19.95 per month (the cost of an Internet service provider account), you might jeopardize your job, or risk your business. Get another account.

With more and more employers being held liable for actions of their employees online (cybertorts), many employers are setting up Internet use policies to regulate their employees' Internet access. Most of those policies prohibit the use of the account by non-employees, and substantially restrict the online activities of employees.

In addition, Big Brother may be watching you. All but a small minority of states permit an employer to monitor electronic communications of their employees, if the employer supplied the equipment and access or the employee consented to the monitoring. (E-mail policies contained in your employee handbook may be deemed consent.) That means that they are permitted to intercept and monitor your e-mail and where you go online. (Or your kids, for that matter.)

If employers discover a misuse of their Internet accounts, they may be able to discipline or fire you. So be careful.

▼ Protecting Your Computer in Cyberspace ... Viruses

A virus is a special computer code, contained within a computer program, that is designed to infect a file and when executed, do something bad to your computer and spread. Your computer may crash, it may not be able to turn on (boot up), files may become corrupted, the entire hard drive may be wiped out ... there are a lot of ways a virus can wreak havoc. If your computer suddenly does something weird, or doesn't do what it's supposed to do, look for a virus before you waste your time doing anything else.

The odds of catching a virus on the Internet are very small. But they can do lots of damage if you do catch one. Most viruses have been especially designed to damage computer systems, and are very successful at what they have been designed to do. They also replicate themselves, infecting file after file once they've imbedded themselves into a program.

Remember Mikey? The kid who wouldn't eat anything? Well, you may also remember the rumor about twenty years ago that he died while eating Pop Rocks (the effervescent candy) when he drank a can of soda and his stomach exploded. Rumors, especially those that sound believable, have abounded for centuries. It isn't any different in cyberspace. Computer virus rumors are just the latest fad of cyber-rumors.

E-mail hoax messages warning me about some new virus hazard arrive in my mail box daily. One night my son Michael sent me a list of supposedly infected files that someone had sent to him at college. The list included the upgrade for AOL, among many other unlikely virus-carrier candidates. This is the typical virus hoax which attempts to frighten people who have already installed popular programs, like AOL. (I reminded him to reread this section before he forwarded the hoax e-mail to anyone else.)

One of the biggest Internet rumors in the last few years was the Good Times virus, which was reputed to infect PCs through e-mail. Experienced Internet and computer users dismissed it as a hoax, because they knew a virus couldn't be passed by reading an e-mail message. A lot of other people were fooled, though.

The far greater danger lies not in Internet-passed viruses, but through sharing infected floppy disks (something kids do all the time) and by running infected programs. When my law firm's website was first being built we were drafting a lot of articles, from home and from our office. We kept the articles on one disk and took it back and forth, sharing it from computer to computer. One morning, none of those computers would boot up. The virus was on the disk, and had infected each and every computer it touched.

▼ To avoid viruses . . . practice safe computing!

Luckily, there are good virus protection programs available that scan your hard drive for viruses and get rid of them. The two most popular for PCs, Norton Anti-Virus and McAfee Anti-Virus, will both rid your system of any existing viruses and scan it regularly for new ones that you may have contracted unwittingly.

I use Norton Anti-Virus. It's easy to install and you can buy it wherever computer software is sold. (It also saved our computer system during that boot-virus event I just told you about.) They also have a good tech support team at Norton to handle any questions. McAfee, though, is the favorite of the teen members of our research team, basically because you can download a trial version, without charge, from the Internet. McAfee's site is at www.mcafee.com/ and the program can be downloaded at www.mcafee.com/down/index.html. I found it very hard to install, though.

Both products update the software frequently to stay on top of the latest viruses. You can update both products from the Web, with free downloads.

Smart and safe computing means being careful. Preventive medicine is the best medicine. You'll be fine if you remember to:

- Use a good anti-virus program on each boot up.
- Run each Internet downloaded document/program through an anti-virus program.
- Check each floppy disk for a virus before loading anything onto your computer.

In order to make sure your computer stays well and virus free, practice, and make sure your children practice, safe computing.

PART 3

Making and Enforcing Your Choices

as Parents

(everything you need to know to make your children cyber-smart and cyber-safe)

CHAPTER 12

Understanding Your Options

A Bird's Eye View—

▼ Teach Your Children Well

▼ Making Your Choices . . . Finding a Fit That's Right for You and Your Kids

▼ What Are Other Parents Doing?

▼ When Is Your Child Old Enough to Use a Computer?

▼ Balance . . . When Do You Know If They've had Enough?

▼ Teach . . . Your Children Well

President Bill Clinton recently announced an expansive plan to build a family-friendly Internet by giving children a "seat belt" for cyberspace. (I knew my idea for the book cover was a good one.) The White House plan calls for cooperation from the Internet industry to provide parents and teachers with "easy-to-use" child protection technology, and promises to continue enforcing the existing laws designed to protect children in cyberspace. To get this all accomplished, though, the plan encourages parents to learn more about the Internet in order to help guide their children in cyberspace.

Of all the tools and tips I'll share with you, the most important one, more important than any software or hardware device you can buy, is that the first and best line of defense is Internet education. You have to teach your children to be aware and careful in cyberspace. Even if you use every technology protection available, unless your children know what to expect and how to react when they run into something less than perfect online, they are at risk. Arming them well means teaching them well. (Now, all together . . . (with my apologies to Crosby, Stills, Nash & Young) . . . "teach . . . your children well . . .")

▼ Making Your Choices . . . Finding a Fit That's Right for You and Your Kids

Your decision about what your children should be able to see and how you'll enforce your choices is a very personal one. It depends on the child, and depends even more on you—the amount of time you're willing to devote to learning about your child's journeys in cyberspace, and how well you and your child communicate.

There's been a lot of talk lately about child protection software. Several different software programs and methods have been developed to restrict and monitor access to, and rate the content contained in, certain sites on the Internet. Many also restrict information being sent from your children to others on the Internet and online services. While they may be helpful, they aren't a substitute for good parenting.

There are three methods currently in use to allow parents to control their children's access to certain information and sites on the Internet. The most popular is blocking and filtering software, installed on your home computer (called the "first-generation software" by members of the Internet industry).

The most popular of these are Cyber Patrol, CYBERsitter, Net Nanny and Surf Watch. (We've reviewed them in this book in the chapter, *Implementing and Enforcing Your Choices*.) Most have predetermined "bad sites," blocked when the program is activated, and screen other sites based upon certain content and keyword preferences set by the software manufacturer or, in some cases, the parents. The database of "bad sites" needs to be updated regularly, and some companies charge for update subscriptions.

Some of these programs monitor computer activity both online and offline as well. Currently three of the four products we reviewed, Cyber Patrol, CYBERsitter and Net Nanny, also provide a two-way blocking feature to prevent your children from sending certain information (like their name and telephone number) to others.

The second method is server blocking, where parental control software is installed at the Internet gateway that allows you access to the Internet. That means you don't install the software on your computer, but your online service provider or ISP does. It's easier to use, since no installation or configuration is done by the parent. It's also harder to by-pass by the children. But, it can't be customized. The most popular of this type, Bess, is reviewed in this book.

The third method, and the one most Internet-savvy professionals are banking on, is PICS (the Platform for Internet Content Selection) standard site ratings, which allow your web browsers or other software to screen sites based on their content ratings, allowing access only to the sites bearing ratings selected by the parents.

Although PICS provides the technology that the web browsers use to screen the rated sites, it doesn't set the rating standards or rate the sites.

The two most prominent rating services are Recreational Software Advisory Council on the Internet (RSACi) and SafeSurf (both are discussed later in the chapter *Rating the Web . . . PICS, the Platform for Internet Content Selection*). RSACi is generally recognized as the industry leader in rating sites using the PICS standard and is typically the default rating system used by the web browsers.

Although both services rate sites using different standards, their procedure for rating sites is the same. Sites submit certain information about their content and are given a rating code to be used at the beginning of the site, to alert web browsers using rating software to identify the site's rating. (Only those with a preapproved rating can be accessed using the web browser.) Sites self-rate, on the honor system, but both RSACi and SafeSurf reserve the right to confirm the accuracy of the rating.

In addition, another parental control program, Net Shepherd (also reviewed in the *Using Technology to Implement and Enforce Your Choices* chapter), has rated sites based upon its own standard and has the largest rated site database available (over 300,000 according to company spokesmen). It limits access to the sites bearing the rating levels you have selected (if it's not rated, your kids can't access the site). Net Shepherd's software doesn't filter sites or information if they haven't been rated.

When I appeared on CNN in March, 1997 to discuss the subject of blocking and filtering software, I was asked if there was a magic bullet on the horizon. There isn't. The software is imperfect, and tech-savvy kids can get around it. But sometimes, even though you're home and seated next to them while surfing, you may need a little extra help. Inadvertently, even the best kids may stumble across something neither you nor they had intended.

Recently, a confusion over the NASA website for the Mars mission brought the problem closer to home for many of us. After you have read this entire book, taught your children about what Internet sites they should be visiting, and are keeping your kids surfing within sight, you still might be in for a surprise or two—inadvertently, your children may stumble across something you'd prefer they not see.

The NASA site (www.nasa.gov, as it's a government site, not a commercial site) had millions of visitors each day while it was broadcasting the Mars mission.

An industrious website operator used the NASA site's popularity and the lack of sophistication of many newbies to feed a pornography website advertising page. (Actually, it had been up for awhile.) The porn site advertised different links, which rotated frequently, by posting banners and links to the advertised sites. The pornographic advertising site's domain was "nasa.com" . . . confusingly similar to the NASA site, and ending with the zone most newbies are familiar with—".com."

Sitting, presumably, safely in front of their parents, thousands of kids typed in the more familiar Web format, "nasa.com," instead of the correct "nasa.gov," and were greeted with far more than anyone expected. (They had expected to learn about astronomy, not biology!) As much as others may argue against filtering and blocking tools, this case proves their value.

But remember, no software can replace trust and communication. The technology shouldn't be the cyber babysitter. It's just another available tool to help knowledgeable parents enforce their choices, nothing more. It's not a magic bullet.

▼ What Are Other Parents Doing?

At the end of 1996, *Family PC* magazine conducted a survey of almost 600 families. (It's reported at their website, www.familypc.com) On the average the persons surveyed were married couples in their late 30's with two children under the age of seventeen. They used Windows 95 on a Pentium PC, with a 28.8 kbps modem, and Netscape Navigator as their web browser.

The parents surveyed were very concerned about their children's online activities. Most parents didn't allow their children to use chatrooms online; a smaller percentage monitored their children's e-mail. Yet, only a quarter of them used child protection software (incidentally, they reported that ease of use and setup is an important factor in selecting such software). All of the families however, set rules for Internet use in the home. ["Families in the World of the Web, Results to our first Family WebTesters Tell All survey help us get to know you." *FamilyPC*, December 1996]

Most of the Internet-savvy parents I know don't use child protection software either, tending to rely instead on education and trust. Representative Zoe Lufgren, one of the most Internet-savvy members of Congress, is a good example. She says she doesn't use it for her 12 and 15 year old children because she trusts them to follow the rules and communicate concerns to her.

But the inadvertent accessing of offensive sites may be a good reason for using child protection software to catch the sites before your kids do. Your child may be searching for *Seventeen Magazine*'s website at the obvious name, "www.seventeen.com." *Seventeen Magazine* doesn't currently have a website, just a forum on AOL (keyword "seventeen"). But www.seventeen.com is a hardcore sexual site.

Representative Lufgren shared a similar story with me about a search conducted by one of her congressional staff on the subject of volcanos. He searched for "eruptions" and found far more than he intended. Child protection software, although certainly not perfect, can avoid a similar problem in your home.

▼ When Is Your Child Old Enough to Use a Computer?

Too often parents get caught up in measuring their children against other children: who is speaking first, walking first, the first out of diapers. I am often asked when children should be introduced to a computer and how to tell when are they are ready. I always give the same lawyerly answer . . . "It depends." It depends on you as well as on your child.

Most children are introduced to computing while seated in our laps, watching us "play" with our computers. My niece, Danielle, would play with a spare keyboard when she was ten months old. She would bang away perfectly safe, far from the computer itself. As she got a little older, she would wander over from time to time to get a peek at the flashing colors and sounds of the monitor. If her mom or dad ignored her for the computer for too long, she would scramble into their laps, needing once again to be the center of attention.

As she got used to the computer, her hand would be guided on the mouse, and she soon learned, at eighteen months, that moving the mouse moved the cursor. She would giggle while the cursor played wildly around the screen.

Software designed for young children made different sounds every time she struck a different key on the keyboard. (My sister used a MAC program called "key wack.") She was learning that the computer could be fun for her, as well as for her parents. By the time she was two and a-half years old, she could sit and play her favorite programs, still learning how to control the mouse cursor. By her third birthday, she could manage the mouse with the best of them.

A few days after her third birthday, in receipt of a new CD-ROM featuring her favorite character, Arthur, she surprised all of us. While my sister was on the phone, she heard the computer whirring to startup. Danielle was seated in front of the computer, having loaded the new CD-ROM, and had begun playing the program. It was the first time she had ever used the computer alone.

Are all children ready to use the computer by themselves at three? Of course not. It depends on the family, how often the child sees family members using the computer, and the child herself. When parents play sports, children are interested in sports. When parents cook, children like to cook. When we enjoy computers, children follow our lead, excited about what makes us excited.

So let your children sit in your lap and touch the keyboard and mouse. Find a few programs that use characters your children enjoy and find a few family sites with their favorite characters too. Often books can be coupled with interactive programs, fostering an interest in reading at the same time they're becoming familiar with the computer.

Guide their hands when using adult-size accessories. You may want to check out what child-size accessories are available for your computer. (Actually, I was surprised how few gadgets there are for young children. I expected to find more products geared for a child's hand and lots of other gadgets.) The right sized accessories can be much more comfortable. They fit the child's hands better and are usually peanut-butter-proof. They're also more colorful than their adult counterparts. (I've listed some products I like in the chapter called *Parry's Picks.*)

As delighted as I am that my genius niece has followed in the family technology footsteps, I do not recommend that she be unleashed unsupervised with my sister's expensive Power Mac. (After I wrote this section, we learned that she had deleted file after file from my sister's computer since she could drag and drop files into the trash can, and Oscar the Grouch would praise her each time she deleted a file. Talk about timely advice!)

Nor do I recommend that she devote all her genius to computing, since I fully expect her to qualify for the Olympics and become Secretary-General of the United Nations after she retires from her second term as President of the United States.

So balancing her computing time is very important. (I've already decided to put her on the waiting list for Outdoor Online, the summer camp that combines outdoor activities with online activities in order to teach their campers to balance the two better. You'll learn more about Outdoor Online in the next section, *Balance . . . When Do You Know if They've had Enough?*) Seriously, this isn't a competition. Your children should use a computer when they want to and advance as fast as they are comfortable. (Just keep an eye on those files . . . and Oscar the Grouch!)

Online activity is less important for younger children than for children once they learn to read and can follow online directions, generally by seven or eight. Even then, online family and children's sites should be visited with the parent or another adult family member. It's a great way to spend time together and share your values and thoughts with them.

Your children shouldn't be allowed online unsupervised until you are sure that they know the rules and will follow them. Fancy child protection software shouldn't be used as a substitute for parental supervision.

New young netizens should be issued a learner's permit to surf, one that requires an adult to surf along with the child until they can pass the test for a full fledged license to surf. You need to set the rules and administer your own test, one designed just for your child and your family. (Read on to learn about Internet use policies.) Only you can make sure your child is ready.

So . . . when is a child ready? When her Internet-savvy parent thinks so.

▼ Balance . . . When Do You Know if They've had Enough?

One of the biggest challenges parents face is making sure their children don't become consumed with computers and Websurfing. We all recognize the benefits of teaching our children to use computers, but we also need to recognize the risks associated with letting them spend every waking hour hiding behind a computer monitor.

A cyber-penpal is a poor substitute for a real live friend. And fingers limbered by typing are poor substitutes for those limbered by throwing a baseball or playing Chopin on the piano. Any parent faced with kids who enjoy video games—and the impossible task of trying to distract them from the video screen—understands how addictive interactivity can be. Yet, knowing how to use and enjoy computers and cyberspace is an important part of our children's development. How can we help our kids maintain a healthy balance?

I stumbled onto one option—Outdoor Online (www.outdoor-online.com). It's a terrific summer camp, devoted to helping parents and children find a balance between computing and the outdoors and other activities. To the untrained eye, it looks like any other summer camp, located at the Kirkwood Resort in California, 30 miles south of Lake Tahoe.

Now in its third season, Outdoor Online offers 250 kids a ten-day combination of responsible computing and outdoor fun. The kids vary between newbies sent to the camp to learn about computing to kids who have to be pried off their PCs before attending this camp—the only sky and clouds they may have seen in recent months having been on their Windows 95 screen saver.

But no screen saver (not even Microsoft's) is a substitute for ten days engulfed in Lake Tahoe's grandeur. The kids kayak and camp and enjoy water sports and hiking. A new program involves the effort of certain campers and counselors in the Lake Tahoe community's effort to keep the lake environmentally sound. They also enjoy sharing their online enthusiasm with a crew of energetic counselors and camp administrators.

I spoke with Mindi Roberts, the multi-talented woman who runs the camp. Trained in a variety of creative fields, she has a wonderful approach to kids computing online. "Everyone wants to get wired," she says "but no one really knows why." It's her job, and that of the camp, to help the children and their parents understand why.

"People," she patiently explains to all the new campers, "are irreplaceable and there's more to interpersonal relations than chatting online." I agree. If you spend too much time behind a computer screen, you'll miss too many important things in this world, like a real sunset, sitting beside real kids, and sharing stories around a campfire.

She also thinks that one of the most important things we can teach our kids is not to believe everything you read on the Internet. The camp is also very concerned about Internet safety, especially for children. The campers build their own websites emphasizing child safety in cyberspace and the outdoor activities they enjoy best. According to one parent, who has sent all three of his children to the camp, there isn't a better program that addresses the critical issues of Internet child safety. And he should know— he heads a local high tech crime buster team.

One young camper was asked by a visitor whether the Internet can and should be regulated. He said that governmental regulation isn't the answer. This boy was ten. Although he probably will follow future attempts to regulate the Internet, he now also knows how to kayak.

Soon after I found Outdoor Online, President Clinton and Vice President Gore did, too. They arrived by helicopter and spent time with the campers and counselors. Mindi thought you'd enjoy some of the photos of the visit. (Many more appear at the site.)

Maybe there's hope for me, too. I wonder if they accept forty-six year old out-of-shape campers? I've always wanted to learn to kayak.

CHAPTER 13

Defensive Parenting . . . Avoiding Problems by Planning Ahead

A Bird's Eye View—

▼ Forewarned is Forearmed

▼ Know Your Kids and Create a Workable "Internet Use Policy" for Them

▼ Educate Your Children About the Dangers in Cyberspace

▼ Forewarned is Forearmed

When children are armed with the ability to decode passwords, scramble our files and locate our credit card information and passwords on our computer systems, it's hard to control them. It's even harder to figure out what they might do next, in order to stay one step ahead of them.

But who said parenting was easy? Parenting is always learning on the fly, having to address the unexpected, having your kids leave a chocolate bar on your sofa cushion in June or spit up on your outfit just as you are leaving for work . . . why should your kids' computer activities be the exception?

Passwords. Don't share your passwords or store them where they can be found: remember that those who control the passwords control the world. Find a password you can remember easily, but one that's not so obvious that your children can figure it out. Also, change your password frequently. When you type it in, don't let them look over your shoulder. Never store it on your hard drive, or preprogram it into your sign on screen. This may cost you a few more seconds when you get online, but may save you plenty of heartaches.

You should also remember that some services, such as America Online, will allow you to charge certain purchases to your account. Since most AOL members have their bills automatically charged to a credit card, or deducted from their checking account each month, this is a more convenient way of purchasing something online than having to type in your credit card information each time. That's another reason to guard your password: it identifies you as the account holder.

Protecting your children when they're not home. Make sure that you and the parents of your children's friends are in agreement about monitoring the children's activities online, and that you use similar tools to enforce your choices. If not, circumventing your parental controls is as simple as your children walking next door and computing at a friend's house. If you can't agree on a joint policy, make sure the other parents honor your wishes and keep your children off their computer while visiting.

Backup or password-protect your files. Don't leave important files on your computer without a backup and password protection if your kids are using the computer unsupervised.

Even the most innocent and experienced computer user may push the wrong keys at the wrong time. I've done it myself. (Far more often than I will admit.) Important speeches or articles are lost with a click of the mouse. The first outline for this book, carefully prepared on my new laptop during a trip to Moscow, was lost completely. The computer shut down, without provocation (I swear I didn't do anything . . .), and the automatic backup didn't work. Jet lagged and exhausted, I had to start from scratch. (So, if you don't like this book, I can promise you that the earlier outline would have been better. If you like it, ignore that thought, thank you.)

So, if you have something important, make a backup copy on a floppy disk. Or better yet, password-protect your files on the computer, in addition to saving important files to a tape backup (a special device which stores copies of your files in special condensed tapes) or floppy. That way, it's less likely that your children will be tempted to snoop through your personal files. Many software programs allow you to password-protect certain information. It's easy and will avoid a myriad of problems.

Credit cards. Don't store your credit card information on your computer. As inconvenient as it might be to have to access it from somewhere else, it creates too much of a temptation for computer-savvy kids and their friends.

By the way, don't be afraid of using your credit cards online, as long as you follow certain safety rules:

1. Only supply your credit card information on secure lines. (Your web browser will warn you if it's not a secure transmission.)

2. Make sure, even if the line is secure, that you're dealing with a reputable company, and that they are who they say they are.

You're already protected, at least for everything over $50.00, if someone else charges on your card without your authorization. (As one Internet expert said, if you trust your credit card to gas station attendants who take your card and process it out of your view, you have no reason to be worried about using your credit card on the Internet.) AOL, as a special service to their members, covers that first $50 for any unauthorized charges on their system with an AOL vendor.

Keep the computer in a central family location, not in your child's room. Make sure that the computer with online access is located wherever the family hangs out together. It's harder for our children to get into trouble right under our noses. (Not impossible, however, just harder . . .) Friends who may be provoking the situation would also have problems provoking it with you around: provocation requires too much energy to be done quietly. You'd notice something is up.

Let your kids know that many people are not what they seem. I remember a comedy skit where a middle-aged beer-bellied man in his underwear was pretending to be a young teenage girl while chatting online with a teenage football jock, who was really a middle-age woman in curlers and a house-dress.

While my kids laughed at the skit, it also brought the issue home. People online are not always what they say they are.

Many kids are lured online by adults masquerading as kids. As disillusioning as it might seem, warning them about this risk *now* may protect them from serious danger later.

Make sure you can see what's on the monitor. And let your kids know you look at it from time to time. Kids can get into trouble under our noses, but knowing that you can see what they're doing,whenever you want to, keeps them on the straight and narrow. (It worked for me when my daughter walked into my room and I was searching for sexual sites to test the software against.)

Check your hard drive and any floppy disks every once in a while. Look for downloaded images stored on your hard drive or on floppy disks. They are easily spotted, because they generally end with either ".jpg" or ".gif."

Let your kids know you're checking downloaded materials. I think that snooping through their private things without letting them know that you might is a terrible violation of their privacy.

Cover your own tracks. If you visit sites you don't want your children to see, check your hard drive for these wayward graphics and make sure your bookmarks don't lead them to those sites. (When I checked my hard drive for an image I couldn't find, I found a pornographic image that had been loaded onto my computer. I'm the only one who uses this particular computer and hadn't loaded the image. I can only assume that some new technology allowed one of the sites I was viewing to drop a graphic onto my drive.)

One of the reasons the First Amendment exists is to let you see what you want without having to worry about whether it's appropriate for children. But be careful about naming your bookmarks, and make sure you haven't stored anything you don't want your kids to see on your hard drive or on an accessible disk.

Don't send them out there alone until they're ready. Screen e-mail when your kids are younger and sit with them while they're in any non-child unsupervised chatrooms. Make sure they know the chatroom rules too, and where to report violations and things that make them feel uncomfortable. Knowing the basic rules will help them surf more safely. The two most important rules, in my opinion, are:

- Make sure your child knows what information can be shared and what cannot be shared with others online; and
- Make sure your child knows never to meet someone in person whom they have met online.

Play an active and interested part in your children's online life. Get to know your children's online friends and correspondents. Your children shouldn't be afraid to tell you anything, so don't criticize them when something goes wrong. Encourage your children to come to you when they are uncomfortable or receive a message that violates your rules or makes them uncomfortable. Secrets can be dangerous. Be the one your children share their secrets with, and be worthy of that valuable trust.

Don't rely on software to prevent a sophisticated computer kid from getting into trouble. Even with all the software devices and tools we have on the market to protect our kids and to keep them from getting into trouble online, a computer savvy kid can get around them. And, the tools are imperfect. Several of them let many sites through that you may not want your children to see. Don't rely on technology to protect your children, that's your job.

You need to know if your kids can be trusted. Educate them on the risks of hacking and other improper computer and online behavior. Teach them good netiquette. Then, if they still can't be trusted, lock your computer and take the key with you. There may be no other way of keeping them out of trouble.

Some basic rules for you to remember as a parent . . . Your cheat sheet

- Make sure your child doesn't spend all of her time on the computer.
- People, not computers, should be their best friends and companions.
- Keep the computer in a family room, kitchen or living room, not in your child's bedroom.
- Learn enough about computers so you can enjoy them together with your kids.
- Watch your children when they're online and see where they go.
- Make sure that your children feel comfortable coming to you with questions.
- Keep kids out of chatrooms or IRCs unless they are monitored.
- Encourage discussions between you and your child about what they enjoy online.
- Discuss these rules, get your children to agree to adhere to them, and post them near the computer as a reminder.
- Help them find a balance between computing and other activities.
- Remember to monitor their compliance with these rules, especially when it comes to the amount of time your children spend on the computer.
- Get to know their "online friends" just as you get to know all of their other friends.
- Warn them that people may not be what they seem to be.

▼ Know Your Kids and Create a Workable "Internet Use Policy" for Them.

Find out what your children's interests are. What do they read? What do they watch on television? If they're already on the Internet, what do they access?

Even without an ulterior motive, it's a wonderful way to get to know your children. Too often we *talk at* our children, rather than *listen to* them. And they have wonderful things to tell us, if we just listen.

Ask them to show you around the Internet. Access their bookmarks with them. Don't ambush them and make it look like you're spying on them. Take this opportunity to share some of their interests. You might be pleasantly surprised to learn some of the things that interest them.

For instance, how do they find their way around the Internet? Do they rely on hyperlinks (links to other sites), or do they use a search engine? If so, which one? Ask them why they prefer one over the other, and how they formulate their searches.

Once you have a better idea about how your children use the Internet, you can start developing a set of rules to govern their behavior online and to guide them into safer waters. Your rules should be designed to help them understand proper netiquette, know what to expect from others online, how to behave when something unexpected occurs and how to protect themselves and you from getting hurt in cyberspace. That's an "Internet use policy." (Some call them "acceptable use policies" or "agreements.")

These rules are mutual rules, and should be constructed by both parent and child, not just forced upon your children. Part of what will make them work is the communication between you when the rules are being designed. Some kids respond well to a written policy signed by both the parents and the child; others would prefer a list to be posted near the computer, as a reminder. You should do what makes you both comfortable. After all, you know your kids best.

The site of the Direct Marketing Association, a direct marketing industry group, (www.the-dma.org) has an automated Internet use policy feature. You answer the questions, making your choices. Then the program prepares a policy customized for you, based upon your indicated choices, which you can print out. You should check it out. (I discuss more about the Direct Marketing Association's site later on in *The Bottom Line . . . What Have You Learned So Far?* chapter.)

▼ POINTS TO CONSIDER IN DRAFTING YOUR OWN POLICY

I have given you some basic rules and you should feel free to change them to suit both your and your child's needs. In the chart below, I've tried to sum up the most important tips to remember. Consider it your cheat sheet in advising your child.

- People on the Internet can pretend to be anyone or anything they want. Don't let them fool you.
- Don't use bad language.
- Don't get into arguments with or answer anyone who uses bad language.
- Don't answer if someone says something that makes you feel uncomfortable or that you feel is "bad."
- If someone is doing something "bad," you should tell your parents right away. But don't turn off the computer or log out of the area where the person is doing something "bad." (The adult can then find the person and report his activities as a terms of service violation.)
- Use a fun name when you're online, not your real name (not even your real first name).
- Don't spend all your time online. Set limits on your computer use.
- Never give your real name, address, school, parents' names, friends' names, where your parents work, anyone else's e-mail address or any telephone number to anyone.
- If anyone asks you for this information, don't answer them, and tell your parents or the adult in charge of the chatroom.
- Never talk to anyone you met online over the phone, send them anything or accept anything from them or agree to meet with them unless your parents agree and are with you.
- Never show your picture online to someone without your parents' consent.
- Don't put any information in your online service profile without your parents' consent.
- There are places on the Internet where people talk about and show pictures of things we don't agree with. If you see something like that, click the "Back" button and tell your parents.
- Don't do anything online that costs money unless your parents say it's okay.
- Never give out your password.
- Never give out credit card information.
- Don't copy other people's material and pretend that it's yours.

I've included a sample Internet use policy in the Appendix. I'll tell you what I tell my clients when they ask me if they should use a form agreement. If it fits all your needs, use it. Otherwise, you should use it as a guide in writing your own.

▼ Educate Your Children About the Dangers in Cyberspace

Out of all the tools and tips I will share with you, the most important one is that YOU are the first and best line of defense in protecting your children in cyberspace.

Having been briefed by the leading Internet specialists, President Clinton agrees. He concluded that "the ultimate responsibility rests on parents' shoulders. Cutting-edge technology and criminal prosecutions can not substitute for responsible mothers and fathers. Parents must sit down with their children and learn about the Internet."

Teaching your children to be aware and careful in cyberspace is more important than any software or hardware device you can buy.

▼ THE SAME OLD THING . . . IN A NEW AND IMPROVED PACKAGE

For some reason, people forget what they always knew when they get online. I don't know why. All the normal stuff applies exactly the same in cyberspace. Use the same lectures your parents gave you: the same ones their parents gave them.

Don't talk to or accept anything from strangers. (See . . . familiar territory . . . .repeat after me . . .) Come straight home. Don't say nasty things about other people. Be polite. Don't tell people personal things about yourself. Don't tell personal things about your family.

If you haven't told your children this yet, I suggest you do it quickly before your children go to school and repeat something from home. I'll share a favorite story with you. My former mother-in-law, whom I adore, was always joking with her children. My former brother-in-law, always the most gullible one in the family, asked her what she did for a living. She was a housewife, in the best sense of the word. But jokingly she told him that she used to be an exotic dancer. (In those days they were called "strippers.") While we all giggled, unfortunately he remembered and when his teacher asked what their parents did, he told her. My father-in-law, then president of the PTA, heard about it during one of the meetings. The moral of the story is . . . .

I told you that you already know this stuff, but just needed someone to translate it into cyberspace terms. Here's the translation:

Don't talk to or accept anything from strangers. Who's a stranger? As I told you before, one of the biggest problems with cyberpredators is that they function in your home. Our kids feel safe with us seated nearby.

There is a sense of intimacy online that cyberpredators count on. They need to convince your children that they are not strangers at all. You need to remind them that these people *are* strangers.

Come straight home. When I was young, I was famous for wandering around after school. Friends always invited me home with them, or something interesting was going on. My mother would panic and I would get the same lecture day after day.

Wandering aimlessly online isn't any different from my wandering around after school. My mother needed to know I was safe, and that I was doing something productive, like homework. Allowing your children to spend unlimited time online, surfing aimlessly, is asking for trouble.

Make sure there's a reason they're surfing. If they are just surfing randomly, set a time limit. You want them to come home after they're done, to human interaction and family activities (and homework).

Don't say nasty things about other people. Saying nasty things about other people in cyberspace is called "flaming." It often violates the "terms of service" of your online service provider and will certainly get a reaction from other people online.

Flaming matches can be long and extended battles, moving from a chatroom or discussion group to e-mail quickly. If your child feels that someone is flaming them, they should tell you and the sysop (system operator, pronounced sis-op) or moderator in charge right away.

Be Polite. There are rules for each online area. Learn the rules first. Chatrooms each have their own rules. Don't barge in and start talking until you've had a chance to see what everyone's discussing. Read the discussion thread for awhile, instead of asking everyone what they were talking about. And be respectful of others and their opinions. Don't post the same message over and over. Other people's time is valuable and they don't want to have to weed through the same messages you posted in tons of places. If someone helps you, say "thank you." Courtesy goes a long way in cyberspace.

Don't tell people personal things about yourself. Don't tell personal things about your family. You never really know who you're talking to. And even if you think you know who you are talking to, there could be strangers lurking and reading without letting you know that they are there. It's like writing your personal diary on a postcard.

With children especially, sharing personal information puts them at risk. Make sure your children understand what you consider personal information, and agree to keep it confidential online and everywhere else.

CHAPTER 14

Ms. Parry's Guide to Netiquette

A Bird's Eye View—

▼ Origins of Netiquette

▼ Ms. Parry's Rules for Correct
Internet Behavior

▼ Origins of Netiquette

In order to understand netiquette, you need to understand the Net. The Net was populated by techies who believed in free expression, the golden rule and generosity (at least that's how they tell it . . .). Commercialism was always frowned upon (and actually violated NSFNet's acceptable use policy) and still is . . . although commercialism is rapidly taking over the Net. It's always good to know the rules before you set forth in a new culture, and the Net is the newest culture of all.

Remember that people from many countries will be sharing ideas, and what is normal and correct for them may be strange to you. The rule of the game is RESPECT.

There's a lot to learn, but don't worry about having to learn all this new stuff at once. We were all newbies once, and you'll soon be a seasoned veteran, laughing at all the inside Net jokes.

▼ Ms. Parry's Rules for Correct Internet Behavior

People do outrageous things when they get behind a keyboard . . . things they would ordinarily never do in real space. Somehow, whether it's the fact that they think they're anonymous, or that the Net brings out personality disorders (<g>— you'll understand this if you read on), I don't know. But please don't fall into the trap of saying and doing things online that you know shouldn't be said or done.

Remember that you can be traced, and nothing is ever truly anonymous online. Everything you say should be said with the understanding that *they* will know, sooner or later, that you said it.

Some of you may be seasoned veterans, but many of you are new to both online services and the Internet. To help, I put together a list of emoticons (sometimes called "smileys") which are shortcut terms that allow the reader to understand subtleties in your posts, as well as some basic rules of netiquette.

Netiquette List

USING ALL CAPITAL LETTERS—it's considered shouting and is hard on the eyes.

"Flaming"—inciting or provoking an argument.

"Spamming"—posting something in many places at the same time. It's also the name for junk e-mail sent to millions of people.

These are all no-no's. Remember that just because you're hiding out behind a big computer monitor, you aren't exempt from correct and thoughtful communications.

Emoticons... laughter in cyberspace. Since people cannot communicate sarcasm, teasing, humor or other emotions online (after all, typing is typing) netiquette has developed emotion indicators . . . they are called "smileys." I've posted some of the more popular ones below, but new ones get added every day. Your kids may want to try to invent a few, too.

<g>	grin
<G>	big grin
:-)	smiley face
:->	very smiley face
;-) or ;->	a wink
:-(	frown
:-P	sticking out your tongue
@----->---	a cyber rose

If you don't understand why these emoticons mean what I say they do . . . turn the book sideways. (If you still don't get it . . . turn it the other sideways.)

LOL	laughing out loud
FOFL	falling on the floor laughing
BTW	by the way
OTOH	on the other hand
PMJI	pardon me for jumping in
IMHO	in my humble opinion
ROFLOL	Rolling on the floor, laughing out loud

Acronyms are also used frequently to cut down on the typing. These are a few of the most common.

Now for a pop quiz! (Just kidding. :->)

CHAPTER 15

United We Stand

A Bird's Eye View—

▼ Build a Solid Team of Parents, Friends, Librarians and Schools

▼ Build a Solid Team of Parents, Friends, Librarians and Schools

As more and more schools and libraries are getting online, teachers and librarians are getting wired too. (No, that doesn't mean that they are doing anything they shouldn't be doing <g> . . . it means that they're getting online.) They're a great resource for parents. They have a chance to get to know our kids and our neighbors' kids, know what they're doing when you're not looking and know what wonderful things there are online.

Ask them to set up a program to try to get parents involved. Do what you can to help; they deserve our support and admiration. (I've said it before, but librarians are our most underestimated natural resource. And, I've been lucky enough to know some really sensational ones.) You should also check out the American Librarians Association's (the ALA) website (www.ala.org). It's a wealth of resources and tips.

The American Librarians Association features a good site called KidsConnect (www.ala.org/ICONN/kidscom.html), which is run by the American Association of School Librarians, a division of the ALA. Through e-mail submitted at the site, kids can send inquiries to the librarians online, and within a couple days get help in locating resources that respond to their inquiries. The kids are then referred to their school library media specialist. KidsConnect helps build teams.

In addition, after you've finished this book and have had a chance to surf around for awhile, you may be able to contribute meaningfully to the plans to get your schools and libraries online. Share the wealth. Let them know what you've learned and let them teach you what they know. (My next book is for teachers, since my daughter entered one of the best technology education programs in the country this fall. Hopefully, all you teachers out there will help us.)

Look over the school's proposed Internet use policies and see if there's something you can suggest to improve them. Volunteer to help teach other parents and share resources and sites you've found. Share keywords.

The only way we can truly protect our children in cyberspace is to build a solid team of parents, friends, librarians and schools. Here are a few tips:.

Team Tips

- What are other kids accessing?
- How much do other parents know about the Internet?
- What kinds of use policies have been set up?
- Coordinating with other parents, agree on a common policy.
- Enforce the joint policy with other parents and respect their values.
- Share new ideas and family website finds with others.
- What software are they using?
- How can you get the best out of the software they chose?
- Plan a few community projects, like a cyber scavenger hunt.
- Use your libraries' tech resources.
- Make sure your librarian is an important part of the team.

The best Internet use policies I have found come from libraries, and the "cream of the crop" seem to come from school libraries. Check with your school librarian and see what they're using.

CHAPTER 16

Using Technology to Implement and Enforce Your Choices

A Bird's Eye View—

▼ Parental Control Software . . .
Added Protection

▼ A Little About the Products

▼ Comparing the Products

▼ Our Awards . . . Please Limit Your
Acceptance Speech to 30 Seconds
or We'll be Here All Night

▼ Parental Controls from Your
Online Services

▼ Server Blocking

▼ How We Conducted Our Review and
Testing of the Software

▼ Parental Control Software . . . Added Protection

Child computer safety products fall into several types. They either block "bad" sites or only allow you to access "good" sites. Most also filter words and phrases, and some even filter them in context to prevent blocking innocent phrases. Some provide alerts when certain sites are accessed, while others block access without letting anyone know they're working.

Certain software can also monitor offline computer usage as well, such as how many hours (and which hours) the child spends on the computer or playing computer games. A few online services (such as America Online) provide their own proprietary products which work only on their systems. Some of the other software can be used with online services, while others are designed only for the Internet.

You can also use software to block certain incoming information entirely, such as e-mail, or filter incoming information, or prevent certain information from being sent by your children to others (such as your telephone number). Online searches can be blocked, as well.

The programs are either customizable or preset by the manufacturer of the software. Some allow you to set different levels of protection for different children, so you can set more restrictions for younger children than their older siblings. Many of the better systems combine the various options, to give you the greatest protection and maximum flexibility.

I've included below a detailed description of the kinds of protection technologically available. Later in this chapter, you'll find a chart comparing the features of each of the leading programs we've reviewed.

Bad site lists. There are products that block certain sites determined (by either the company or the parent) to be undesirable. These types of software have lists of "bad sites" (updated on a regular basis) compiled by the software company, and access to anything on these lists is automatically blocked. Some also allow the parent to add or delete names from that list, allowing it to be customized for your child.

With the purchase of a product, you usually get a subscription for updated lists for a certain period of time. The cost of updates after the subscription period has expired varies, as do the frequency of updates. Given how rapidly websites are being added to the Web, the more frequent the updates the better.

Before you jump on the "bad site" blocking bandwagon, however, you should know that there has been substantial controversy over how the "bad sites" are selected. Inconsistent determinations, improperly trained or untrained reviewers and lack of real quality-control can result in an unreliable list, either limiting too many sites, or not enough.

A few of these programs allow you to review the list of blocked "bad sites." If you can, you may want to check out the sites and see if you agree with their classification.

Access only to preapproved "good" sites. Some manufacturers, recognizing that they can never keep up with all the new sites being published on the Web, have opted for a list of preapproved, prescreened sites that are considered child-friendly. Each manufacturer screens the sites based on its own criteria, and while a site may be on one manufacturer's good list, it may not be on another's. While using an approved list addresses the problem with "bad" site blocking, not being able to list all the new sites, or even all sites already existing on the Web, may limit your child's access to terrific sites that haven't yet been reviewed and approved.

These programs also include a subscription to the approved list, which the manufacturers frequently update. As with the "bad" site software, there is often a charge for updates after the subscription period has ended, and the frequency of updates varies product by product. The problem with quality control of "bad" site screening also exists with the "good" site screening, since sites may not be included in the approved list based upon inconsistent standards and the application of these standards by often improperly trained or untrained individuals.

Rating Services—PICS. The people who know the most about the Internet have set up a rating system. Unfortunately, it hasn't caught on as fast as it should. Perhaps with the fact that the CDA was found to be unconstitutional, it may gain greater acceptance and usage.

PICS, the Platform for Internet Content Selection, is a technological standard which allows web browsers to read the rating labels for, and block, sites based on their rating. Website operators submit their site for rating by a third-party rating agency. Based upon the information voluntarily submitted by the website operators about content at the site, the site is rated. PICS then sends them a code that must be added to the HTML coding at the top of their site. While this code is invisible to us, it is read by your browser and allows or denies access to the site, depending upon the rating criteria set in your browser. Microsoft's Internet Explorer versions 3.0 and higher support PICS and Netscape's next version of Navigator will include PICS capability too. That allows good site accessibility, and bad site blocking.

Unfortunately, since so few sites are rated, selecting this software means your children can only access the rated "good" sites. Only 40,000 are currently rated. Limiting access to only preapproved sites may err on the side of being overly protective over your children's access to content on the Internet, but if the choice is between allowing your child to access only preapproved content, or not permitting them to be online at all, there's no choice. Even limited access is better than no access.

Until more sites are rated (an effort we support), we recommend using another parental control system, hopefully, one that supports PICS compatible ratings.

*Keywords and phrases (**either in context or not**).* Certain words tend to be used in most of the sites that contain content you want to screen or block. The technology allows you to block access to any sites that contain these words. (Some products allow you to add words to the list, or delete words from the list.) But if a site contains inappropriate graphics which are not described with any related keywords, or if the site is in another language, these filters may not work.

Choosing effective keywords isn't as easy as it sounds. You'll have a better sense of how to choose them once you've been online awhile, but in the meantime, get as many suggestions as you can from others. Share certain keyword lists with other parents, once you've found some good ones. At our site, we will try to list the keywords you have found and have sent us. (But we will have to do it carefully, or you'll screen out our site!)

One of my favorite inadvertent blocking stories was shared by an Internet father and co-designer of Kids of the Web. (I've discussed the site at length in the chapter *It's a Wonderful (Online) Life.*) When they moved their website to a new ISP, www.hooked.net, they found that most of the parental control software programs blocked their site. It was a sub-domain of www.hooked.net, and "hooked" was blocked as a drug term.

Some of the words typically chosen are "tobacco," "smoking," "wine", "drugs", "sex," "breasts," various vulgarities, and other descriptive terms and slang terms for sexual activities and organs. Unfortunately, unless your software is smart enough to block these words only when they are used in context with certain other trigger words, let me show you what happens (I made these examples up):

BLOCKED: "John, a young slave, looked down the **tobacco** road, wondering why he didn't have the freedom to keep walking until he found where he wanted to be."

Blocked: "Jim Carrey's movie, *The Mask*, proves that he's really **smoking!**". (No comments please on whether some of Jim Carrey movies, like *The Cable Guy* and *When Nature Calls*, should be blocked as a matter of course . . . we're only talking about protecting our children from serious dangers, not bad comedy.)

Blocked: "Welcome to France . . . enjoy this site and your tour of the **wine** country."

Blocked: "Parents of **sex**tuplets have problems coping with the workload."

Blocked: "Perdue's fresh roasted chicken **breasts** make preparing dinner much easier for working couples."

Blocked: "You can buy this comic book at your local **drug**store. "

That's why you want a software that screens keywords only in context. That means the keywords are blocked only when they are used in combination with other words. (They also block using algorithms, but I won't bore you with an explanation of how that works. Just trust me.)

You should know, however, that certain adult sites have learned how the keyword blocking works, and have started misspelling words commonly blocked by parents. They'll use words like "penus," and begin words that correctly begin with an "f" with a "ph." They may also add an extra "k" on the end of certain words. It's hard to argue that certain adult site operators aren't seeking a younger audience along with the adult audience when they do things like this. (Of course, the explanation may be as simple as the fact that they just can't spell. . . .)

Alerts. Some of the software lets you know when it's working, others don't. Some alerts tell you when the site has been blocked by the software, "This site has been blocked by _."

Other programs block access, but don't tell you that's why you can't access the site. I don't like that feature. Make sure your kids know what steps you're taking. The Internet is still too finicky for users to know that the reason they can't load the site is because of the software, rather than a problem on the Net. Your kids will spend lots of time trying to get it to work. Why frustrate them unnecessarily?

Monitoring access, with or without blocking. Some of these programs keep track of where your kids have been. They either block access to sites based on criteria you've set, or just let you know that your kids have been to those sites. I like this feature, especially with older children. When you want to be able to educate your children about risks in cyberspace and then trust them to look out for those dangers on their own, this let's you know what they're doing. It gives you the information you need to modify your choices and add or subtract from the parental controls you had already chosen. It's the "fly on the wall" parents always wished they had.

Again, make sure your children know they're being monitored. It's a matter of respecting them and earning their trust. If they still want to see whatever was blocked, first view the site alone, and if it's okay, let them access it too.

Works with a certain online service. Some blocking software only works with a specific online service (like AOL or MSN), while others work with all online services. Even though the most popular online services have their own parental controls (most are based on Cyber Patrol), you may want to customize the parental controls beyond what is offered by your online service. If you use ISP direct access, rather than an online service provider, you don't need this feature.

Works only on the Internet. Many of the programs work only on the Internet but not on online services like AOL or MSN. If you've read the first section of the book, you already know that the Internet includes more than the World Wide Web. It includes Gopher, IRCs, Usenet and FTPs. The blocking programs work on these other Internet areas as well. But don't buy a program that is Internet-only if you use an online service.

Works both on and offline to monitor all computer usage. Some programs also offer monitoring of offline computer use, like games, in addition to monitoring online use. These programs can tell you how much time your kids are spending on the computer and what they're doing. I like this feature, especially with younger children (10-13 years) who spend a lot of time playing computer games. It's also a Godsend for working parents who don't have childcare for those few hours the children are home after school. It lets you know if the kids are sticking to the rules, and also lets you know if their friends are too.

Customizable for more than one child at a time. Some products allow you to make different settings for different children in your household. Otherwise, you're back to your one size fits all setting, where your fourteen-year-old has to live with the same controls as your six-year-old.

Incoming Screening. This is an important feature. Many of the dangers are being home-delivered these days. E-mail messages can have HTML coding that links you directly to adult sites, and people who you don't want to reach your children can send them e-mail and other messages that you don't want them to receive. Incoming screening screens all inbound information, including e-mail. Once your kids are using e-mail on their own, this may be an important tool to help screen out undesirable information and certain e-mail senders.

Outgoing Screening. If I had to chose one feature, this would be it. Outgoing screening prevents your children from sending anyone their telephone number, address, real name or anything else you decide to block. It's particularly helpful when you are dealing with younger children, who might be fooled into disclosing the personal information you agreed shouldn't be disclosed. It also keeps them from being able to fill out most of the registration and survey forms that children's sites want them to complete. They'll need you to help them do that, which gives you control over what information these sites have about you and your children.

Actually, these work by adding your personal information to a blocked keyword list. You have to be smart when you add the info to the list, and remember to list your phone number as both (111) 123-4567, 111-123-4567 and any other variation that your kids might use. Get your kids' help in selecting the keywords for blocking.

In increasing levels of control, I've done a quick review of the types of protection parents can offer their children—from trusting them and educating them to never letting them use a computer. As you gain more control, you limit more information your children can access, both good and bad, and rely less on trust. That's the balance you'll need to strike. And, it's your choice.

Levels of Control and Protection
(in increasing levels of protection)

a. Trust and education
b. Tracking use and duration
c. Filtering
d. Blocking
  i. server proxy
  ii. customizable local blocking

e. Parental controls on online services
f. Limited children-only areas online
g. Locking the computer when you're not home
h. Living in a computerless home and community

Note that there is no way to make sure your children are 100% protected (unless you choose option "h") and decide to live computerless. Recognize that everyone should be accepting some level of responsibility for safe surfing and sometimes things will get through that you wish hadn't. It's a risk we have to learn to live with—to minimize, but learn to live with nonetheless.

▼ A Little About the Products

We selected four of the most popular brands of parent control software currently on the market to review: Cyber Patrol, CYBERsitter, Net Nanny and Surf Watch.

Cyber Patrol, from Microsystems Software, Inc.

Cyber Patrol undoubtedly has the most features, and protects more areas than any of the other products. This is reflected in the difficulty in setup. Although it gives parents lots of choices, newbies and even some more experienced computer users will have problems configuring the product. (If you know any local computer geeks, this is a good time to call them and beg for help.)

But the feature choices may be enough to outweigh the setup difficulties, since Cyber Patrol has the best features of any of the programs we reviewed. It can be configured for up to nine different users, so your 16-year old won't be stuck viewing sites approved for your 8-year old. It has bad site and good site lists, and can be customized to add or delete certain sites to either. There are multiple content filtering categories (check them out on our chart). The program works in chatrooms, newsgroups and on the Web, and also on and offline.

Our kid testers told us that it was the hardest to crack of all the locally-installed products we tested. (Locally-installed means installed on your computer, not on the server, like Bess, which we'll get to in a moment.)

Parents can control the number of hours and times of day their children are using the computer, and can generate reports detailing usage. Best of all,

Cyber Patrol has addressed parents' privacy concerns with their "ChatGard" feature, which allows parents to choose certain information that their children shouldn't be sharing online with others, and block attempts to send it. Whenever anything from the blocked list is typed in, the letters are replaced with "Xs." This also helps remind kids what information they shouldn't be sending out.

Cyber Patrol is PICS compatible and supports both RSACi and SafeSurf's rating systems. It is offered, without charge, to users of Microsoft's Internet Explorer, as well as to members of CompuServe and Prodigy. AOL uses its technology. Just before we went to press we heard that AT&T would be offering it to their members as well.

CYBERsitter, from Solid Oak Software

CYBERsitter's controls allow parents to filter websites, newsgroups, chatrooms and two-way e-mail.

CYBERsitter's privacy controls offer a special feature over those of its competitors. Its Advanced Phrase Definitions Capabilities lets parents select certain word combinations, to maximize blocking of outgoing private information.

Its bad site list is not customizable, which is a problem. But the program supports the PICS standard, and ratings using that standard.

Two of CYBERsitter's best features are its keywords in context system, which prevents accidental blocking of innocent sites, and access to inappropriate ones, and its ability to log the sites accessed by your kids while not blocking them. This is a particularly good feature for your older kids and teens, when you just want to keep an eye on where they're going even if you choose not to block their access.

Net Nanny, from Net Nanny Ltd.

Net Nanny uses a parent's input to form the access filtering and blocking database. The program comes with a sample dictionary of filtered keywords designed to be customized by the parent. It can control access to both chatrooms and the Web, and Windows and DOS programs offline. It screens incoming and outgoing messages, and can be customized to filter certain private information your child may attempt to supply to others online. One of their best features (one that my sister could have used when her three-year-old got carried away with Oscar the Grouch's trash encouragement) is the blocking of your children's ability to delete files on your computers.

Net Nanny also logs attempts to access blocked sites, for reports to parents. And, if a parent selects its special feature, the computer will shut down after a set number of attempts to access blocked sites.

Surf Watch, from Spyglass Inc.

Of the most popular locally-installed parental control programs, Surf Watch has the largest database of both good and bad sites, which can be customized by the parent. Surf Watch protected the best out of all the products we tested against our own list of sites, by blocking 75 percent of the sites tested. (This is compared with the 19 percent blocking results of the other three programs.) In a face-to-face comparison in March, 1997 CNN found Surf Watch the most effective in blocking offensive sites as well.

Surf Watch screens websites and chatrooms using both a bad site list and keyword blocking. In its new release, Surf Watch 3.0 allows parents to block their children's access to chatrooms entirely unless they are accompanied by their parent. It doesn't, though, block outgoing personal information. Representatives from Surf Watch explain that outgoing filtering is too easy to bypass to be effective, but it's a feature I miss. (Its new chatroom blocker was designed to avoid the problems associated with children giving out information in chatrooms, but doesn't address children filling out forms and surveys online with personal information.)

In addition, Surf Watch blocks access to the general search engines, if parents select the "SearchWatch" feature, limiting their searches to Yahooligans!, Yahoo!'s search engine for kids. Parents who are afraid of inadvertent gaps in filtering can select an "Allowed Site" function that allows their children only to access approved sites, and those selected from Yahooligans!

Of all the locally-installed programs (those installed on your own computer, as opposed to your ISP's server), Surf Watch is also the easiest to set up. It's the one newbies find most user-friendly, even without some of the privacy features other programs supply.

▶ Comparing the Products

ON-LINE "BLOCKING" SOFTWARE: FUNCTIONS AND OPTIONS

Programs	Blocking Capabilities — Words & Phrases	Words "In Context"	Web Sites	Newsgroups	Chat Rooms	Outgoing Information	Possible Actions — Warns/Blocks	Masks Words	Monitors Activity	Application shuts down	Offline Controls	List Customizing — Add	Delete	Customizable (# of Children)	On-line Service Compatibility — CompuServe	Prodigy	AOL	Available for OS — Windows	Macintosh	Number of Sites — Good	Bad	Topics Covered
Net Nanny 3.1 $39.95	✓	✓	✓	✓	✓	✓	✓	✓	✓	✓	✓	✓	✓	1	only compatible if user manipulates thru cutting & pasting			✓		600	20,000	anything "inappropriate for kids"
CYBERsitter 2.11 $39.95	✓	✓	✓	✓	✓	✓	✓	✓	✓	✓	✓	✓	✓	1	✓	✓		✓		N/A	50,000	1. sex 2. illegal/illicit activities 3. bigotry 4. racism 5. drugs 6. pornography
Surf Watch 1.6 $50.00	✓		✓	✓	✓		✓					✓	✓	1	✓ free	✓ free	✓	✓	✓	15,000	50,000	1. sexually explicit 2. violence and hate crimes 3. gambling 4. illicit drugs and alcohol
Cyber Patrol 3.30.007 $29.95	✓		✓	✓	✓	✓	✓				✓	✓	✓	9	uses technology		uses technology	✓	✓	4,000	20,000	1. partial nudity 2. nudity 3. sexual acts/text 4. gross depictions 5. Satanic/cult 6. intolerance 7. drugs & drugs culture 8. militant/extremism 9. violence/profanity 10. questionable illegal/gambling 11. sex education 12. alcohol & tobacco

Number of Sites as specified by manufacturer—some companies may be more explicit in defining blocked areas

▼ A QUICK RUNDOWN . . . COMPARING EACH PRODUCT,
   THE GOOD AND BAD

Cyber Patrol (v. 3.30.007)
Microsystems Software
Sales: (800) 828-2608
$29.95

Features	GOOD	BAD
	• easy installation	• difficult set up
	• message is clear when it blocks	• cannot be used on the same computer with any other filtering programs
	• can monitor hours online	• does not log hits
	• customizable for up to 9 children	• user must pay for updates

Updates: $29.95 for 1 year subscription, $19.95 for 6-month subscription available weekly (see "New Version" below)

Technical Support: available 8:30 a.m. –11 p.m. EST, 10 on staff

Customizable for More than One User: yes, up to 9 users

New Version (v. 4.0, available September 1997):	• daily update feature
	• a little faster
	• improved filter technology to be even more precise
	• ability to use *any* PICS rating system, including new ones as they come out

CYBERsitter (v. 2.11)
Solid Oak Software
Sales: (800) 388-2761
$39.95

Features	GOOD	BAD
	• easy installation	• cannot be used on the same computer with any other filtering programs
	• easy set-up	• does not consistently give message that it is working to block a site or search
	• free updates	• can't see list of blocked sites
		• not compatible with Macintosh
		• no "good site" list
		• not customizable for more than one user

Updates: free, updated daily

Technical Support: available 9:00 a.m. –5 p.m. PST, number of staff not available

Customizable for More than One User: no

New Version (available now):	• CYBERsitter 97 allows third-party filtering and can access filter files of other organizations
	• Will never give message that it's working

The Best Way to Protect your Children and Free Speech on the Internet.

Net Nanny (v. 3.1)
Net Nanny, Ltd.
Sales: (800) 340-7177
$39.95

Features	GOOD	BAD
	• easy installation	• 19 percent effective—allowed access to 13 of 16 adult sites tested
	• easy set-up	
	• only software tested with a "Shut Down" option	• must cut and paste site list into a words and phrases list in order to be compatible with AOL, CompuServe, and Prodigy
	• free updates	• incompatible with Macintosh
		• not customizable for more than one user
		• very small "good site" list

Updates: free, updated twice a month

Technical Support: available 8:00 a.m. –5 p.m. EST, staff of 3

Customizable for more than one user: no

New Version 3.1:
- V. 3.1 has customized integration with Internet Explorer and uses PICS
- Now working on changing lack of compatibility with AOL, CompuServe, and Prodigy
- V. 4.0 will look at words in context and will be customizable for more than one child

Surf Watch (v. 1.6)		
Spyglass, Inc.		
Sales: (888) 6-SPYGLASS		
$49.95		

Features	GOOD	BAD
	• easy installation	• monthly updates; fee after first year
	• easy set-up	• cannot block outgoing personal
	• gives clear consistent	information
	message that it is	• does not log hits
	working when it	• must pay for updates
	blocks	
	• 75 percent effective	
	allowed access to	
	4 of 16 sites tested	

Updates: free first year, then $30.00 per year thereafter, available monthly (see "New Version" below)

Technical Support: available 7:30 a.m. –6 p.m. PST, staff of 6

Customizable for more than one user: no (but see "New Version" below)

New Version:	• automatic daily updates
	• can completely eliminate chat rooms
	• can customize for more than one user

▼ Our Awards . . . Please Limit Your Acceptance Speech to 30 Seconds or We'll be Here All Night

I hesitated to give awards. Everyone was always asking me which product was best, and I couldn't give them an answer. Instead, I'd have to ask them questions. How much do you know about computers? Are you willing to take the time to customize options? How well do your kids listen? Only then could I recommend the best . . . and it was a "best fit," not a "best product."

Therefore, I can't choose a "best overall," because there isn't one. Instead, I've focused on certain important criteria.

When it comes to choosing the right product, there are three main criteria I felt were the most important. The first is ease of set-up. The second is the best variety of features and options. The third is how effective they are in blocking and filtering the things you want blocked and filtered.

▼ EASE OF SETUP (DRUMROLL PLEASE . . .)

Hands down, the easiest one to set-up was Surf Watch. All of the tech support people were terrific at each of the software companies, but we didn't have to use tech support to set-up Surf Watch. I suspect that over the years since its release, they've worked out most of the set-up bugs.

▼ Best features and options

And the winner is . . . (as the envelope rips open and a tall spokesmodel smiles into the camera) Cyber Patrol! Cyber Patrol has, unquestionably, the best features of all the programs we reviewed and tested. One of the things we liked best about Cyber Patrol is that you can use different settings for different children. It has up to nine different settings. It also monitors time spent online, restricting children to certain hours of the day or the time spent online, as a whole. Cyber Patrol can also block access to parents' applications like your finance manager.

Cyber Patrol is an interesting product. Relatively new to the market, it has taken the online services by storm. Each week there's another announcement about someone adding Cyber Patrol to their parent control arsenal. The most recent was AT&T's announcement that it was offering Cyber Patrol to its ISP subscribers.

Cyber Patrol has terrific features. It obviously has its thumb on the pulse of parents. I wish it were easier to set up, though.

The new release, Cyber Patrol spokespeople promised, is much easier to install and customize. I'm sure that they'll address this concern in the same professional way they do all the others.

▼ MOST EFFECTIVE IN BLOCKING AND FILTERING

I'll cut to the chase, since I'm running out of witty things to say. Surf Watch blocked 75 percent of all the sites we selected for our testing. Surf Watch has been at this the longest, and has the largest database of good sites, and (next to CYBER-sitter which only has a "bad site" list) the largest database of bad sites. (I wish that Surf Watch allowed parents to block outgoing personal information, since that is one of the most important features in our opinion. It is the only one that doesn't have that feature. Surf Watch . . . are you listening?)

The information relating to test results of the other software programs is set forth in "How We Conducted Our Review and Testing of the Software."

▼ MISS CONGENIALITY . . .

There are several options and features I want to draw to your attention. As long as I'm handing out awards, I thought I'd give out a few more.

Best updates.

When it comes to updates, the more frequent, the better. Also giving free updates is better than charging for updates (I'm just venturing a guess . . . but I suspect you might agree with me on that last one . . .)

Surf Watch's new version has free daily updates, too.

CYBERsitter
Free daily upgrades

Net Nanny
Free semi-monthly upgrades

Best single feature. It's a tie.

Net Nanny prevents children from deleting files. Cyber Patrol won two separate single best feature awards: Cyber Patrol has nine different user settings; and Cyber Patrol controls the times when your child can use the computer.

▼ Parental Controls from Your Online Services

Each of the online service providers offers some type of parental control feature for no additional cost. These range from children and teen only areas and the ability to block e-mail and instant messaging features, to providing Cyber Patrol (or its technology), for their members' use.

▼ KIDS ONLY AND AOL'S PARENTAL CONTROL

 America Online (AOL) parents can restrict their children to their "Kids Only" forum or a teens level of access, with prescreened content and monitored chatrooms. Parents can also prevent their children from receiving e-mail or instant messages, and may prevent them from entering chatrooms or accessing the Web. AOL also provides its members with Cyber Patrol technology at no additional cost.

Strict terms of service enforcement has also helped AOL maintain a safer environment. (Remember when my account was closed for my daughter's friends' flaming match?)

▼ PRODIGY'S PARENTAL CONTROL

 Prodigy provides parents with the option to control access to its individual bulletin boards, chat areas, or newsgroups. Parents can also block complete access to the Web for certain users.

Prodigy offers kids and teens their own chatrooms, as well as special Web areas exclusively for them. Prodigy also makes Cyber Patrol available to its members. Within Prodigy's monitored chatrooms and public forums, users are prevented from posting items deemed unacceptable for children.

Prodigy's kids' online area is located at http://kids. prodigy.net. (Don't all rush there. It's only viewable by Prodigy members.) Prodigy has designed its kids area to appeal to kids of all ages.

▼ Compuserve's Parental Control

CompuServe offers parents the option of controlling which areas members of the family can enter by using passwords. No chat areas are available for children. Parents have the option of having e-mail sent to them first for screening before a child receives it. CompuServe also makes Cyber Patrol available to its members.

▼ MSN child protection

The Microsoft Network uses RSACi ratings. When you open your account, you are asked to designate which rating levels you prefer. If you fail to make a selection, the system automatically uses the most restrictive levels of RSACi ratings as your default setting. You can, of course, choose not to use any rating blocking, and need to click on that option when registering your new account, or the default setting will be used. MSN is a strong proponent of RSACi ratings, and uses them as a default setting in their Internet Explorer releases 3.0 and higher.

MSN doesn't have any special areas only for children, other than Disney's Daily Blast. But it does prescreen certain newsgroups based upon their hardcore sexual content or the fact that they promote criminal activities, such as computer piracy or pedophilia.

▼ Server Blocking

Server blocking or filtering is when the parental controls are installed at the ISP or online service company level, not on your computer. That way, you're blocking or filtering at the source. With server-level blocking parents don't have to worry about updating lists or setting up the software either. Most serve blockers, however, aren't customizable.

▼   BESS

Bess is a server-based filter, which is installed at your Internet access server. Bess is purchased by your ISP, and offered as their parental control. It doesn't require any installation, and can't be customized by the parents. It filters incoming and outgoing e-mail and newsgroups and prevents all access to chatrooms.

Bess is also tamper-proof, since it's not located on your computer. It is the easiest of all the products to use, since like parental controls on AOL you only need to turn it on and it's working. There's nothing to configure.

Also, Bess is updated automatically, which allows Bess staff to update blocking for all its users quickly. Bess performed better than all the others in blocking access to links from Nasa.com. Many were already blocked, while the others were blocked within an hour of the news leaking out about the site. (The automatic updating also saves newbie parents from having to struggle with downloading update lists from the Internet, or installing updates from disks.)

One of the best features of Bess is that it gives parents the ability to contact them directly when a site is blocked, should the parent feel that the site shouldn't be blocked. I hope that it will also make a form available to its users when they encounter an offensive site, to request that a site *should be* blocked. Many parents and teachers have worked together with Bess administrators to help review sites and individual pages.

The biggest problem with Bess is that it's not being used or offered by ISPs for server-level blocking. I wish its public relations were as good as its product. (Hint . . . hint)

▼   NET SHEPHERD

Net Shepherd rates sites using its own system, classifying sites as "general," "child," "preteen," "teen" and "adult." It also uses the PICS standard, which allows the software to block or allow access based on RSACi or SafeSurf ratings.

Currently it only works on websites, not chatrooms or newsgroups, although the company expects to add a newsgroup feature soon. It also cannot filter unrated sites for content or keywords.

It does, however, block access to all unrated sites, as well as use a "good list" system of allowing access only to those sites selected by the parent. It currently has the most rated sites out of all the programs reviewed, estimated at 300,000, relying on volunteers to help rate the sites, and its own rating system.

Net Shepherd is available for use as a locally-installed program (for installation on the family's computer), but is also a very good product for ISP server-level blocking. It is updated automatically, as more sites are rated.

▼ How We Conducted Our Review and Testing of the Software

Throughout this book, I have tried not to sound like a lawyer, but unfortunately need to put my lawyer hat on for a moment or two. I want you to understand what the review and testing represents and what it doesn't. In order to do this, I've described the test settings and how results were obtained. Your experience may differ from ours.

▼ WHICH SOFTWARE WE SELECTED FOR TESTING

We selected four different brands of child protection software, Cyber Patrol, CYBERsitter, Net Nanny and Surf Watch, and one server-blocking software, Bess, and Net Shepherd (which defies categorization).

We tried to select the most popular products, although many companies refused to disclose annual sales or sales to date. As far as we can judge, Cyber Patrol, CYBERsitter, Net Nanny and Surf Watch are the most popular. Of the four, Surf Watch has been on the market longest and claims the most users (approximately 3.5 times as many as its nearest competitor). Cyber Patrol, though, seems to have captured the online service market and is catching on with certain ISPs.

▼ HOW WE CONDUCTED OUR TESTING

In order to test each software, we installed them according to the manufacturer's instructions and used the default settings (the ones that came with the software), rather than customizing the programs. Each was tested on the same Pentium 133 machine, with 16 MB RAM and a 28.8 kbps modem. The computer used Windows 95 as its operating system. All programs were installed on the same computer at the same time, and deactivated while the others were being tested.

The same person conducted all the tests. Each software was tested against 16 sites we selected at random based upon their sexual content or provocative value (as in the case of an organization that encourages adult and child relations). We also tested each against the nasa.com site, when that controversy was announced. (A list of the sites used has been provided to the software manufacturers so that they can review those sites and take any action that they feel appropriate. I will also supply the list to any reader who requests a copy, in writing, and includes a self-addressed stamped envelope. All requests should be mailed to my attention, c/o Aftab & Savitt, P.C., East 80 Route 4, Paramus, New Jersey 07652.)

In addition, random testing was done with each product searching for offensive sites (including topics other than sexual content claimed to be blocked or filtered, using the default settings, like drugs and alcohol). We surfed using each software, testing its effectiveness with sites and links from those sites. The actual effectiveness rankings were done only with the 16 selected sites and each product was tested against those sites repeatedly to confirm consistency.

▼ THE RESULTS OF OUR TESTING

Although we believe that our test results are accurate, under the conditions tested, Cyber Patrol has informed us that their product does not work properly when installed on a computer which has another filtering product installed also. (Their product instructions, however, do not warn of such a problem. I have suggested that they add that warning to avoid parents having the same problem that we did. Since we suggest that parents shop around, and try different programs in order to find the one best suited to their needs, this problem is likely to occur frequently.) CYBERsitter informs us that, like Cyber Patrol, their product doesn't work properly when other filtering programs are installed on the same computer. (Unfortunately, they do not warn their users of this problem, either.)

Cyber Patrol's company representative also informed us that 12 of the 16 sites we tested were on their blocked sites list as of the date our tests were conducted, and that their product, if installed alone on our computer, should have blocked access to those sites. Had Cyber Patrol actually blocked those sites in our test, it would have tied with Surf Watch for our Most Effective in Blocking and Filtering Award. We have elected not to redo the award, since it was given for the products as they performed under the test conditions. Because CYBERsitter works differently from the other programs, in that it does not rely heavily on a blocked site list, we cannot determine how many of the tested sites should have been blocked on the test date, had it been installed alone on the computer. However, CYBERsitter informs us that as of September 19, 1997 it blocked all but three of the sites (one site was no longer available).

This testing is only a small sampling and may or may not be indicative of a larger sampling. Other groups have conducted much more extensive testing and if you have the time and patience to review their test results, I suggest you review Karen G. Schneider's site for the Internet Filter Assessment Project (she's working on a book on filtering) www.bluehighways.com/tifap. In addition, good reviews of the programs appear at the *FamilyPC* site, www.familypc.com, and are also available at the website www.neosoft.com/parental-control.

In the chapter *A Little About the Products,* I've provided the information on how many sites are rated and included in their good and bad lists by each of the major software companies. Our test results were consistent with that information. The companies with the largest databases blocked better.

But don't base your decision on our test results alone. All of the companies will provide a demo version, and we've listed all their websites (as well as linking to them from www.familyguidebook.com). Try them out and decide for yourself.

CHAPTER 17

Rating the Web ... PICS, the Platform for Internet Content Selection

A Bird's Eye View—

▼ PICS ... What is It?

▼ The Recreational Software Advisory Council's Labeling System for the Internet (RSACi)

▼ SafeSurf's Labeling and Rating System

▼ Net Shepherd Rating System and Software

▼ Microsoft Internet Explorer and PICS

▼ PICS . . . What is It?

 In response to governmental and parental concerns regarding the amount and quality of content on the Internet, many of the leaders in the Internet and computer industry joined W3C (the World Wide Web Consortium) to create PICS (the Platform for Internet Content Selection). The members of PICS are: America Online, Inc. (AOL), Apple Computer, Inc. , AT&T, The Center for Democracy & Technology (CDT), Compuserve, IBM Corporation, Information Technology Association of America (ITAA), Interactive Services Association (ISA), INRIA, MIT's Laboratory for Computer Science and W3C, MCI, Microsoft, Netscape Communications Corporation, NewView, Inc., Open Market, Prodigy Services Company, Progressive Networks, Providence Systems/Parental Guidance, SafeSurf, Spyglass, Surfwatch Software, Time-Warner's Pathfinder and Viacom's Nickelodeon.

PICS is a couple of computer code specifications that allow content to be both self-labeled and labeled by third parties. But PICS is not a rating service. PICS just governs the format of the rating code and how the codes are transmitted. Think of it as a food product label law, which specifies how big the lettering has to be, where on the product it has to appear and what color the label has to be. Otherwise, the food product manufacturer labels its own product, just like the rating companies do.

Many of us are betting on PICS to help ease the pressure on governmental groups to censor the Internet. The hardest part about getting the rating concept to work, as promised, is getting the sites rated.

Familyguidebook.com has a special e-mail that can be sent from the site to website operators asking them to rate their sites. Hopefully the search engines, as President Clinton requested, will help too. I suggest that Web hosting companies commit their help as well

Many rating companies are already using the PICS standard to come up with new products and services to address the needs of special interest groups.

▼ The Recreational Software Advisory Council's Labeling System for the Internet (RSACi)

We rated with **RSAC** *i*   The Recreational Software Advisory Council (RSAC) runs RSACi ("RSAC on the Internet"), a content rating labeling system that rates sites on the Web (www.rsac.org). RSAC is the non-profit organization that developed a content-rating system for the level of violence contained in computer games. They have taken their extensive experience and applied it now to the Internet. RSACi uses a rating system similar to the one used to rate computer game violence to rate Internet sites for nudity, sexual content, violence and vulgarities.

Parents can select the types of content and levels of ratings appropriate for their children. As with movie ratings or food labels . . . parents become the informed decision-makers. Using content ratings allows you, not the software blockers or government censors, to decide what and how much your children should see.

The RSACi rating system has been available since April 1, 1996, and has rated approximately 40,000 web sites. There is no charge for getting rated, and any website operator can submit a questionnaire at RSAC's website to obtain a rating label. The questionnaire asks a series of highly specific questions about the level, nature and intensity of the offensive language and graphic content used on the site. (Although currently based on the honor system, RSACi reserves the right to confirm the accuracy of the rating.)

The RSAC server processes the questionnaire and produces HTML advisory tags, which the website operator codes into the site. Your web browser then reads these tags, allowing or blocking access to sites with specified ratings.

Cyber Patrol, Surf Watch, Net Shepherd, Microsoft's Internet Explorer 3.0 and Microsoft Plus! for Kids currently support the RSACi ratings system, and RSACi's ratings are the default standard for their browser. Netscape reports that it will be adding PICS support to its next version of Netscape Navigator.

RSACi rates sites using the following categories and levels.

	Violence Rating Descriptor	Nudity Rating Descriptor	Sex Rating Descriptor	Language Rating Descriptor
Level 0:	None or only sports related	None	None or innocent kissing; romance	None
Level 1:	Injury to human being	Revealing attire	Passionate kissing	Mild expletives
Level 2:	Destruction of realistic objects	Partial nudity	Clothed sexual touching	Moderate expletives or profanity
Level 3:	Aggressive violence or death	Frontal nudity	Non-explicit sexual acts	Strong language or hate speech
Level 4:	Rape or wanton, gratuitous violence	Frontal nudity (qualifying as provocative display)	Explicit sexual acts or sex crimes	Crude, vulgar language or extreme hate speech

RSACi provides help in determining which rating level applies to the content of the site. When website operators complete the questionnaire, they are given a definition of the terms used in the form. For example, "frontal nudity" includes "any portrayal of a nude being which shows public hair or genitalia, excluding known animals in their natural state of undress." That means that nude female human breasts do not qualify as "frontal nudity." Nude breasts qualify instead as "partial nudity."

Unless you are familiar with the definitions, you won't be able to intelligently choose permitted rating levels. You can find the RSACi definitions at http://register.rsac.org/def.

▼ SafeSurf's Labeling and Rating System.

 SafeSurf, formed by concerned parents in 1995, uses its own rating standards, as well as the PICS standard. It rates the type of content and its level of intensity. It has many locations mirrored around the Web where website operators can fill out the questionnaire for a rating. If you have your own site, and support SafeSurf, you can request to be a mirror site yourself. That would allow other website operators to rate their sites using SafeSurf right at your site. It's an interesting grassroots concept, and may help get sites rated. It will also certainly raise the rating consciousness on the Web for all your website visitors.

SafeSurf can be licensed by ISPs for server level blocking as well. Web browsers that support the PICS standard will support SafeSurf.

SafeSurf has become the second most popular rating system. Most programs which use RSACi as a default, make SafeSurf a rating choice.

SafeSurf uses more rating categories than RSACi. The categories and levels used by SafeSurf are set forth below, and are more subjective than RSACi.

For each category—profanity, heterosexual themes, homosexual themes, nudity, violence, intolerances, glorifying drug use, other adult themes, and gambling—SafeSurf ranks the content into one of nine levels. The nine levels are strictly age-based. I've set them out below.

Age Range:
1) All Ages
2) Older Children
3) Teens
4) Older Teens
5) Adult Supervision Recommended

6) Adults
7) Limited to Adults
8) Adults Only
9) Explicitly for Adults

Profanity:

1) Subtle Innuendo
   Subtly Implied through the
   use of Slang
2) Explicit Innuendo
   Explicitly implied through the use
   of Slang
3) Technical Reference
   Dictionary, encyclopedic, news,
   technical references
4) Non-Graphic-Artistic
   Limited non-sexual expletives
   used in a artistic fashion
5) Graphic-Artistic
   Non-sexual expletives used in
   a artistic fashion

6) Graphic
   Limited use of expletives and
   obscene gestures
7) Detailed Graphic
   Casual use of expletives and
   and obscene gestures.
8) Explicit Vulgarity
   Heavy use of vulgar language
   obscene gestures.
   Unsupervised Chat Rooms.
9) Explicit and Crude
   Saturated with crude sexual
   references and gestures.
   Unsupervised Chat Rooms.

Heterosexual Themes:
1) Subtle Innuendo
   Subtly Implied through the use
   of metaphor
2) Explicit Innuendo
   Explicitly implied (not described)
   through the use of metaphor
3) Technical Reference
   Dictionary, encyclopedic, news,
   medical references
4) Non-Graphic-Artistic
   Limited metaphoric descriptions
   used in an artistic fashion
5) Graphic-Artistic
   Metaphoric descriptions used in an
   artistic fashion
6) Graphic
   Descriptions of intimate sexual acts
7) Detailed Graphic
   Descriptions of intimate
   details of sexual acts
8) Explicitly Graphic or Inviting
   Participation
   Explicit Descriptions of
   intimate details of sexual acts
   designed to arouse.
   Inviting interactive sexual
   participation. Unsupervised
   Sexual Chat Rooms
   or Newsgroups.
9) Explicit and Crude or
   Explicitly Inviting Participation
   Profane Graphic Descriptions
   of intimate details of sexual acts
   designed to arouse. Inviting
   interactive sexual participation.
   Unsupervised Sexual
   Chat Rooms or Newsgroups.

Gambling:
1) Subtle Innuendo
2) Explicit Innuendo
3) Technical Discussion
4) Non-Graphic-Artistic, Advertising
5) Graphic-Artistic, Advertising
6) Simulated Gambling
7) Real Life Gambling without
   Stakes
8) Encouraging Interactive Real
   Life Participation with Stakes
9) Providing Means with Stakes

Homosexual Themes:

1) Subtle Innuendo
   Subtly Implied through the use
   of metaphor

2) Explicit Innuendo
   Explicitly implied (not described)
   through the use of metaphor

3) Technical Reference
   Dictionary, encyclopedic, news,
   medical references

4) Non-Graphic-Artistic
   Limited metaphoric descriptions
   used in an artistic fashion

5) Graphic-Artistic
   Metaphoric descriptions used
   in an artistic fashion

6) Graphic
   Descriptions of intimate sexual acts

7) Detailed Graphic
   Descriptions of intimate details
   of sexual acts

8) Explicitly Graphic or Inviting
   Participation
   Explicit descriptions of intimate
   details of sexual acts designed to
   arouse. Inviting interactive sexual
   participation. Unsupervised
   Sexual Chat Rooms or
   Newsgroups.

9) Explicit and Crude or Explicitly
   Inviting Participation
   Profane Graphic Descriptions of
   intimate details of sexual acts
   designed to arouse. Inviting
   interactive sexual participation.
   Unsupervised Sexual
   Chat Rooms or Newsgroups.

Other Adult Themes:

1) Subtle Innuendo
2) Explicit Innuendo
3) Technical Reference
4) Non-Graphic-Artistic
5) Graphic-Artistic
6) Graphic
7) Detailed Graphic
8) Explicit Vulgarity
9) Explicit and Crude

Nudity:

1) Subtle Innuendo
   Subtly Implied through the use of composition, lighting, shaping, revealing clothing, etc.

2) Explicit Innuendo
   Explicitly implied (not shown) through the use of composition, lighting, shaping or revealing clothing

3) Technical Reference
   Dictionary, encyclopedic, news, medical references

4) Non-Graphic-Artistic
   Classic works of art presented in public museums for family viewing

5) Graphic-Artistic
   Artistically presented without full frontal nudity

6) Graphic
   Artistically presented with frontal nudity

7) Detailed Graphic
   Erotic frontal nudity

8) Explicit Vulgarity
   Pornographic presentation, designed to appeal to prurient interests.

9) Explicit and Crude
   Explicit pornographic presentation

Violence:

1) Subtle Innuendo
2) Explicit Innuendo
3) Technical Reference
4) Non-Graphic-Artistic
5) Graphic-Artistic
6) Graphic

7) Detailed Graphic
8) Inviting Participation in Graphic Interactive Format
9) Encouraging Personal Participation, Weapon Making

Sex, Violence, and Profanity:
1) Subtle Innuendo
2) Explicit Innuendo
3) Technical Reference
4) Non-Graphic-Artistic
5) Graphic-Artistic

6) Graphic
7) Detailed Graphic
8) Explicit Vulgarity
9) Explicit and Crude

Intolerance - (Intolerance of another person's racial, religious, or gender background):
1) Subtle Innuendo
2) Explicit Innuendo
3) Technical Reference
4) Non-Graphic-Literary
5) Graphic-Literary

6) Graphic Discussions
7) Endorsing Hatred
8) Endorsing Violent or Hateful Action
9) Advocating Violent or Hateful Action

Glorifying Drug Use:
1) Subtle Innuendo
2) Explicit Innuendo
3) Technical Reference
4) Non-Graphic-Artistic
5) Graphic-Artistic

6) Graphic
7) Detailed Graphic
8) Simulated Interactive Participation
9) Soliciting Personal Participation

▼ Net Shepherd Rating System and Software

Net Shepherd isn't either fish or fowl. It's a rating system that complies with the PICS standard, but parents have to download it and install it on their computer to use it. I think that it works best as a server level blocker, where an ISP licenses the product, and parents can turn it on or off, and set the controls for various levels of content and classifications of content.

The beauty of Net Shepherd is that it has more rated sites than anyone else. They've managed to do this by working from AltaVista's site registry, and hiring people to rate sites. Their site ratings are based on maturity (the maturity levels of the persons who should be viewing the site. Note, that doesn't mean understanding the site, it only means viewing it. A site describing a nuclear reaction experiment would be okay (although understandably boring) for most people, and would get a more general viewing rating.)

Their Maturity definition system is set forth below.

Rating	Definition
General	Content appropriate for all ages
Child	Content appropriate for ages 6-9 yrs.
Pre-Teen	Content appropriate for ages 10-12 yrs.
Teen	Content appropriate for ages 13-17 yrs.
Adult	Content appropriate for ages 18 yrs and over
Objectionable	Content may be objectionable for any age group

They also rate on quality of the site, using a star system the way a restaurant would be rated.(One star is "poor" and five stars "excellent.")

Breaking away from the pack, Net Shepherd has gotten into the topical directory business. All sites, in addition to the maturity and quality ratings, receive a topical classification.The topics range from "Arts & Literature," "Sports & Recreation" and

"Business" to "News," "Kids & Family" and "Personal Websites" (among others). Using these topical classifications, you can limit your searches to those Net Shepherd topics. That way, it becomes a directory-type search engine for Net Shepherd users.

Taking this feature one step further, Net Shepherd has announced that it will join forces with AltaVista (the largest indexing search engine) to create special interest search engines for special interest groups, on a case-by-case basis. For example, if a religious group wants to commission a special search engine for its members, where only preapproved sites would be listed, Net Shepherd, together with AltaVista, would prepare a special interest search engine just for that group.

Even more relevant is the fact that Net Shepherd can prepare a special family-friendly search engine of prescreened sites. That way a parent can limit their children's surfing to sites referenced by that search engine, each of which would have been rated by Net Shepherd as safe for all ages.

▼ Microsoft Internet Explorer and PICS

Microsoft Internet Explorer versions 3.0 and higher work with PICS. I've set out some screen shots which show you how easy it is to setup the PICS controls on Microsoft's Internet Explorer. It uses RSACi as the default, but can be configured to use SafeSurf, instead.

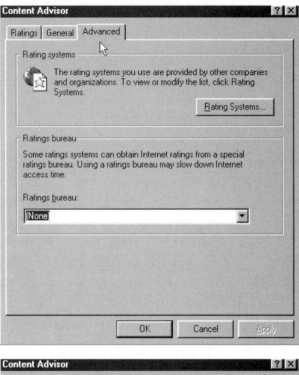

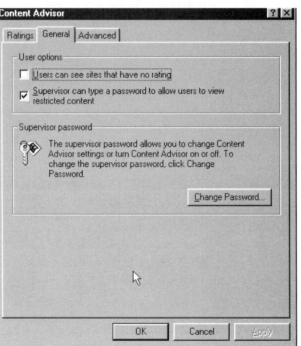

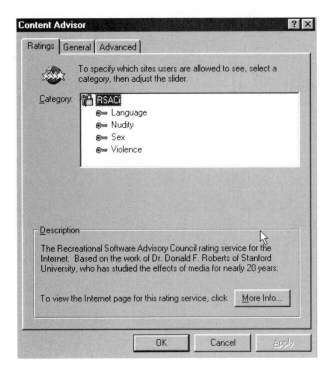

CHAPTER 18

What Have You Learned So Far?

A Bird's Eye View—

▼ What? You Never Told Us There Was Going to Be a Quiz!

▼ How CyberSavvy are you?

▼ What? You Never Told Us There Was Going to Be a Quiz!

Remember when I promised you there wouldn't be a quiz? I lied. (You should be used to this by now.) This CyberSavvy™ quiz was put together by The Direct Marketing Association, in conjunction with CARU and Call For Action. It's a terrific example of how the industry is trying to self-regulate and keep parents informed.

By now you should be "CyberSavvy."

▼ How CyberSavvy Are You?

1. How can our family communicate with other people on the Internet?

    A. E-mail
    B. Chat rooms
    C. Newsgroups
    D. Listservs
    E. All of the above

Answer: E. There are many ways people communicate online—through e-mail (sending and receiving messages to and from specific people), chat rooms (speaking directly to other people online in real-time), newsgroups (posting messages in online "bulletin boards" for everyone to see and respond to) and listservs (automated e-mail communications to large groups of people). It is important for families to discuss what is and what is not appropriate to communicate online. Some parental control software now helps families block the transmission of specific words and phrases, including names, addresses and telephone numbers.

2. Who uses the Internet to communicate directly with other people?
  A. Kids
  B. Adults
  C. Schools
  D. Businesses
  E. All of the above

Answer: E, all of the above and more. Clubs, organizations, even governments use the Internet to communicate directly with other people. Many post information about their organizations and activities online, and some sponsor their own online discussions, chat areas, newsgroups and listservs.

3. Are people able to talk directly to us online, even if we don't know them?

  A. No
  B. Yes

Answer: B. The Internet is just like any other public place. You can communicate with other people from around the world, even if you do not know them person-ally. Many people meet new friends while they are online, but it is very important that your family discuss and create your own rules about talking to people you do not know on the Internet. The CyberSavvy Family Pledge [available at the DMA site]may be a good starting point for your family to establish these types of fam-ily policies.

4. Is talking with someone over the Internet the same as having a private conver-sation?

  A. Always
  B. Never
  C. Sometimes

Answer: C. As you know, people use the Internet in many different ways to communicate with each other. Sometimes, people speak to a lot of people at the same time in newsgroups and listservs, while other times, they communicate one-on-one, usually through e-mail. It is important to know that people you meet in chat rooms and newsgroups may want to have a private conversation or send you a personal e-mail. Your family should discuss your own rules for having those types of conversations and for determining what is and what is not appropriate to talk about. Remember, you should never give out personal information to strangers online.

5. Why is it that some companies request that I complete a questionnaire or survey before I can move through their Web site?

    A. To learn more about the people who visit their sites
    B. To gather information for marketing and customer service
    C. To provide a better service to customers
    D. All of the above

Answer: D. There are several reasons why companies like to know information about people who visit their sites. Generally, it helps companies provide a better service to all customers. If a company learns that people of a certain age tend to visit their site most often, then they can tailor the information they provide to that age group. Some companies may use this information to communicate with you about their products and services. If you have a specific question about a survey or a questionnaire you find online, you should contact the company directly.

6. How do I know if a World Wide Web site belongs to a business?

    A. Because I have visited the site
    B. Because the domain name in the World Wide Web address, .com, indicates
      that a business operates it
    C. Because I have heard of the company

Answer: B. You'll learn more about domain names and URL addresses in the upcoming tour. But for now, a simple rule to remember is that .com in a site's address usually means the site is a owned by a commercial business. [Actually, I got this one wrong when I took the quiz, since personal sites use the ".com" zone too. If you have any questions, go back and reread the *CyberSpace . . . A Map for Non-Geeks* chapter.]

7. Are there places on the Internet that are designed especially for children?

    A. Yes
    B. No

Answer: A. Thousands of schools and organizations have created Web sites specifically for children. Many sites provide interesting information and games that are easy for children to understand. Some services also provide "kids-only" areas just for children. One of the best ways to find interesting sites for children is to listen to the sources you trust. Schools, parenting magazines and newspapers are all beginning to offer more information about "kids-only" online areas.

8. What kind of information could a Web site automatically read about our family when we first click onto that site?

    A. Information about our computer system, browser and the general location of our Internet service provider
    B. Information about our online purchases
    C. Specific information about family members
    D. No information at all

Answer: A. Most computers have stored information that can be read by some Web sites when you click onto their site. Those sites may be able to tell what kind of computer system you have, the company you use to access the Internet and the site you visited just before reaching their site. It is important for families to remember that their online visits are not unnoticed.

9. Can browsing the Internet change or alter the information on the hard drive of my computer?

    A. Yes
    B. No

Answer: B. No, the data on your hard drive is generally safe. But your browser(software that lets you surf the World Wide Web) does record where you've been on the Internet in a "history file," and some Web sites send an extra bit of data for your browser to store in a special file called a "cookie file." "Cookies" help Web site managers (or "Webmasters," as they are usually called) track and record information about individual visits to their Web sites. Tracking people's activity and preferences online enables Webmasters to keep their sites easy to navigate and relevant for viewers. It can also help make your activity online easier and quicker because some information about your interests is already stored and ready to use if you visit a site regularly.

10. How can we make our family's time online even more meaningful?

    A. Spend time online together
    B. Establish family rules for online behavior
    C. Explore parental technology options
    D. All of the above

Answer: D. Parents can do all of these things and more. Generally, the best way to ensure a meaningful experience online is to surf together. Sometimes, this isn't possible, and some parents will let their children explore online alone if the family has an established set of rules and policies in place. Parents can also employ helpful technology, such as parental control software, which allows parents to block access to sites that may have content the parent deems inappropriate for children. As we discussed before, some software stops the computer from sending out specific words or phrases, including names, addresses and telephone numbers.

This quiz has been generously provided to us by The Direct Marketing Association, CARU and Call for Action. Their booklet, *Get CyberSavvy*, can be found online at www.the-dma.org/pan/intro.html. Copies are also available by writing to The Direct Marketing Association, Ethics and Consumer Affairs Department, 1111 19th Street, N.W. Suite 1100, Washington, D.C. 20036-3603.

Hopefully, you got them all right! (Or know why you didn't.) Congratulations! You have now earned the right to graduate—to the next section . . . The Good Stuff!

PART 4

The Good Stuff . . . 99.44 percent pure
(enjoying your family time online)

CHAPTER 19

It's a Wonderful (Online) Life . . .

A Bird's Eye View—

▼ Johnny Can Write (and Research)!

▼ Shopping Online

▼ Let the Web Entertain You

▼ Traveling the World

For far too many pages, I've talked about the dark side of the Internet and the need to protect our children online. But, as I've told you over and over . . . the Internet is a terrific place with thousands of interesting sites for families and children. It opens up a whole new world to us parents, and to our families.

I share a few ways you can enjoy the Internet as a family, and some examples of how other families have used the Internet for fun and learning. Our family reviewers and resources recount for you, in their own words, some of the ways they use the Internet every day to enhance their lives.

Children improve their communication skills online and meet people from other countries and cultures, sharing information, photos and stories with the world and other family members, and learn not only to be creative, but to share their creativity. Children can research school projects right from home, and families can plan vacations online. And students can keep in touch with teachers, even after graduation.

Family members provide support for each other in tragic and trying times, and share their joys in good times. New parents learn parenting skills, and can always find an answer to their questions and someone willing to help. The list goes on and on.

Hopefully, you'll share your stories with me too, so I can share them with others at our website, www.familyguidebook.com. After all, we're all in this together!

▼ Johnny Can Write (and Research)!

▼ W R I T I N G

When I was growing up (if you ask my kids, in the days before electricity and indoor plumbing . . .), writing was something we did because we *had* to. We *had* to write thank you notes for birthday gifts. We *had* to write essays for school. Writing was painful and formal. (Maybe that's why it took me so long to write this book!)

No wonder everyone complained that Johnny couldn't write. But, that must have been before Johnny got online. The Internet and online services have changed all that. Kids have to write to communicate. It's how they "talk" online.

Many families are building websites for themselves and their kids. and these sites are first rate! One of my favorite kids' sites written by kids (and judging by the awards they've received . . . a favorite of many others as well) is Kids of the Web (www.hooked.net/~leroyc/kidsweb/index.html). Three kids, Brian (age 14), Mark (age 12) and Amanda (age 6), and their dad, Leroy, have designed a site to highlight other sites written by or about kids, and it has been visited by over 100,000 people. Obviously, they're doing something right!

Actually, this shows more than how talented families can create something together. The Kids of the Web project demonstrates how people can use something like building a website to help build a family. Leroy isn't Brian, Mark or Amanda's birth father, having married their mom several years ago. But the site has helped bring them closer, and has given Leroy an opportunity to show them how much he loves them.

If you want to see other websites written by kids, try KidWeb (www.teleport.com/~rhubarbs/kidweb), which also collects sites written by kids and families. If you design a site together, you can register it with KidWeb too.

Kids are contributing to important sites online as well. World Kids Network (www.worldkids.net) uses kids to help craft their site: over 80 percent of the site is "put together and/or run by children."

Kidzine, ABC network's news site for kids on AOL (keyword "kidzine" or "kids") is written largely by kids too. Susan Treiman (streiman@aol.com) designed and runs Kidzine, and will soon take over the ABC.com site as well. (In my humble opinion, that's a smart move on ABC's part, since Susan has managed to increase activity at the Kidzine site to over 9 million hits a month!)

Susan sees the entire world as subject matter for her kids' reporting.

They write about topics as far ranging as the current baggy clothing craze, or dealing with an alcoholic parent. But in addition to building a wonderful resource, there's a method to Susan's madness. While learning to write news, kids are also learning about the news. The site offers "Children's Express," a weekly e-zine about current events. And Susan tells me that most of the kids who take the news quiz at the site get all the answers right.

In addition to reporting news, the kids are collaborating in writing fun things online too. The kids wrote a joke book with over 700 entries available at Kidzine. They're even getting excited about science. Susan brought Michael Gillan on board as "Dr. Universe." He takes the kids on online science field trips, which have become a very popular feature.

Children's Express (www.ce.org) also uses kid reporters to research and write the stories for the site. It has more of a global flavor and has produced some wonderful reporting.

If you just want to share some artwork or something special your children have written, there are sites for that as well. They're called "refrigerator door sites" because you can post things you would normally place on your refrigerator door at home. The Global Show-n-Tell Museum (www.telenaut.com/gst) is a great place to post your children's artwork online. You can also just look at the artwork supplied by other children from around the world.

Undoubtedly, though, KidPub (www.kidpub.org) is the leading refrigerator door site, with over 500,000 visitors and thousands of stories written by children from all over the world. Originally begun as a place where the hosts' nine-year-old daughter could show her work, it fast became a place where everyone else's daughters and sons could show theirs as well. In an interesting FAQ, the host explains that his daughter only contributed one article to the site. Lucky for us that he kept the site running anyway.

Want even more proof that the computer helps make kids literate? I asked children around the country to help me review children's websites and online areas. The youngest reviewer is three years old (dictated to her mother), and the oldest one is eighteen. Other than correcting their spelling and some obvious grammatical errors, I left their reviews unedited to make a point. These children, and all others who use e-mail and communicate online, are writers. It's a more informal writing style (almost like a conversation), but they are sharing their ideas and making themselves easily understood. They can write!

▼ RESEARCHING

In addition, our children are learning how to find things on the Internet. They're finding information as diverse as academic research, travel options, college data and consumer product and source information. The term paper, which used to contain a bibliography gleaned from the local library, now contains sources from all around the world. To get you started, I've recommended two research sites I like a lot:

One, The Study Web (www.studyweb.com), was specifically designed for helping with homework research, with a database of over 17,000 research quality URLs. (And remember the problem with source reliability I raised in Part 2? This site prescreens research sites for reliability. So if you're looking for Elvis sightings, you may have to look elsewhere . . . sorry.) Kids can research using keywords, or by topical indices. (They're also rated with RSACi.) The Study Web even ranks information by school grade levels, so ten-year-olds won't have to muddle through research information appropriate for sixteen-year-olds. Printable images and downloadable materials are clearly marked as well.

The other great research site, the Internet Public Library (www.ipl.org), contains everything you could ever want in a research site, and more. It has special sections for teens, which include advice columns, and sections for "youths" as well. The teen section is steered by an advisory board actually comprised partly of teens. The site is designed to be responsive to the needs of teens, and it shows. The teens we had explore the site were uniformly enthusiastic about its contents. One of their favorite pages was the "Career" page, with career choices that include biographies of people working in each field.

The youth section contains a page that helps younger children learn about the world and cultural differences, as well as book reviews written by children and audio books online.

Kid-friendly, it's stocked with lots of information, but it's a fun site: one page teaches you how to say "hello" in over 30 different languages. It also features a list of sites on the Web, organized by Dewey Decimal System categories, so librarians on the ground can help younger kids frame their research projects for cyberspace. (Remember that librarians are the secret weapon of students—and lawyers—everywhere.)

In addition to researching for school projects, kids are also researching schools themselves. Teenagers can check out prospective colleges, and can even apply right online, and parents can learn about college financial aid and the application process.

There are three college prep sites which we recommend, Princeton Review's website (www.review.com), Petersons' website (www.petersons.com) and The Stanley Kaplan website (www.kaplan.com).

Of the three, I think that Princeton Review's site has the most information, in the most user-friendly format. The site has 1 million visitors, who view a total of, roughly, 3 million pages each month! The three sections of the site I thought were the best were their new parents' discussion boards, "Parents Only," where parents can share our "I have no clue what to do when my child applies to colleges" neuroses with other similarly situated parents; their "Counselor-O-Matic" page, where your children can submit their credentials and find colleges likely to admit them based on these credentials; and "Find-O-Rama," which helps find colleges that meet your children's criteria. It's a great place to start learning about the college application process.

When my daughter, Taylor, applied to colleges last year, we used Petersons' site. I also bought their guides and thought that their *The Ultimate College Survival Guide* was an extremely helpful resource for both teenagers and for parents. (It's still the bible, as far as Taylor is concerned, and we compiled our college shopping list right from the book.) I also recommended it to other parents, and still do. It's the best single source of college-specific data we've found, and luckily, you can buy it online.

In addition, the Petersons' site has an instant inquiry section from where you can send an e-mail to any college in their database. It also has video clip tours of many campuses, and news updates from a large list of colleges. I found that using The Princeton Review site first to help narrow the choices based upon both eligibility and preferences, and then checking out more about the specific schools using the Petersons' site was the most efficient and effective way to get the college search started.

The Kaplan site was more fun, but not as informative about colleges. It is directed more at the preparing-for-the-entrance-examination market. They use games at the site to help kids sharpen their test-taking skills, which is what Kaplan is all about. (The schedules of classes to prep for the SATs and other examinations are available online too.) The kids enjoyed the "Beach Blanket Brain Drain" section, although it's fun, not substance. Parents can laugh and learn from the "Tuition Impossible" game too, especially as tuition deadlines draw near.

FinAid (www.finaid.com), for financial aid assistance, does it all. Maintained by Mark Kantrowitz, the author of *The Prentice Hall Guide to Scholarships and Fellowships for Math and Science Students* and sponsored by NASFAA (the National Association of Student Financial Aid Administrators), it's not very colorful and doesn't have glossy graphics, but is incredibly informative. You can learn about financial aid scams, calculate aid contributions, and find special interest aid all at one site. Using this site will save parents a lot of time and money, and they won't need a separate scholarship search service.

Recognizing how well our kids can navigate the Web, many families I spoke with now research their vacations online. Most airlines have websites and so do most hotel chains. Lots of discount travel services are available on the Web too. Many families even assign their family vacation research to their teenagers. They research a few travel locations, ways to get there, things to see and where to stay.

Chrissy Peters, my law firm administrator and dear friend, is an Internet newbie and mother of one of our kid reviewers. She recently planned a trip entirely on the Internet and AOL, as is recounted here:

The Peters' Family Vacation, by Chrissy Peters

Recently, in preparation for a family vacation to Washington, DC (if you could call it a vacation... all that walking) I went to AOL's Travel section. I found it very helpful—all kinds of information about the Hyatt Regency on Capitol Hill, the hotel we were going to stay at. At the time I was looking, Washington, DC was the featured spot of the week! What luck. I was able to get a ton of information from AOL, and I also went on the Web and picked up all kinds of information on where to go, what to see, what time things were open, and how to obtain VIP tickets for early tours (8:00 a.m.) with no waiting lines at the White House, the FBI and the Capitol!

I could have bypassed my travel agent (and probably should have) and made the travel arrangements myself. We took Amtrak, and Amtrak's webpage gives you all the information you need and allows you to make your own reservations, purchase tickets, the whole nine yards. After we came back, I looked over the FBI webpage (www.fbi.gov)— I thought it was, as the kids say, "pretty cool"! I never would have thought to check that Web site out before going to DC, but since the webpage address was on the cap my daughter bought, I had to see it! Next, I'll check out the White House website. I wish I had done that in advance too, but since we never got to see it in person, my daughter can take the "Socks tour" for kids at their website.

I frequently use the Internet for our family vacation information. I've earned a reputation for accomplishing the impossible, often, with some of the "finds" I've located online.

Last year, by searching websites about Arizona and its National Parks, I was able to book a suite with a balcony right on the edge of the Grand Canyon on a couple weeks' notice—it's usually booked years in advance. Watching the sunrise over the Grand Canyon while sipping tea in lounge chairs is something neither my best friend, Lanell, nor I will ever forget. Being able to reach people on the ground with local expertise and contacts is a great advantage! And you can do it all from the comfort of your family room.

▼ Shopping Online

Shopping is much easier on the Web, too. Most of the major retailers have glossy and easy-to-navigate websites, and many are offering consumers the ability to purchase online. This is a particularly useful service for working parents and parents with younger children, who don't have the chance to get out and shop as often as they would like. (These sites all offer secure transmissions for your credit card information.)

The two sites my kids and I use the most are Spiegel's and J. Crew's. Both are easy to navigate and have everything organized well for online shopping (since they're both catalogue retailers, that makes sense). Spiegel can be found at www.spiegel.com and J. Crew can be found at www.jcrew.com. (With two kids in college, I have just decided to turn over my entire paycheck to J. Crew each week. Just think of the paperwork they'll save . . .)

▼ Let the Web Entertain You

You can even check out local movie listings, theaters and Broadway shows and buy tickets online. The Web has many movie sites. At least two are parent-friendly. Moviephone's website, Movielink, is at www.777film.com. That site has a Parent's Rating Guide, which explains why each top movie was given its rating (e.g., "brief mild language"). Also, you can search for movies by type, and one of the choices is "family." As with Moviephone, the Movielink site gives show times and theatres, and offers for many the option of purchasing the tickets online.

The site designed expressly for parents is www.screenit.com. That site contains reviews of movies, music and videos, rated in several categories. The categories include "alcohol/drugs," "profanity," and "sexual content," among many others. Each reviewed movie has a chart that summarizes the rating in each category. The best thing about the site is that it then goes on to explain in detail the contents of the movie with respect to each category (for example, a rating of "mild" profanity may be explained as "the word hell is used three times"), so that parents can judge for themselves if a movie (or video or music album) should be off-limits.

All the information you need to plan your theatre-outing can be found at www.playbill.com. It contains listings of shows and theatres not only on and off-Broadway, but also regional theatres around the country, and theatres in Canada and London. In its "Theatre Central" area, it has links to other performance-related sites by name of celebrity or category of performance. The "Theatre Listings" section lists the plays. If you don't know what play to see, you can search by type. There's even a search that finds only those shows that are suitable for children. The listings include a brief synopsis, cast list, show times and prices, a street map with the location of the theatre, and in many cases a seating chart. If you register, you can also join the Playbill Club, which entitles you to get discount tickets to certain shows and theatre-related merchandise.

To purchase tickets, playbill.com links to NetTicks, www.telecharge.com. At Telecharge's site, you can order tickets online. NetTicks also gives information about the shows, including information for parents that playbill.com does not have. That information is in each show listing, under "Audience." There, NetTicks gives its analysis, noting, for example, that a particular show "may be inappropriate for children 12 and under." The listings also remind parents that children under four are not admitted to any Broadway show.

▼ Traveling the World

The Internet is global, remember? That's one of the best things about it. It's also a terrific way to get your kids ready for their future. The days are over when the world was broken into little fiefdoms. All business is global. Even the mom-and-pop grocery stores are buying international goods, and your local businesses are selling to, buying from, or sharing expertise with, other businesses around the world. What better way to teach your kids global thinking and painlessly prepare them for their careers than letting them speak to the world right now?

Want to travel to a different country each month? Do it from your computer chair at World Surfari (www.supersurf.com). It's a great way for your family to learn about the world together. The site features information about history, society and the people of the country of the month.

Interested in learning about kids worldwide? World Kids Network (www. worldkids.net), as I've mentioned before, is one of my favorites. It's glossy, and packed with information about kids worldwide. It has a wonderful links page, too.

It's fun to try to find international penpals and sites, and especially if your child is studying another language. It's a great way for them to practice communicating in it. World Kids Network is a good place to meet kids from around the world. So is KidsSpace (www.kids-space.org), a particularly good site for finding international pen pals. They also have very strict terms of service designed to protect kids from adults masquerading as children. Kidscom.com (www.kidscom.com) will be adding foreign language options shortly. It also is very world conscious.

KidLink (www.kidlink.org) is a site developed internationally for children from all over the world, where they can converse in listserv discussion groups (conducted by e-mail) in sixteen different langauges, although English appears to be the base language for the site. In order to participate in the discussion groups, children have to register and answer five questions relating to how they see their role in the world and how they hope to improve it. What a wonderful way to get your children started in a global community.

CHAPTER 20

A Family Project . . . The Web Can Bring You Together

A Bird's Eye View—

▼ Let Your Children Teach You . . . Learning to Listen

▼ Your Own Soapbox . . . Creating a Website Together

▼ Family Sports—Take Up Web Surfing Together

▼ Let Your Children Teach You . . . Learning to Listen

Throughout their lives, children are being taught and lectured to by adults. Teachers, parents and family members all know more, and are constantly proving that to children. Guess what? Most of our kids know far more about the computer than we do. Proficient with computer games of problem-solving mazes with dragons and spaceships that boggle our minds, they spend hours honing their skills. Few adults have the hand-eye coordination necessary to kill off the monsters and retrieve the treasures. But our children do. They can point and click with the best of them.

Give them a chance to level the playing field. Armed with this book, so you won't appear too ignorant, sit down in a comfortable chair and let your children show you around the family computer.

If they are already online, ask them to show you their favorite online forums, chatrooms and sites. Check them out. In addition to helping you understand your child better, and giving you a good simple tour of the online world, it will help you begin to understand how to help balance your values and your children's preferences.

Even if you're an experienced websurfer, let your child lead the tour. Let them talk and teach you for a change. Make it an "us" afternoon or evening. This exercise will help you to see the computer as something that brings you together instead of something that pulls you apart.

There are two sites which might be interesting to surf together, while you're exploring with your kids. One of my favorite websites, Games Kids Play (www.corpcomm.net/~gnieboer/gamehome.htm) is a terrific and non-glossy page with lots of games (the old fashioned ones we used to play) for families to play . . . like Mother May I? Showing them what we used to do for fun (in the days of horses and buggies . . .) is a good way of sharing stories about when we were younger. It's all about communication.

The second site, Just for Kids (www.eagle.ca/~matink/kids.html), has every conceivable site any family could want to access, from animal links, to dinosaur links, to educational sites, to those "just for fun." It's a good place to explore together.

Aside from surfing together, feign interest in the newest computer game to capture your child's imagination. (Many of you have been waiting for an excuse to play these games anyway, so grab the opportunity. That way, when found playing the football game, *NFL* 98 for twenty consecutive hours, you can blame me and this book.)

You'll be amazed at their skill. Although there are plenty of space and sports games for simple enjoyment, there are far more problem solving games, where your children must break through levels of the game by solving problems and discovering clues. Take the joystick when it's offered. This will be one game that you won't have to let them win. You don't stand a chance against the new generation of computer-savvy kids we're raising.

When you look at their faces while they are teaching you, and their extraordinary patience with your ineptitude, you'll understand why I suggested this in the first place.

In addition, if you use parental control software, and your children want to visit sites blocked by the software or not yet rated by a PICS compatible service, take the time to visit those sites with them. It will help build trust between you.

▼ Your Own Soapbox . . . Create a Website Together

Anyone can set up a website. You create it to say what you want to share and design it to say it the way you want. It's your own personal soap box. You can add photos, graphics, sounds and animation, and share stories about your family pets, your friends and your favorite brands of cookies. It's yours, and you can do anything you want with it. (Well . . . almost anything. Read the section about what's illegal online first.)

Personal sites comprise a large part of the Web. They range from sites that preach a political point of view to those making fun of other sites, and share things as diverse as family photos and biographical information about the website operators. While a majority of the commercial sites are designed professionally and at substantial cost, most of the personal sites are designed by the website operators themselves. Many of the website operators, especially the younger ones, have designed some very special sites, filled with the latest in Internet technology.

Building a website teaches your children to be creative and how to communicate their ideas. I've often tapped into this rich lode of creativity and graphic and design talent for technical help in designing our sites.

▼ Family Sports—Take up Web Surfing Together

Now that you're ready to navigate around the Web, I thought I'd share my favorite family-friendly and children's sites with you. All of these are free. (There are a few family-friendly services which cost a monthly fee. I've mentioned these too, but think that with all the free children's content on the Web, no one should have to pay for it.)

You can start with a few we've recommended here, or start out on your own. But find something you can all research and learn about together. What about a family vacation you need to plan? It's a great way to plan and make sure everyone's involved.

Here are a few interesting sites.

ESPNET-Sportszone (**www.espnet.sportzone.com**)
ESPNET offers the most abundant site for scores, stats, and exclusive articles written by ESPN's expert analysts on the Net. On this site, all the major sports—baseball, basketball, football, and hockey—have a page devoted to the breaking stories, trades, and profiles relevant to these respective games. If the "big four" aren't the fruit of your interest, Sportszone offers similar pages from Auto Racing, Golf, and Bowling to Figure skating. Sportszone is a must "hit" for any sports fan as either a casual spectator or a subscriber and offers the best coverage of any sports page on the Net.

As a subscriber, for $4.95 a month, or $39.95 for the year, you are granted access to a multimedia library, a sports almanac, and discounts on sportscenter's fantasy leagues.

Kids.com (**www.aha-kids.com**)

Kids.com is a site engineered for kids between the ages of two and twelve. By providing links to stories, games, and challenges separated by skill, Kids.com proved to be a winner among other sites. "Emmy award-winning producer, Al Hyslop (Captain Kangaroo, Sesame Street, and 3-2-1 Contact), has brought forth a bright and fun web site for kids of different age groups," claimed Parentsoup, itself a premier site geared at finding safe and fun places for kids on the Net. Aside from providing a toy department (ugh!) so that kids may purchase their favorite Kids.com merchandise online, they provide a parents link so that parents can review the basis and content of the site before they allow their children to become a regular visitors

For children between the ages of two and five, Kids.com presents DDog, your child's "first online host". In this section your children can select one of a number of options, including DDog's diary and Cowboy Jim Bob's "read to me" bedtime stories.

For children between the ages of six to twelve, Kids.com offers Mia Miaow's Mysteries and Wuhnik's Science for kids. Mia Miaow is in the tradition of the old serial stories, where a continuation will be posted every week. Aside from offering a standard tale of mystery, Mia's tales are also interactive, allowing your child to pick the designated route for the characters. Wuhnik's Science for kids offers daily questions to which your children can post their answers and presents photos in a "guess what this is" format.

Certain magazines, like *Parenting,* (www.parenttime.com) *Family PC* (www.familypc.com) and *Home PC* (www.homepc.com) have great site lists too, broken into age levels. Try a few of those. Then explore. Try checking out sites linked to from those sites, and sites those sites link to, and so on and so forth. Whenever you find a site you like, remember to bookmark it (I've explained how in Part 1) so you can go back and visit them again.

If you find a site you really enjoy, write a brief review telling other families why they'd like the site and e-mail it to us at the www.familyguidebook.com site. We'll post them so they can be shared with other families.

▼ FAMILIAR BRAND NAME SITES . . . FOR AGES 1 TO 100

With the thousands of sites now up on the Web, there is something for everyone, regardless of age. It's like a big game that you never grow out of. Also, many sites are designed especially for family use and are meant to be viewed by parents and kids alike. Often, they are put up and managed by well known corporations such as Disney, Nickelodeon, and Fox so you are guaranteed G-rated material.

Disney's site is located at www.disney.com. It offers many pictures, sounds, and movie clips of Disney movies and TV shows. Many of these multimedia downloads require one or more plug-ins. (Plug-ins are additions to your web browser that allow you to get the most out of special multimedia online). Also, many of these clips and sound bytes are quite large and require a long time to download.

This site is especially loved by young children—even if they can't read yet, they'll be able to identify with the cartoon characters on the screen. Disney also runs another site at www.family.com which provides parents and children with different activities and games that the family can do together, which I've also reviewed.

Nickelodeon's cable TV content is devoted to kids (as you probably already know); their site at www.nick.com is no different. The site does use a cookie, but it is only used by the same site. Many of the games and areas require VRML and Macromedia's Shockwave plug-ins but are worth the download time.

There are pictures and clips from Nickelodeon's shows for younger children and games for slightly older ones. The trivia games ask questions covering a large range of topics. Thus, they teach as well as entertain. All of the areas are brightly colored (as in a cartoon) and cover topics that interest kids: jokes, snacks, TV shows, problems, etc. There are even places that kids can hear and trade other kids' jokes.

Even cereal companies like Kellogg's have kid's sites. At www.kelloggs.com, the kids' areas have games that focus around their cereal products. Many of these games also require the Macromedia Shockwave plug-in and load a cookie but the games are worth it. Although adults may find that these shoot-the-Corn Pops are pointless, kids seem to love them.

Fox is another TV Network that has a great site for kids. While Fox's site is www.fox.com, they run a separate site, www.foxkids.com, for kids. This site revolves around the kids' shows on the Fox Network and have downloadable pictures, sounds bytes, movies clips, etc. about these shows.

The Family Channel (www.familychannel.com) has some interesting features, along with resources for parents. In addition the ABC Network has a wonderful site at www.abc.com. The site is available on AOL (keyword "ABC") and on the Web. The site has content from a myriad of shows from the ABC Network.

Many of our family and kid reviews recommended these sites. Here's a review, as described by the mother of Karylie, a five year-old girl.

Karylie's favorites, by her mom

My oldest daughter's name is Karylie and she just turned six in May. She has been using the computer since she was 5. She mostly uses the Paint program or the interactive storybook programs. She is quite competent at manipulating the mouse and knows where she is going with it. We have just recently found Nickelodeon on-line and Disney on-line. She said what she likes best about Nick on-line, is being able to pull up the pictures of the people or characters from the show—Keenan and Kel for example. She loves being able to access them at her own will. She can't read too well yet, so almost everything she accesses is from the picture clues on the home page.

With Disney on-line, she has been able to explore, in depth, due again to the picture icons. Disney also has a lot of interactive activity. She especially likes being able to print the colorful pictures that present themselves. She enjoys the ability to access all of the Disney stories and movies.

Older kids and teenagers may wish to visit the regular TV network sites. The only trouble is that since many of these TV shows are aimed at more mature audiences, the material at the site also contains material that may be inappropriate for younger children. Of course, there's no hardcore sexual content at any of these sites. But, anything that might be said or shown on TV might turn up at the site.

CHAPTER 21

The Wonders of E-Mail . . . Families Keeping in Touch

A Bird's Eye View—

▼ Parents Talking to Children . . . Love Notes to Your Kids

▼ Creating Teams

▼ More Than E-Mail . . . Keeping An Eye On Your Family

▼ E-Mail Can Be Used to Accomplish Many Things

It's estimated that over 44 billion e-mail messages will be sent from home computers this year, for an average of 52 per week, per household. It's fast becoming an inexpensive and convenient alternative to using the telephone, and a faster alternative to snail mail.

When I asked other parents to tell me why they use e-mail to communicate with their children and other family members, they shared these ten reasons. We've shared their stories with you below, too, just in case you need further incentives to get online.

I've shared some of the benefits to using e-mail, below.

The Hidden Benefits of E-mail

- It's the only way you can make sure your kids are listening to what you have to say, instead of their interrupting or contradicting you, mid-thought.
- You're always in the mood to "talk" when you send an e-mail (unlike getting a phone call).
- Time differences, mail delays and telephone charges make international communication, other than e-mail, difficult.
- It's convenient—no stamps, no envelopes and no addresses other than a simple e-mail address (which you can store in your computer's address book).
- Kids use it as a diary, and can share all their daily activities with their parents.
- It makes it easier for parents to help with homework and school assignments.
- It's so easy for you to share all the little things you want to, not just the general things that letters usually contain.
- You can send photos, audio messages and can forward documents and other things you've found online.
- You can share one message with many people at the same time, just by adding them to the mailing list.
- It's a great way to move one word-processed document from location to location. If your child left her report at home, you can e-mail it to her at school.

▼ Parents Talking to Children . . . Love Notes to Your Kids

I'm an original sentimentalist. (I even cry at a good AT&T commercial, and anything having to do with grandparents will do me in.) Given the number of hours I work, and the stress of my everyday practice, my time with my children has always been limited. In trying to find ways to communicate with them, I've tried to come up with ways to tell my children that I love them and am thinking about them, even when I'm not home.

I used to write notes on their blackboard each night so they would find them first thing in the morning. I also used to leave short handwritten notes in their lunch boxes. They would respond with their blackboard messages back to me, and by leaving notes on my pillow.

But as my practice took me out of town more often, I found it harder to leave them little indications of my affection. I wasn't home to write my messages, or receive theirs. Somehow phone calls were strained if I made them during the hours they were home and still awake, and by the time I was ready to enjoy a conversation with them, they were already asleep. Trips to other time zones made it even harder to coordinate our schedules.

In addition, as my children got older, these tried and true measures lost their effectiveness. My children no longer took their lunches to school, and outgrew the blackboards. Their calls to me usually coincided with my busiest time of day, and my calls to them ended up with my leaving messages on their answering machines. Their busy schedules and mine made communication harder.

Technology helped solve both problems, and my children and I learned to share love notes and information via e-mail. In e-mail, schedules and time zones are irrelevant. You send it when you can, and the recipients reply when they can. You can also "talk" when you're in the mood. The Internet is always open, around the world. It's also much more affordable than transnational and international phone calls.

E-mail lets me review my children's homework and school assignments too, even while traveling. I can review their reports and term papers for school, making suggestions for improvements and calling certain resources to their attention. It may be a poor substitute for family dinners and working side-by-side in the family-room, but given the demands on parents with their careers and community activities, and those on children with their own activities and responsibilities, it works.

And it works both ways. As my children found information they wanted to share with me, they began to attach articles and other information to their e-mail messages. My son, in particular, has used e-mail to forward jokes to me and to his friends at the same time, by using an e-mail broadcast list. When my daughter needs advice on how to respond to an e-mail she has received from a friend who in turn needs advice, she shares the e-mail with me for my suggestions. The former panic usually associated with my leaving for Moscow is gone. I'm never further than my e-mail, and we each check it several times a day.

Even when I'm home we coordinate schedules and handle the normal family administration via e-mail more often than not these days, especially when we need to involve my son, now at college. And, every now and again, we send each other love notes, reminding ourselves of days of the blackboard messages and lunch box notes. In my lunch box note tradition, a great site for kids and families is the Post-card site maintained at MIT (http://postcards.www.media.mit.edu/postcards). You can select from many postcards and send them to friends and family for free.

▼ Creating Teams

E-mail is particularly helpful when children need to work together in teams. They can share reports and ideas via e-mail, and can set agendas and share information, making working together far more efficient. Interesting resources and electronic documentation can be sent with the click of a mouse across town or around the world.

This is particularly helpful when the only other option is to drive the children across town in the pouring rain. Even the most technology resistant among us will recognize the advantages of having the library open 24 hours a day from your own home computer, especially during that rainstorm.

It also helps them stay in touch. Al McWhirr is a technology educator in New Jersey. He uses e-mail to stay in touch with his students. It's inspiring.

How One Teacher Uses E-mail to Stay in Touch
by Al McWhirr, a high school teacher

My kids brought me into the computer age. I fought it for the longest time, only using the computer and accessories when absolutely necessary. Now that I use it, I don't know how I got along without it. Without my e-mail capabilities, I would be lost. I use it just about every day, and I enjoy it. As a teacher, I am able to keep in touch with many of my former students who moved on to college. Prior to this, it would be a hand written letter sent on occasion. I seem to have a better relationship with these students because they feel that I am taking an interest in their life beyond high school, which, in fact, is the case. I feel that I am on the same "electronic" level as they are.

Occasionally, students of mine will e-mail me for clarification on assignments. This is great, since I don't have to give out my phone number. (I have yet to receive a harassing e-mail note). From college, my daughter was able to e-mail her high school calculus teacher. It was the night before an exam, and her professor was not available to help her with her question. Her high school teacher solved the problem.

▼ More Than E-mail . . . Keeping An Eye On Your Family

While on a recent trip to Moscow, I was watching CNN International. They ran a piece on "I See You," new technology developed by IBM that permits photos, updated every 30 seconds, to be posted on a secure website. The technology was being tested at a daycare center in Connecticut. (There are other similar projects and products being used around the country, too. You can check out a website for KinderCam at www.kindercam.com.) The parents can check in on their kids from work, merely by accessing the website and using their special security passwords. (Making sure that these are really secure pictures is important to the children's security.)

Just think about how terrific this is. Parents can see what their kids are doing throughout the day, and their kids know they can show things throughout the day to their parents. Even more exciting is the fact that other family members, like grandparents who live in other countries or other states, can watch the children at play.

You're never out of touch. It's a terrific way of sharing memories. Now I can cry at "I See You" sites as well as AT&T commercials.

▼ E-Mail Can Be Used to Accomplish Many Things

Outdoor Online teaches children how to get the most out of e-mail communication. I asked Mindi Roberts to share some stories about how campers, and their families, have used e-mail.

Mindi Roberts Shares Some E-mail War Stories from Outdoor Online

A camp mom with "computer phobia" learned e-mail from her husband before her son went to camp. Everyday, it was the highlight of her day to receive her child's e-mail and she got over the "computer phobia" fast. It helped her deal with separation anxiety and gave them a great way to stay in touch.

An 11 year old female camper taught her elderly next door neighbor about e-mail and computer skills to help her find companionship online.

At camp, campers are told that e-mail is monitored by the system administrator. Once, a couple of campers who decided to date during camp e-mailed each other a place to meet secretly. They arrived to find some counselors waiting, and the word got around camp.

On a good note, the camp has a dance at the end of each session. Campers e-mail their song requests for the last dance, perhaps with a wave file, to lobby for the last dance.

Here's an example how one family used the Internet to deal with a family dispute, from Melissa, a member of our research team who shall remain nameless to protect her identity and her life.

My Family Saga, by Melissa

In my family, e-mail has played a large part in resolving family conflicts. E-mail has been used to resolve arguments between family members when the parties did not want to actually speak to each other. At the beginning of the summer, my sister-in-law (the co-gossiper), fed up with her brother (not my perfect husband, the other brother) over an issue involving their mother . . . and a chair . . . and who paid for it . . . and if it was even paid for . . . and why wasn't it paid for . . . and when would it be paid for . . . and it was wrong that it hadn't been paid for . . . and who was the one who ever said it had been paid for in the first place . . . (you get the point), finally decided to air her opinion to her brother, but was uncomfortable speaking about it in person or even over the phone. She felt that she was not "good on her feet," and would not be able to clearly make her points. She decided to e-mail what was bothering her to her brother. She had time to carefully craft her letter and was able to organize her thoughts.

Well, her e-mail brought about an e-mail response from her brother, who explained his position. The content of his response angered her even more. So she proceeded to write an e-mail to end all e-mails. This e-mail basically mentioned every single thing that he had done wrong in the past four years—no stone was left unturned. Needless to say, he was none too happy, and e-mailed back a "sweet" little note of his own. At that point, for about the next month, communication of any kind between them ceased.

Then my brother-in-law, perhaps realizing that this last e-mail from his sister contained a good deal of truth, e-mailed back a friendly letter to his sister, basically saying that by-gones should be by-gones. My sister-in-law, who was never one to deal well with tension, gladly agreed, and then actually picked up the phone to call him. Everything was back to normal (actually no one in my husband's family is normal) thanks to the ability to communicate via e-mail. The back and forth communications were helpful in resolving problems and resentments that otherwise probably never would have been spoken about.

And, by the way, my mother-in-law paid for the chair herself.

CHAPTER 22

And Now ... A Special Word From One Grandmother ... My Mom's 2¢

A Bird's Eye View—

▼ A Grandparent's Guide to the Internet ... and How to Enjoy Yourself in Cyberspace

When you ask your mother to share a few of her thoughts about how grandparents can use the Internet, and she sends you a whole chapter . . what can you say but "Thanks, Mom." My mother is a grandmother of four, extraordinarily talented (she worked on her PH.D until last year), and is funny too. Here 's what she gave me, word for word. I don't know anyone brave enough to edit her mother. Do you? So here it is . . .

▼ A Grandparent's Guide to the Internet . . . and How to Enjoy Yourself in Cyberspace

There's a whole new world out there. Some call it Cyberspace. Others describe it as the Internet, "surfing the Net," or "searching the Web." Call it what you may but unless we seniors get acquainted with the new technologies, we might as well sit down in our rocking chairs and wait out the rest of the century.

Several years ago my children wanted to "modernize" my ways—they said that a typewriter was not the "way to go" any more. I had signed up for a summer course at the local community college and was assigned a lengthy paper. My typing mistakes were driving me mad—extra copies meant a trip to the Xerox machine at the library or a local Office Max, and changing script during editing for final copy was literally "cut and paste"—I mean with scissors and tape! Then the text had to be recopied.

Soon Christmas came and under the tree there was a gift for "Mom." It was a heavy box and a complete mystery to me. I opened it slowly, and panicked when I realized that it was a laptop computer, complete and ready to go! The kids told me that I was now up to date, would be able to change paragraphs in my papers, print extra copies, use the spell-checker and save all of my original text. (They must have thought I'd be taking college courses for the rest of my senior life.)

Well, I plugged in the "machine," connected the cords and other "things" and just sat there and looked at it. Real panic had set in by now. I couldn't admit defeat but glanced around for my trusty old typewriter. That night I didn't sleep. I came down into the den and turned the laptop on. Disks! I read the instructions and all new jargon came tumbling into my world of complacency. I really needed help and fast!

The admissions office at the college told me about a computer literacy course that would be starting the next week. Curious, I visited the Computer Lab to see for myself. There was a demonstration going on at that time and as I walked around, I noticed that there was another student "online" with Internet. He had visited the "mail room" for his E-MAIL, joined his favorite "chat room" on the Politics Corner and scanned the New York Times for the morning news. Sometime during all of this (there were several windows open on his screen) he "downloaded" the best sellers from a world famous bookstore in New York. If you've ever felt intimidated, this was it, big time!

What was this new technology? I had to find out. Because I was a "senior citizen" I was not going to be left behind. That happens, you know. CYBERSPACE! Wow! I was going to learn to surf the Net and keep up with the world. Well, I signed up for the computer orientation course and when I arrived the first day the classroom was filled with people just like me—seniors!! All were anxious to get on the Web. "Settle down everybody—first things first," the instructor told us firmly, "first you have to learn to turn the computer on!" Laughter filled the room and we all settled down. Then a whole new world opened before our very eyes.

It didn't happen overnight. I had to complete the course to use my own computer effectively and even then when I did write papers, letters, etc. I kept the 1-800-hot line open many hours every day. I did learn, however, that the most important procedure in my experience was the command "save." I had lost too many papers before I mastered that dumb process. There were many different computers. I learned on the Apple; it seemed a little easier for me.

Actually, getting on the Internet isn't as complicated as it seemed. There are many on-line services out there. America On-Line, Prodigy, etc., which all help you gain easy access to the Internet. I can't begin to describe the many interesting activities that are available. After you subscribe to a service you'll receive software to install. My Internet server offers a post office, travel agent, homework helper, shopping mall, movie critic, library, newsstand, just to name a few.

You're probably thinking right now, "I'm not going to spend a thousand bucks on a computer just to get on the Internet." Well you don't have to—there are several alternatives. There's a gadget in the computer stores you can buy—it looks like a little black box and comes with a cordless keyboard. You connect the box to your television set and zing! You're on the Net with a full menu. Any computer store carries this unit and if my memory serves me correctly, it costs less than $500. Way to go! [My mom is referring to WebTV.] And if you don't want to do that, just visit your public library. They have many computers set up and will show you how to access the Internet. Personally I love the convenience of having this online "stuff" set up in my own den. Many a night when I can't sleep I find my way downstairs to the computer. Funny, but the Internet is "open all night" too.

Well, you might ask what I'm up to lately. I have started a book about my family history. I'm not sure anyone will ever want to read it, but the Internet is there for me every step of the way—access to the Harvard Library, data from the National Geographic, maps and pictures of the 17th Century shipwrecks, and material from the British Museum.

By the way, I have a friend who is in her 80's and never a day goes by that she doesn't sign on in her cooking chat room to say hello and exchange a recipe or a joke or two. She's never met any of these people, but I'll tell you it keeps her mind sharp and makes her feel a "part of things." A part of the bigger world out there— a part of the CYBERSPACE, on the Internet. Way to go seniors! Get with it. Get with it with us all. And by the way, I remembered to save this. If you're wondering about my work at the college, I did register formally and finally received a degree. Gotta go now; time to sign onto the Internet. Why don't you join me?

CHAPTER 23

Special Families . . . Special Kids

A Bird's Eye View—

▼ Looking for Inspiration?
Try Lisa's Page

▼ Exceptional Children, Special Needs

▼ Adoptive Families and Foster
Parenting Online

▼ Single Parenting and Step-Parenting

▼ Parenting Twins and Other Higher
Order Multiples

▼ Grandparents Parenting (Again)

Parenting can be isolating. This is especially true as we find ourselves fractured into different roles, at work, and home and in our community. The olden days, where parents could sit around, compare stories and chat over a cup of coffee, or over the back fence, sharing ideas, visions and worries are long gone. We barely have the time and energy to get a load of laundry done, or get our kids to soccer.

When families have special needs, the isolation is magnified. Adoptive parents need to be able to talk to other adoptive families. Single parents (no longer a minority in our society, but carrying a special burden nonetheless) need to be able to share with other single parents. Grandparents who find themselves as primary caregivers to their grandchildren need someone to talk with in order to get them up-to-speed on parenting (and grandparenting) this generation. And parents with exceptional children (disabled and seriously ill) need to be able to reach others with similar children and needs. Stepfamilies and foster families have special needs, too, and need to share them with others who have been through these things already. Parents are a great resource for each other, but until now, finding other similarly situated parents has been very hard.

They can all find help and support online, 24/7 (as my kids say, which means 24 hours a day, 7 days a week). It's the new backyard fence and community center, and families with special needs are finding more support online than anywhere else. And, they don't need to leave their home to get it.

Most of the large parenting sites have special areas for special parenting needs. Some of them standout, though. Family.com (www.family.com), the family site run by The Disney Company, has put a lot of time and money into developing a parenting page that provides resources for every special parenting group and it was clearly money well spent. ParentsPlace.com (www.parentsplace.com) hosts a lot of sites for many special interest parenting groups. So do Parent Soup (www.parentsoup.com) and Parent Time (www.parenttime.com).

It's not only the parents who can share with others like them using the Internet, either. Kids can find resources designed just for them, too. Remember, in cyberspace we have no skin color, wear no special costumes, don't need to be able to walk or run, or see, or hear . . . it allows us to be what we are under all these physical imperfections—just plain people.

▼ Looking for Inspiration? Try Lisa's Page

One of the examples of this I found is a website written for a six-year-old girl, Lisa, by her father. Lisa is a very special little girl, with a special message. Lisa's Home Page (www.geocities.com/Heartland/8580) contains great links for other kids, and special sites for exceptional children. You see, Lisa has cerebral palsy. (She's also inspired me to set up a foundation to help children like Lisa get connected, but I'll share more about that later on.)

From the moment I first found her site, I was hooked. There is something about Lisa's Home Page which strips away all the gobbily-gook, and is very touching.

Lisa, although still pretty young for cyberspace, had a lot of input into her page. She chooses the background and the color scheme. She is also always look-ing for links to add to her site. A typical first grader (she's repeating first grade again this year due to the time she lost because of the surgery), Lisa is into teddy bears, Barbie and cartoons.

She's also into Michael Jordan. (Lisa's Page contains a link to a popular Michael Jordan site.) Not only because of his extraordinary athletic talents, how-ever, but because he uses the same electrical muscle stimulator that Lisa uses each night. (She spotted him on television one night, while he was nursing a pulled hamstring muscle using the stimulator unit.) Think of how empowering it must be for a little girl who can't walk to have anything in common with the great hero of sports!

I asked Lisa's father, the website designer and webmaster, why he designed the site for Lisa, and what it means to them to be able to communicate online. I couldn't say it any better than he did, no matter how hard I tried. Here's what he said.

Why did I build Lisa's Page?

There are many reasons why I wanted to put together a web page for my daughter. First I wanted parents in the same situation as ours to realize that they are not alone. That was a major hurdle for my wife and me to overcome. We felt that we were the only people in the world to have a handicapped child.

Since then I've received E-mail from people all over. We've swapped stories and shared experiences (both good and bad).

There has been a lot happening in my daughter's life in the last few months—surgery, followed by an extensive inpatient therapy program.

I just haven't had the time to add it all to her page. Instead, I've spent time answering e-mail from "web friends" who want to know how everything went.

My feeling is that we're all equal in cyberspace. There are no handicaps . . . no wheelchair ramps. No one is looking or staring when you wander through the web the way they do when you shop at the mall.

I know people mean well. In fact I think that they are really impressed and amazed at how this little girl drives her power wheelchair around with all the skill of an Indy race car driver—maneuvering around clothing racks and racing over to the toy department.

The second main reason for her page is because I am so proud of her. Lisa is so bright! She is a very loving child—very sensitive and caring. She is really quite an amazing six-year-old (soon to be seven).

Lisa can read and write and does everything that any other first grader can do, except walk. That is why I'm glad that she loves computers so much.

The good thing about computers is that they can be adapted to be operated by anyone no matter what their situation may be.

The thing we love the most . . . and what really gives Lisa a feeling of equality is that when they're computing—everyone else is sitting down too!

Al Kandziorski

Lisa's and her father's goal is to one day make Lisa's Page the "one stop shop" for information on kids with cerebral palsy. I intend to help them accomplish that goal.

Inspired by the courage and energy of Lisa and her family, I've set up Roads Without Ramps, a charitable foundation to help get kids in wheelchairs and with other disabilities connected to the Internet. A portion of the purchase price of each book sold will be donated to Roads Without Ramps, and we hope to get others in the computer and Internet industry involved as well. (I've already volunteered my sister, Deanna Aftab Guy, M.D., to help and will put more information about Roads Without Ramps at the www.familyguidebook.com website.)

▼ Exceptional Children, Special Needs

Special needs differ from child to child. Seriously ill children (who have no mental or physical disabilities) have very different needs from children with serious physical and/or mental disabilities). The parents of these children have different needs too.

Many of the big parenting sites have good sites for parents of children with special needs. I've highlighted a few here, but you should check out the other ones and see what they have to offer as well.

I've tried to break the sites I've found into special need categories, but many of them overlap. In addition, knowing that other sites exist where children who are exceptional (and their parents) can share good and bad things with others who understand their concerns can inspire parents of all children. So, I've jumbled them all together here, in one group, without trying to categorize them. You should check each of them out. They inspired me, and I hope will inspire you.

The Mining Company (www.homeparents.miningco.com/) has a great general site for parents, and a few wonderful sites devoted to parenting children with special needs. The featured areas include medical discussions and some help parents deal with day-to-day issues of parenting special children.

Our Kids (www.rdz.stjohns.edu/library/support/our-kids/) is a website (actually, it's a list serv) designed to give support to parents of disabled children. (Actually it's to all caregivers, but since this book is written for parents . . .) Randy Ryan, the one who keeps the Our Kids site going, explained that primary caregivers of a severely disabled child (who is cognitive enough to want entertainment) find it extremely hard to network with other parents. The listserv offers the advantage of the ability to participate on their own schedule plus get input from "a LOT of other parents that have already gone through the same things as [the parent is] asking about, far more input than [they] would be able to get via "live" networking. And support is always just a keyboard away."

The average subscriber to the Our Kids list has a child with long term disabilities and 99 percent of them have children with mental/behavioral issues in addition to a physical/genetic disability. The site focuses on broad interest in physical/medical/behavior issues. It's a great place to go when you need the support and help of other parents of Our Kids.

There are a few special parent resource sites I want you to know about, also.

Family Village (**www.familyvillage.wisc.edu**) is a "global community of disability-related resources." It provides resources for mentally retarded people and people with other disabilities, and their families, and their caregivers. It contains great resources, especially for recreation and leisure, including information about the Special Olympics.

Parents Helping Parents (**www.php.com**) is also an all purpose resource site for parents of children with disabilities or special medical conditions. There is a database of resources searchable at the site. They also have a list of support groups listed by medical condition or disability. Its a very special site with a lot of information.

Apple Computer Inc.'s sites (www2.apple.com) are a rich source of support for parents and children with special needs too. One site, The Disability Connection (www2.apple.com./disability/welcome.html), lists equipment available to help adults and children with disabilities use computers and get online.

Another site sponsored by Apple is their Convomania site for children battling serious illnesses (mania.apple.com). It features live chats, cybercolumns, Ask

"Margot" (the "Dear Abby" of the seriously-ill kids set) and discussion groups. It's written by kids for kids, and it shows.

In addition, they have a refrigerator door page, where kids can submit artwork responsive to the topic of the month (a recent topic was expressing pain, through artwork). Convomania then posts the submissions at the site.

Apparently (and thankfully) I wasn't the only one to notice this very special site. In Spring 1998 a musical theater production of Convomania opens. Based on the life stories of the Convomania kids themselves, a script is being prepared using comments and ideas submitted by the kids at the site. Anyone can add ideas for improving the script and developing the story line. It'll be fun to watch the script develop . . . like a story built around the campfire. I want a front row seat.

Another resource, just for kids with hearing disabilities, Internet for Deaf Cyber Kids (dww.deafworldweb.org/kids/internet.html) is a list serv for deaf kids, from ages 3-19. It also sponsors an IRC channel for deaf kids chats twice a week. I've heard only good things about this community for deaf kids.

It's hard enough trying to find toys that make our kids happy, but to find them for exceptional children is next to impossible. A good resource for toys for exceptional children is the Dragonfly Toy Company, Inc. site (www.dftoys.com/). Dragonfly produces toys for children with special play needs. At the site you can either search for a toy that matches your child's needs or register (like a wedding gift registry) for toys your child would like to receive.

WOW Online (www.wowusa.com) is a website maintained by Winners On Wheels, a non-profit organization for children who use wheelchairs. This isn't a site for parents, it's for the kids themselves. The sites contains some very good basic Internet skill training. In addition, kids can post their artwork or writing at the site and find cyber penpals across the United States.

If you're looking for hard to find products and devices, I've found another very helpful site. Disability Information and Resources (www.eskimo.com/~jlubin/disabled.html) isn't a glossy site with a lot of graphics, but it is loaded with a lot of information. Everything from special computer accessibility products to exercise devises are listed at the site, in an easy to read list. It also has a searchable list of links to other sites for disabled and special needs resources. This is a good site to use first when you're looking for a site for special needs kids.

▼ Adoptive Families and Foster Parenting Online

Barbara Kalish is president of the New Jersey chapter of the Adoptive Parents Committee, a not-for-profit education and support group for couples and singles who have adopted (and those interested in adoption). The Adoptive Parents Committee home page is located at www.wp.com/apc/home.htm and provides useful information, dates of upcoming meetings for adoptive parents and hosts some interesting chat groups as well.

Barbara and her husband learned the issues faced by adoptive parents first hand. They have two terrific children whom they adopted. Even though both she and her husband are lawyers, the adoption maze proved a challenge, even for them. As many other families in their situation had already learned, the most useful person to talk to is another adoptive parent. But unless you already know some adoptive parents, finding them can be a real headache. The Net makes that simple. It is often the quickest mechanism to locate another adoptive parent sharing the same or similar challenges at the same time.

Asked to help me find reliable adoption information on the Internet, Barbara also reviewed them for this book. I appreciate her help and support.

Adoption.com (www.adoption.com) is the largest of all the adoption websites. In its first month of operation alone, more than a million people logged onto the site. Among its many options are family chat groups, parenting information, links to adoption-related professionals, and a World of Love page with information on international adoption. It also has its own search engine, Adoption Search, which helps locate birth relatives. (This can prove very useful where serious medical issues arise and a "blood relative" could help.)

Another useful site is The National Adoption Information Clearinghouse (NAIC) site (www.calib.com/naic/). NAIC is a service of the Children's Bureau, Administration for Children and Families, U.S. Department of Health and Human Services. It was set up by Congress to provide information and other assistance on all aspects of adoption. NAIC site contains an extensive database of laws, expert adoption agencies and other adoption-related information and services. (It's just one of the terrific Federal government sites available to parents.)

I asked Mary Sullivan, NAIC's project director and the person responsible for the NAIC site, to describe some of the highlights of the site. She was particularly proud of their new "An Adoption Guide to the Internet" with almost 120 pages of Internet listings in 10 major categories and 34 sub-headings. The "Adoption Guide" is designed to help adoptive families, adopted adults and their families (both birth and adoptive parents), as well as adoption professionals, locate relevant sites quickly and efficiently.

She explained that the NAIC site is a primary information resource for prospective adoptive parents by providing them with "how to" information. It is also a wonderful resource for adopted adults interested in birth parent search issues, as well as birth relatives interested in reuniting with children who had been placed for adoption. (Its database of adoption documents is available online without charge, 24 hours a day, seven days a week.)

I have personally found the NAIC site to be particularly helpful to parents of adoptive and fosterchildren with special needs, as well. My best friend, Lanell and her husband, Clarence, adopted two half-siblings, at birth. Kelsey (my Goddaughter) is 5 years old and Kylie is 3 years old. (Kylie was originally considered a foster child, until the parental rights were severed, and she could be adopted.) Lanell and Clarence faced a special problem, since both Kelsey and Kylie were born drug-dependent because of the birth mother's drug use. (The doctors suspected that Kelsey was cocaine-dependent and Kylie was heroin-dependent.)

Parenting these children required that Lanell understand the effects, both short term and long term, of drug dependency on their development and behavior. I turned, as usual to the Internet for information Lanell needed. I found everything we needed at the NAIC site, and shared that information with her. It made a big difference.

In addition to websites devoted to adoptive parenting, the online services have special adoptive special interest areas as well. AOL has scheduled chat groups for adopted parents. These take place at 7:30 p.m., 9:00 p.m., and 10:30 p.m. EST. Typical topics include: parenting toddlers/pre-schoolers who were adopted, and a China Chat (for those who adopted from China, a popular source for adoptive children). (To get there AOL subscribers use the keyword "adoption." Then, click on "Parenting Conference Center." Once there, choose "The Back Yard.")

In addition to those reviewed by Barbara, I found an adoption site that I recommend, as well. Adoptive Families of America (www.adoptivefam.org), the publisher of *Adoptive Families* magazine, has a great site for adoptive families and families of foster children.

Many of the adoption sites also have good information for fosterparents. My favorite site devoted exclusively to fosterparenting is Foster Parenting Community (www.fosterparents.com). It contains great resources and has recently added a network page for other fosterparenting associations to use when collaborating and sharing resources.

Most of the parenting websites we reviewed also offer good discussions and chats on adoption and fosterparenting. Many of them also have special areas for children with special needs, which is helpful to some adoptive parents. You should check each of them to find your favorites. When you find things about those sites you want to share with other parents, feel free to post them at the familyguidebook.com site.

▼ Single Parenting and Step-Parenting

Single parenting can be tough. Step-parenting can be even tougher. I know, first hand, because I've done both. It is generally accepted that over 75% of second marriages end in divorce. I suspect that problems associated with step-parenting contribute to this high divorce rate. It's always helpful to have others to talk to, and share solutions with and not always so easy to find them.

I've found several sites that are dedicated to different groups. Some are directed to specific groups, like custodial fathers, while others are more general. Some other sites offer support to several specific groups at the same time.

Stepfamily Foundation (www.stepfamily.org.) is a terrific site with everything a stepfamily needs to know.

Single Parent Resource Center (rampages.onramp.net/~bevhamil/ singleparentresourcece_478.html) has everything a single parent needs, all in one place, from fathers' single parenting to parenting surveys. It is a great site for parents who are new at single parenting.

Daddys Home (www.daddyshome.com/index.html) is a site for fathers who are primary caregivers and either work at home, or single-parent. Great information about parenting, and even better information about handling the role of primary caregiver when you're the dad, and dealing with the "Mr. Mom" label.

Steve Kennedy's Parenting Links (www.apc.net/steveknndy/parent2.htm) is designed by Steve Kennedy, a single father, but offers links for all parents. I think the material on single fathers is particularly good. Steve's sense of humor comes through.

The Divorce Central Parenting Center (www.divorcecentral.com/parent/) has many different discussion areas on divorce and helping your children deal with the problems associated with their parents divorcing. If you're divorced, considering divorce or related to someone who's getting divorced (I guess that's everyone . . .), this is a great resource. (It's also a great resource for grandparents.) They even give legal tips.

▼ Parenting Twins and Other Higher Order Multiples

Multiply the number of children, and you multiply the parenting concerns. (At least that's what my friends tell me.) According to Twins Magazine, 120 sets of twins are born in the United States each day. Luckily there are some terrific sites for parents of twins and other multiples (triplets. etc. . . .) online.

ParentsPlace.com has the best selection, in my opinion, of information on twins and multiples of all the general parenting sites. It hosts the site for Twins Magazine (www.twinsmagazine.com) which includes the table of contents for each month's issue as well as selected articles from that issue.

One of my favorite sites is The National Organization of Mothers of Twins Clubs, Inc. (www.nomotc.org). The National Organization of Mothers of Twins Clubs, Inc. (NOMOTC) is a network of local clubs representing over 21,000 parents of twins and higher multiples. It's run entirely by volunteers and Linda Dreyer (their national past president) has done managing and designing the site. (Until last year, NOMOTC was hosted by ParentsPlace.) The most popular feature at the site is the expectant and new parents area, where parents can get help locating local support groups. It's a great place where parents are helping other parents. (They even have an annual convention each year!)

Parents of twins, and expectant parents of twins, tell us that NOMOTC is the best twin resource online and on the ground.

As much as I love the NOMOTC site, I have one I like even more—Twinz Unlimited (www.twinz.com). Twinz doesn't have any chatrooms or discussion boards. It just has interesting information about twins, parents of twins, famous twins and my most favorite—cartoon twins. In case you didn't know, Marge Simpson has twin sisters, Patty and Selma Bouvier. More multiples? What about Huey, Dewey and Louie? And, for all the members of our children's generation, there are Phil and Lil DeVille, from Nickeloedon's Rugrats show. This is a great site to visit with your children.

▼ Grandparents Parenting (Again)

More and more grandparents are primary caregivers to their grandchildren, and the numbers are increasing each year. According to 1994 U.S. Census over 1.3 million children were being raised exclusively by their grandparents. (And that was over a 25 percent increase from the number of children being raised by their grandparents the previous year.)

Grands R Us (www.eclypse.com/GrandsRuS) is a great site designed just for grandparents who are raising their grandchildren. (According to statistics reported at their site, over 3.7 million children are living with their grandparents (some with and some without their parents residing there as well.) It's a great resource and has been around for awhile. Grandparents can post their comments on a bulletin board recently provided to Grands R Us when they joined the ParentsPlace.com group. (Again, ParentsPlace.com is a great resource for special parenting and grandparenting needs.)

Family.com also has a great site for grandparents (www.family.com/WebObjects/Boards). (What else would you expect from a Disney company?) It's user friendly and easy to read.

I'm going to break my rule about trying to supply only Internet resources, because two of the most helpful resources I found don't have a website yet. If enough of you call, I'm sure we can get them wired, but in the meantime, you should have this information:

AARP Grandparent Information Center
(Newsletter & Resource List available
   upon request)
601 E Street, NW
Washington, D.C. 20049
(202) 434-2296

Grandparents Reaching Out (GRO)
Mildred Horn
141 Glen Summer Road
Holbrook, New York 11741
(516) 472-9728

CHAPTER 24

Some Great Family Websites and Parenting Resources

A Bird's Eye View—

▼ Parenting Sites

▼ The Moms on the Internet . . .
  Cybercelebs All

▼ Fun Sites for Kids

▼ Parenting Sites

I've found some favorite parenting sites, and there are new ones daily. They are a wonderful resource for parenting tips and can help you when you're feeling all alone, as parents. There are two sites that I think parents should be bookmarking before any others, Family.com and FamilyPC.com.

Family.com (**www.family.com**)

This site has taken over the old Family Planet site and added Disney pizazz. It's clear that a lot of thought has gone into making it easy to navigate and user-friendly. It contains something for every family. Want an activity for your 6-year-old? Insert your child's age, and click. Voila! Thinking about adopting? . . . no problem. Planning a family vacation? You've got it. Everything for everyone.

Disney's cornering the children's market continues into cyberspace with this site filled with activities and subjects ranging from Learning, Travel and Food, to general parenting. This site is filled with a number of useful family tools including free electronic greeting cards and reference sites to help kids with homework and other projects. A separate message board and chat section add an interactive aspect to the site giving parents and kids alike the opportunity to comment and converse with other visitors to the site.

FamilyPC.com (**www.familypc.com**)

This is the website for *FamilyPC* magazine. Robin Raskin, whom I mentioned before, is "Internet Mom" at the site and the magazine's editor-in-chief on the ground. The site provides answers to all of your online computing questions. When friends ask me something I don't know . . . I send them there for answers. (That way I can still take the credit for providing them with a good online resource.) Fun and interesting to read, the site is also very easy to work through.

Then surf around and find your favorites from these terrific parenting sites.

Parenttime (**www.parenttime.com**)

A spokesperson from Parenting said that the format will probably mirror that used on their AOL Thrive site. Although nothing is firm yet, I'll assume that the chats and boards will remain the same. Currently, there are chats in the site for expectant moms of every month. They even have a nurse midwife, behavioral specialist (counselor), family therapist, an ob-gyn and a nutritionist. There's a teen chat as well.

Although Parenttime is still under construction, it has considerable online experience and talent behind it. Formed as a joint venture between Colgate-Palmolive and Time Warner, and using Pathfinder as a resource, it expects to quickly rival the other parenting sites online. We'll have to wait and see. Though if my sister, Deanna Aftab Guy, M.D., stays with them, they can't go wrong.

Mom and Pop Get Wired (**www.mompop.com**)

This site bills itself as the hippest parenting site on the Web. It may be right. In addition to live chats and lots of discussion groups, it's joined forces with Yahoo! to bring you the latest news stories of interest to parents. Are you a frustrated author? The site gives you a special 'zine just for parents. Submit your manuscript, or whatever you want, and they'll publish it. (Well, at least anything you submit within reason . . .)

Parent Soup (**www.parentsoup.com**)

This site has live chats and a terrific selection of discussion groups. In its Q&A sections you can contact experts on discussion boards or sift through the archived questions on pediatrics, family counseling, nutrition, colleges, and activities for tots. You'll find information about special parenting situations as well as the meat and potatoes stuff. The nutritionist not only answers questions about how to eat right, but also how to handle the preferences of picky eaters.

You have to register at the site to access their discussion boards and live chats. (You can download a chat server plug-in right from a link at the site.) If there's something you want to share, want to try, or want to talk about that's related to parenting, I guarantee you'll find it here (and if you don't, you can become the leader of your own group).

The site recognizes that parents have a life outside of their role as parent; there's tons of information on topics like marriage, dealing with a dysfunctional family, depression and marriage, and finding a great book to read or vacation to take. (After all of that, you'll need one!)

Foster Parent Community (**www.fosterparents.com**)

One of the most informative foster parenting sites I've found. It has articles ranging from medical and health tips to those by foster children. It has adoption information too, as well as grandparents raising grandchildren.

In addition to great articles, the site has a chat channel, where foster parents and others can chat with each other, live. (You'll need an IRC program, though.) It also has great links, resources and information about foster parenting and adoption by state and country. Finally, you can sign up for a list serv on foster parenting.

Got a question you want a professional to answer? Try Parenting—Q&A (**www.parenting-qa.com**) It's run by the parenting publication leaders, Parents Plus, Inc., who usually answer questions posted by visitors to the site within a few days. It's a particularly good site for parents with younger children who have lots of questions about what to expect and when to expect it.

Another favorite is ParentsPlace.com (**www.parentsplace.com**)

With 250 separate discussion boards, there's nothing that relates to parenting that hasn't already been discussed here. I've shared more about ParentsPlace in our "Special families . . . special children" chapter, but it has great areas for parent-to-parent chats and advice. You'll always find someone who's been there and done that . . . it's comforting to know you're not alone. And, you're never alone in ParentsPlace. They have over 500,000 visitors a month.

The content is always fresh at ParentsPlace, with at least four new articles added daily to the home page. The most popular areas include "Expecting Clubs," "Trying to Conceive Community," "Breastfeeding," "Parents of Toddlers," "Marriage" and "Frugal Living" forums. David Cohen and Jackie

Needleman (husband and wife) run the site from their home, assisted by seven other parents from around the U.S.

Folks Online (**www.folksonline.com**) is a good starting place for newbies. It has a special feature called "Net Newcomer," just for newbies, and many other areas that are helpful when you're first getting started online.

Parenting on the Web (**www.geocities.com/heartland/9530**)

This is a great site, where parents review other sites and resources for parents on the Web. Maybe because it's written by other parents, I thought their reviews were relevant and thoughtful. I found myself in agreement with the reviewers most of the time. It is also a good source of parenting links.

The Daily Parent (**www.dailyparent.com**) is loaded with articles and resources for parents. Their topic finder gives you a choice of many topics relating to parenting, and will search for articles on the topic you select. It's an easy way to navigate a big site, especially for newbies.

Parent News (**www.parent.net**) is a terrific site packed with simple and easily accessible information for parents. I especially like their book and movie reviews. They have a weekly article about parenting (which I always enjoy) and a daily parenting tip. Their daily homework site resource is a good feature, one that many parents check daily with their children.

Sesame Street Parents (**www.ctw.org/parents**) is a good general parenting site. There are parenting discussion areas, reviews of products and one of my favorites—Our Family Journal, where Jahnna and Malcolm share their family stories in ways other parents can truly appreciate. Its an easy site to enjoy.

Parenthood Web (**www.parenthoodweb.com**) is a very complete site, with live chats, articles, weekly spotlights and a free weekly electronic newsletter which is delivered to you by e-mail. It has a product recall list and lots of child safety and medical tips.

Home and Family (**www.homeand family.com**)

This site is an extension of The Family Channel's (www.familychannel.com) popular TV show. It contains a show diary and interesting features on parenting, relationships and health. If you fill out a "viewer profile" they will e-mail you to alert you to special show segments of interest to you. They also promise to use the profile information only to provide this service, and not to disclose it.

Steve and Ruth Bennett's Family Surf Board (**www.familysurf.com**) is a fun and informative site for families. The site contains recommended websites for kids and one of my favorite features—the children's Internet Activity Center. The Children's Internet Activity Center is a terrific start for your family web-surfing. Steve Bennett also has a column he writes for Cleveland Parent about parenting challenges in this technological age. You can also find some great demo of new software in their Demo Depot.

▼ The Moms on the Internet . . . Cybercelebs All

Multimedia Mom (**www.multimediamom.org**) Bonnie Scott formed the Mult-Media Mom Network as a place where parents and educators can join forces to review and evaluate children's media. They review children's products "with a keen eye to issues of gender, culture and violence, and are very choosy about what [they] approve." The reviews are posted monthly. Bonnie also operates a list serv, which you can subscribe to from the site.

Bonnie told me that although everyone is talking about how cyberspace is changing parenting, no one realizes how much parenting is changing cyberspace. She's right. Just look at the ways families are using the Internet and how much rich content there is providing support to parents of children of all types and special needs. In taking us into the future, the ease in which parents can share experiences with other parents takes us back too . . . back to when parents could rely on each other for assistance and support.

When you check out the MultiMedia Mom site, you can spot the amount of creative talent devoted to the site by Bonnie and her volunteers. Bonnie has a background in award-winning children's videos, many of which were widely acclaimed. MultiMedia Mom was the result of years of Bonnie's research into what children learning media works best for kids. Bonnie also appears weekly on Debbie Nigro's talk radio show, Working Mom on the Run, with her MultiMedia Mom minute.

Her mission statement says it all:

> I . . . wanted to make a difference. The true heroes of our world are not alien-fighting ninjas or mutant anything, rather the true heroes are those men and women who model peaceful coexistence and cooperation. Facts are the essential tools of a child's imagination, and a rich imagination is the key to a happy, healthy child. Our job, as parents, is to provide opportunities that enrich our child's imagination, to passionately encourage its growth and to cherish its wonders.

CD-ROM Mom (**www.cd-mom.com**) Wendy Dubit is the publisher and editor (and the "Mom") at CD-ROM Mom, a family site with information about multimedia and computer activities. Wendy shares that the site (and CD-ROM's which she proposes to market) is "designed to bring the family together in activity, education and fun[.] . . . CD-ROM Mom is a place where appropriate technology and meaningful content meet—bringing us to a greater understanding of ourselves, our families, our communities, our world."

Net-mom (**www.netmom.com**). Jean Armour Polly is undoubtedly one of the most famous and successful of all the Internet moms. In fact, she invented the term "surfing the Internet" way back in 1992, in the days before the Mosaic web browser, and just about the time when Berners-Lee released HTTP on the general population to form the Web.

Jean Armour Polly is best known as the author of the best-selling children's book *The Internet Kids Yellow Pages*, published by Osborne/McGraw-Hill ($19.95 ISBN 007-882-197-5). Her newly updated and expanded edition, *The Internet Kids & Family Yellow Pages* was recently released. My local Barnes

& Nobles store tells me they can't keep enough of them in stock, they're so popular. (I've got to learn about marketing from that woman!)

Her yellow pages collection is more than a mere list of sites. Jean has reviewed every single site to make sure it's family and kid friendly. Her net-mom.com site has updates and sample sites from the book. (www.net-mom.com/ikyp/index.htm) You can even order the book online. The net-mom.com site also offers a free newsletter that is e-mailed to you each week describing family-friendly sites and pointers.

A librarian by training, Jean is very proud of her involvement with the landmark "Project GAIN:Connecting Rural Public Libraries to the Internet" study. In 1993 Jean also became one of the first two women elected to the Internet Society Board of Trustees, the most prestigious organization in the Internet industry. She's an extraordinary woman. I could devote an entire book to describing how much she's done for the Internet and for families online.

Interactive Mom (**www.interactivemom.com**) Kolene Tanner is Interactive Mom. She has a nice touch, with lots of "down home" advice for parents. She also deals with serious issues, like juvenile delinquency. She endeared herself to me by her choice of photo for her bio section. (Where she's licking a spoon from an obviously delicious, and now totally empty, roasting pan.)

Internet Mom (**www.familypc.com**) Robin Raskin, whom I've talked about relentlessly throughout this book, is Internet Mom. She's also the editor-in-chief of *Family PC* magazine.

Her online columns on the trials and tribulations of raising kids in this computer age are one of the best things about the familypc.com site. She manages to cut to the heart of the issue, with humor and insight few can match. Respected as a leader in the emerging field of children and technology, Robin was also a key spokesperson before the FTC on the recent hearings on privacy and child protection.

While many people are jumping on the children and the Internet bandwagon, this isn't a new fad for her. Robin has been writing about kids and computers for over 15 years. As a freelance writer trying to break into publishing while juggling the task of raising kids at the same time, she submitted an article titled "How I Learned About Computers to Save Our Marriage"—the story of learning UNIX to keep pace with her husband, which started her on this unwaivering course.

Before coming to *FamilyPC*, Robin was Editor of *PC Magazine*. She has written two books on kids and computers, and recently served as Series Editor for three new family computing books from Hyperion.

She has three children ages 17, 15 and 11 and lives a highly "connected life" in both New York City and the beautiful Hudson Valley.

SGT MOM's Kidz (**www.sgtmoms.com**) Kathleen (Kathy) Motteler is SGT MOM. Kathleen is an army wife and mother currently stationed at NAB Little Creek VA. SGT MOM'S is a website devoted to the special needs of families in the armed forces. It's a very popular site, with thousands of visitors daily. Kathy first dreamed up the idea for SGT MOM'S when she felt a need for a more casual form of support that couldn't be found in official channels. Being an army wife meant losing friends every time they moved.

When she moved one time too many, she found that although she treasured her children dearly, she craved friends and adult conversation. In her own words, I'll let Kathleen tell you how she wandered around cybersapce, clueless about where she was going or how to get there. It'll also show you how nervous she was getting online. And just look! A few years later and she's one of the leading "moms" online. It'll inspire even the most fearful among you.

SGT MOM... In Her Own Words

[After we got our computer] my husband tried and tried, dragging me kicking and screaming to the keyboard, but I was not at all interested. I was also sure if I touched the computer I would somehow explode it or melt it into a puddle of technocolor goo.

Finally boredom took over, and while the girls napped one day, I got online. But, I had no idea what to do! I just wildly moved the mouse around and clicked constantly. The screen began flipping and changing and suddenly I saw something that said "parents chat." I had accidentally clicked my way into ParentsPlace!

I saw "chat with other parents" and stopped to read what it said! Then I noticed that certain words were underlined and colored and when I moved the mouse cursor over them a hand popped up! So I clicked! Don't ask me how, but I made it through the registration process and started chatting that day! I loved it! And the other chatters took pity on newbies like me! I didn't say much, I was too shy, but I listened and took notes . . . I literally had a notebook and inkpen writing down stuff they said!

The other chatters had homepages, and after visiting a few of them I decided this is what I was looking for! I just had to figure out how to create my own home page! No easy trick . . . but I was determined and committed! I wanted to create a place for military spouses. Some place where we could meet others in the same boats. My idea was that if they signed up for keypals, someone coming to their area might read it and they could make a friend before they got to their new dutystation! They could also get good information on the housing, the schools, and the neighborhoods. Something welcome packets never tell you!

They would also not be so lonely during all the deployments and Temporary duties. I felt there were many other military spouses out there like me that for whatever reasons were slipping through the cracks, and I knew this was the way to reach them! As I continued to chat, I started meeting them.

After being on line two weeks and chatting every afternoon during naptime, I had followed a link on someone's homepage to a place that offered e-z and free homepages made on line. I leaped at the chance and even though I had no clue HOW to make the homepage, I knew WHAT I wanted on the page!

I learned HTML rather quickly and soon at the urging of another chatter who created the SGT MOM logo, my husband downloaded an editor for me. I began playing with it, taught myself how to use it (without reading the directions . . . don't understand techno babble at all) and started redesigning SGT MOM'S. In 6 weeks' time, I had created something I was proud of and we loaded it to the server. It was an instant hit.

I began getting letters from military spouses all over the world! Soon after I started getting letters from active duty, vets, extended family, and brats. All wanting me to include them in my site too. It has been since January 1996 and I have learned much along the way. My site has evolved many times over too.

Today I work full time on SGT MOM'S, often times putting in 40-60 hours a week or more. Recently, following my latest move, it was time to accept the offers of volunteer help from my two closest cyber pals and military spouses.

I still do the vast majority of all work on SGT MOM'S. Carrie a Navy spouse is answering the general mail, and Ker an Airforce spouse is helping behind the scenes.

▼ Fun Sites for Kids

This isn't a website yellow pages (I'll leave that to Jean Armour Polly and her best-selling books), but in surfing to research the book, I found places I loved that our kid testers loved too.

For Girls:

G.I.R.L. (www.worldkids.net/girl/welcom2.htm)
>A pen pal club for girls between 8 and 14 years of age. There's also a newsletter and activity list for G.I.R.L. members.

Cyber Sisters (www.worldkids.net/clubs/CSIS/csis.htm)
>Is for girls between the ages of 6 and 18 and provides a resource for pen pals and worldwide communication with list servs.

For Boys

Guys (www.worldkids.net/clubs/guys)
>A pen pal club for boys between 7 and 17 years of age. There's a sports discussion group and other activities for boys.

For Everyone

Kids-Page—Multnomah County Library (www.multnomah.lib.or.us/lib/kids)
>This site is for everyone and is everything a public library site should be. It has wonderful online resources, and still encourages the kids to get a library card to be able to participate in a scavenger hunt about books. I wish I lived in Multnomah County!

Star Wars Page at Texas A&M (www.aero25.tamu.edu/~swpage/index2.html)
>A great site for you Star Wars' fans . . . with lots of information about the "prequel" and everything else any diehard fan would want.

The Dinosaur Society (www.dinosociety.org/homepage.html)

A great site for dinosaurs. The Dinosaur Society handled the tour of the Jurassic Park dinosaurs around the United States, and has lots of information about it.

The Metropolitan Museum of Art
(**www.metmuseum.org/htmlfile/education/ kid.html**)

The Metropolitan Museum has designed a page for families and kids. It's the best way to tour a museum when the kids are small, from your arm chair.

Family Internet (**www.familyinternet.com**)

This is a great site for teenagers. Glitzy and glossy, it speaks their language. With movie stars, TV stars and rock stars leading the way, your teens can surf the site and learn a few things (okay . . . nothing terribly substantial, but a few things nonetheless . . .) Our teen testers tell me it's great for anyone over 12 years old.

Headbone Zone (**www.headbone.com**)

Older kids a problem? Too old for Sesame Street and Arthur, but too young for teen sites? I found a great site, The Headbone Zone, with lots of games and featuring the Gigglebone Gang. It has an interactive costume site, where, after installing Shockwave, a free plug-in for your web browser, your child can dress Elroy in costumes and disguises. It's a great site for a rainy afternoon— or a sunny afternoon—if your children are between 8 and 12 years old.

CHAPTER 25

Our Kids' Reviews

A Bird's Eye View—

▼ What Our Kids Think and What
Our Kids Like

▼ What Our Kids Think and What Our Kids Like

Our kids reviewers have reviewed their favorite sites, in their own language (although we fixed their spelling <g>). They come from all over the country and range from 3 years old (dictated to her mom) to 18 years old. All of the reviews were submitted to us via e-mail.

▼ AN INCOME OF HER OWN
URL—http://www.aioho.com
by Amanda, 16 years old

An Income of Her Own is about making girls aware—of themselves, of business, of a community of young girls out there with a brain and a future; they are big on trying to connect young girls through seminars, e-mails, and camps. Girls are not made into victims here, with articles like, "How girls are being objectified by the media/men/CEOs/miscellaneous scum of society." Rather, they focus on empowering women by cultivating their minds, not their bitterness. They disguise serious entrepreneurial brainstorming with games and competitions. They encourage women to do what they like, not what looks good in a powersuit; there were articles in abundance on entrepreneurs of make-up businesses or fostercare organizations (though I think they could inject a little more ruthless drive into their site). The distinct lack of substance in certain areas (read: the incessant promotions of their camp and competitions) was irking but never turned me off.

Notable Notables

1) They have a Q&A with different, successful female entrepreneurs every month. They encourage girls to ask them (good, intelligent, mature) questions and furnish them with information on these womens' success stories.

2) They have tips and studies interspersed between their newsletters about everything from why it is good to save a business card to the correlation between good parenting and financial security.

▼   CORNELL UNIVERSITY
URL—www.cornell.edu
Sagar S. Mungekar, 18 years old

[And he's too modest to tell you he is also his high school's valedictorian and Cornell's lucky to have him!]

Towards the middle of junior year in high school, I started to give serious thought to the college I wanted to attend. There were literally thousands out there, and hundreds had begun sending me pamphlets and information. Even after I narrowed my list down somewhat, there were close to twenty universities. I knew I couldn't visit all of them, and even if I did, I wasn't sure how much that would help in choosing the ones I would apply to. The best way, I found, to learn about the college, its programs, requirements, and such was over the World Wide Web. Every college that I was even remotely interested in had their own website at www.college name.edu and each page of the sites was filled with useful information.

The one that I found most informative and best laid-out was Cornell University (to which I was accepted and will attend in fall '97. As a prospective student, I was able to take a virtual tour of the campus (complete with pictures and textual information). By clicking on the admissions area on the opening map, I was led to a number of links that answered my every question. The pages explained the differences among the various colleges at Cornell, how financial aid was managed, the different majors available, the student activities that were available, and much more. When I decided to actually visit the campus, I was more prepared in asking questions at the information sessions and on the tour since I already had some background knowledge.

The website was as just as useful after I was accepted. During the summer, I was able to look at the map of the campus and find out exactly where my dorm was. I was also able to look at what classes were offered to freshmen and start to make up my schedule. It seemed as if any question I had, I could find an answer to. I'm sure that once college starts, I will be able to utilize other areas of this informative website.

▼   DISNEY.COM
URL—www.disney.com
By Danielle, 3 years old (as dictated to my sister, her mother)

I love Disney. I can watch movies like Lion King and Toy Story and sing the songs. When the song is over, you can play it again. I have the Disney animated storybooks too—Lion

King, Dalmatians and Winnie the Pooh. I like the Dalmatians the best and read the book with my own words "—there goes Cruella's car! . . . The puppies are cute."

▼ (ADULTS AND) KIDS ONLY
By Emily, 10 years old (with some help from her mother, Beth)

My favorite place in AOL is Kids Only, where there are games, chats and trivia games that are supposed to be like the name says, for Kids Only. My parents are constantly chasing me off of their favorite sites and games and telling me to go get where I belong, in a kids area. Like the good kid I am, I go. (But I have to admit, Hollywood Tonight and Trivial Pursuit are fun when I can sneak into them!)

My favorite place to go in Kids Only is Cartoon-Network Trivia Toon-Up. This is a really fun trivia game where kids compete against each other, answering questions about different cartoons on Cartoon Network (the T.V. network). The questions test your knowledge on cartoons like The Jetsons, Penelope Pittstop, and lots of others. The whole game consists of 20 questions flashing on the screen. You have to click the answer (1, 2 or 3) and do it fast. The faster you give a correct answer, the more points you get. You get one hint that tells you right away what one of the wrong answers is. However, waiting for the hint gives you less total points, even if you are correct. Speed counts.

I love playing this game, and I'm good at it. I even won once! I thought, "Oh my gosh, I won against all these kids!" (And let me tell you, sometimes up to two hundred people are playing at the same time). I was so happy, and wanted to see if I had beaten any boys. (Boys always think they are so smart!) That's when I discovered a secret, and I'll let you all in on it. One person I had been neck and neck with the entire game was almost twenty-two years old!

I was so upset! Not that I won, of course, but that adults were invading the Kids Only chat areas, and not allowing us kids in theirs. There should really be some kind of security or something. This is totally unfair! My parent's won't let me in certain areas because of my age. Why can adults come into ours?

I'll tell you one thing—our areas are more fun, and I think my parents and other adults must agree! The other night, after I logged off and went to my room, I heard my Mom laughing online. Being an average American kid, I tiptoed back into the room. I peeked over to see where my Mom was. Was it Moms Online? Parent Soup? Just what was so funny? And what do you think I saw? My Mom was playing Cartoons Network Trivia . . . and loving it. I'm warning you, guys. Kids Only isn't going to be just for kids much longer!

▼ VIDEO GAME SPOT
URL— www.videogamespot.com
by Justin, 13 years old

For many years I have been infatuated with the World Wide Web. I remember coming up to my dad and asking him to find me codes for my favorite video game, Mortal Kombat. Back then, he was using Gopher.

Since then, I have been glued to the Internet. When I was 10, I made my first web page, it was called "The Mortal Kombat Kompanion." It never really made that much progress, but it was a start. At eleven, I made my own complete video game home page for everybody to use. It consisted of maps, codes, cheats, hints, reviews, even sound clips that I made with my own computer microphone.

About a year ago, a new video game site was released. It descended from the original computer games site, "GAMESPOT." This web page was, and still is the most factual, most used, and most up-to-date video game site I have ever seen.

It has colorful backgrounds and graphics, very appealing to the eye. Children from five to fifteen and older who play video games, all use this site as a number one reference for hints, cheats, codes, reviews, movie clips, and much much more.

It also has info on all the hot new systems like, Sega's Saturn, the Sony Playstation, and the hot new goody, Nintendo64 (A.K.A. N64 or Ultra64). This helps the kids to look at the games they enjoy, and see other people's opinion on them before cleaning out their (preferably their parent's) wallet of $60, $70, or maybe even with the N64 game cartridges, $90 dollars on one video game!

Not everyone enjoys video games, and many people think they're "stupid" or the famous quote for us generation X'rs, "a waste of time". I totally disagree. Video games can be educational. Some are violent and weird, but games like "RPGs" (Role Playing Games) are very educational. VideoGameSpot is just one of many websites that emphasize this idea or theory and helps video game players throughout the world.

▼ ARTS OF AVALON
URL—www.poseyent.com/index1.htm
By Kelsey, 5 years old

I like to play dress up. I make my costumes and like to be a fairy princess and a dancer. I have a site that shows all different costumes, which I want. Sometimes I pretend I am wearing them. I like the princess dress and the indian princess dresses best. I also like the genie costume. If I had a genie costume, I would give everyone their wish, because I can do magic, like in I Dream of Jeannie on tv.

▼ THE BOLSHOI THEATER, BALLET, AND OPERA
URL—www.alincom.com/bolshoi/index.htm
by Kelsey, 5 years old

I love dancing and ballet dancing. Aunt Parry is my godmother, and finds me special places to see ballet pictures on the computer. We don't have a computer, so I have to go to the library to see what she found for me. When I grow up, I want to be a ballet star and dance on a stage. I want to wear beautiful costumes. I only saw ballet dancing on television. When I come to New York, Aunt Parry will take me to see a real ballet, with real ballet dancers and costumes.

I like the pictures of the ballet dancers at this site. I know that Aunt Parry works as a lawyer in Russia where these dancers live. She saw them dance on a stage. Someday she will take me to see them in person. Maybe I will dance with them too.

▼ CAPEZIO CAFE
URL—www.capezio.com/cafe/cafe.html
by Kelsey, 5 years old

I want to be a ballet dancer. I like to look at this site because I can see what ballet dancers wear. It also tells my Mom about ballet dancing, so she can help me when I'm bigger to be a ballet dancer. Other ballet dancers talk to each other, and you can read what they say. When I'm older, I will talk to other ballet dancers too.

▼ "KIDS ONLY" ON AMERICA ONLINE
Keyword— ("kids")
By Maggie, 8 years old

I like to go on AOL and go on Kids Only. I don't like Ren & Stimpy—its a good show, but its not a very nice one—the way they put it is just weird. I like the sections on Kennan and Kel, Shelby Woo and RugRats. My favorite section out of all of these ones I like is Kennan and Kel because I can chat with them. I like to go in the chat rooms, but I don't have a lot to say so I read what other kids write. Sometimes they are really funny and they make me laugh a lot! It's fun to play the games on AOL because I never give up on the quizzes.

I like the Kids Only chat rooms on AOL a lot—the graphics to go in the chat rooms are cool—lips with braces are neat—I want braces—I like ZUZU on the Web—the art gallery has colorful background and there are audios to listen to the answers to jokes that kids send in—there is poetry also and I like to read other kids poetry—kids age 6—12 would like ZUZU.

You get on Blackberry Creek from AOL to the Web—the Creek has Highlights for Kids Magazine stuff on it—you can learn what other kids like from it—the graphics are great and also some kids draw really well—even kids that are 4 years old would like the Creek a lot!

National Geographic is interesting and colorful—kids my age and older would like it—but not kids younger. AOL has games and I really like the Quest Tests—when you lose the man comes on and says "what the heck happened" and when you get the right answer, you hear cool music—the Crystal Ball area is great—it lets you ask a question that you can get a yes or no answer from—that's really cool—Kids Only on AOL is good for kids younger than me and even some teenagers would like parts of it.

I guess that wraps it up.

▼ MOVIESOUNDS.COM
URL—"http://www.moviesounds.com"
by Michael, 15 years old

The Internet access from AOL is good, too. I go to AOL's Web access and search for things off the 'Net. On the Web I go to www.moviesounds.com to download quotes and songs from movies. I put these sounds on the control panel so when I start up Windows 95, exit Windows95, or even minimize things I hear a sound. However, the Moviesounds website is probably better for ages 13&Up because of some offensive language used in some of the sounds.

▼ "SPORTS" ON AMERICA ONLINE
Keyword—("sports")
by Michael, 15 years old

I am an AOL user and enjoy my access to the service. Despite some frustration with the speed of AOL at times, I still enjoy it. I like Instant Messaging my "buddies," too. I have

85 people on my buddy list so it is fun chatting with them. I like receiving mail from my friends as well.

On AOL, I do many things . . . I go to my "Favorite Places," which include Baseball Weekly, USA Today Sports, Duke Sports, Yankees.com, ESPNET SportsZone, and MovieSounds and other websites. I enjoy baseball and basketball a lot so I go to these sites to keep up-to-date on how the professional teams are doing such as the New York Yankees and New York Knicks.

On these websites such as the USA Today Sports—I use the in depth team matchups for additional information on upcoming games. In these in depth matchups, it tells how the one team pitcher does against the other team, how the batters perform against the pitcher of the opposition. I also find the up-to-date news in sports. I look at the sites to find the team standings and statistics. Another thing I do on USA Today Sports is look at the "Roger Maris chase"—the chase for 61 HR's. They have the top three candidates who have the best chance in breaking the single season HR record. On EspnetSportsZone, I read the articles about what the analysts are thinking on certain subjects in sports today. I do not read all of those articles though because then I'd be online like all day. I like going into these sites because I can get information about my favorite sports easily. Those sports websites I mentioned are good for all ages.

Finally, America Online is not only entertaining, it is educational as well. The search engine comes in handy during the school year especially. For instance, during my English class we were reading Silas Marner and I used Barron's Notes off the Internet for help with the book.

▼ Universities online
URL—www.universities.com
by Tim, 18 years old

In an age where attending college is a bare essential, the choice of which college or university to attend becomes very crucial. There is a great deal of stress involved in the college process, and there are only a few places to turn to for reliable information on the topic. One of these sources is universities.com, a Web page that contains a search engine that can and will locate any of 4,000 colleges and universities all over the world.

The page is a very simple one to operate. Simply type in the name or location desired, and a list of results will appear on the page. From there, all you need do is browse at any page that appeals to you, and you have begun to look at schools. Through this page, you can get a good look at colleges all across the world and from there make plans for which schools you are interested in. The page's ability to find almost any school makes it highly useful if you are looking for a smaller name school, or one with a small enrollment. The engine is also more than capable of finding multiple sources on larger name schools, and more renowned ones. Overall, universities.com, can help make the college process a whole lot easier!

▼ POLLSTAR
URL—www.pollstar.com/homenf.htm
by Tim, 18 years old

This website claims to be "The Internet's most accurate, comprehensive and up-to-date concert tour database" and that is exactly what it is. Pollstar is a website capable of finding any one of 2,044 artists or 26,986 events in its contents. By using the page's "Concert Hotwire Search Engine," a music fan may discover the next showing and location of his favorite artist. The search device asks you to specify either the artist, the city or the venue in order to find what you are looking for, and Pollstar always brings back the results to find the shows!

Along with the helpful search engine, the Pollstar homepage also shows a list of all newly announced concert tours, five articles that usually pertain to concert going and a sample of sound bytes for the music fan. There are many links from the Pollstar homepage to other music related pages as well.

▼ NATIONAL GEOGRAPHIC
URL—www.nationalgeographic.com/
by Taylor, 18 years old

The National Geographic site provides tons of fun for parents and children together. This site offers hours of exploration through features such as "Save the Environment," the "Media," the "Society," "Passport," "Resources," "Kids Only," and the National Geographic store.

The site provides education and enjoyment, at the same time, for families, ranging anywhere from taking trips on-location around the world with an actual National Geographic photographer, introductions to the Committee for Research and Exploration, photo biographies, all the way to articles and photos of ancient shipwrecks found deep in the Mediterranean.

The "kids only" area was the best part of the adventure. I explored games, such as Make-A-Mummy, voted on next month's cover, took a geo bee quiz, signed up for an international pen pal, and became a jr. member of the National Geographic society.

This interactive site has a lot to offer families, teenagers, and children. This is, by far, one of the best sites that I've seen!

▼ KELLOGG'S CEREAL CITY
URL—www.kellogg.com
by Aaron, 12 years old

This is the ultimate fun page! It's got everything from cool recipes made from cereal, to interactive Macromedia games. The site features Tony the Tiger as your guide, leading you through all the different parts of site. Different features include "Company Info," the "Recipe Center," and the "Kellogg's Racing Arena." The site emphasizes on informing you about new products and to have fun. It's colorful, highly decorated pages make it a five star eye pleaser.

My favorite part of the site is the "Corn Pop" section, mainly because of the Macromedia Shockwave Games available. If you have the plug-in for your browser, you can play any of three really cool games. The only problem with this page is the long download time due to all the graphics. A must see!!!

Aaron's Scoring System: Terrible: * Poor: ** OK:*** Cool:**** Awesome:*****

The site's scores:
Aesthetics: *****
Info Provided: ****
Kid Friendly: *****
Adult Friendly: ***
Features: *****
Estimated Load Time (28.8): 2 mins per page
Overall: *****

▼ DISCOVERY ONLINE
URL—www.discovery.com
Aaron, 12 years old

The Discovery Channel's homepage is very well designed, but lacks some aesthetic touches that would make someone want to go back to it just for the fun of it. The information it provides is extensive, giving more information about anything that was on the network in the past week.

Topics range from information about sharks, to how to raise a barn, the Amish way! The easy to read menus, always present on the side of the page, are a godsend to people who often get lost on the web. The only problem I have with this page is its kid section. It doesn't provide any real information, just the times that their child-oriented shows air. No real helpful info. I would not recommend this page to a kid looking for info on a school project.

Aaron's Scoring System: Terrible: * Poor: ** OK:*** Cool:**** Awesome:*****

The site's scores:
Aesthetics: ***
Info Provided: ****
Kid Friendly: **
Adult Friendly: ****
Features: *****
Estimated Load Time (28.8): 20-30 secs.
Overall: *** and a half

▼ THE WHITE HOUSE (AND THE WHITE HOUSE FOR KIDS)
URL—www.whitehouse.gov
Aaron, 12 years old

The White House Page is actually a very nice piece of work. The general look of it reminds me of a 19th century decor, using a cursive font, and a mellow speckled background. The animated flags you see on the top are also a nice touch. The page itself offers information about recent press releases, the history of the Whitehouse, and general information about the United States.

The site also has a very nice kids' section, which you are guided through by Socks the Cat. You can view a special newsletter for kids or take a tour of it. You can also get sound bytes of Socks himself! My personal favorite is the link that allows you to actually write the president.

Aaron's Scoring System: Terrible: * Poor: ** OK:*** Cool:**** Awesome:*****

The site's scores:
Aesthetics: *****
Info Provided: **** and a half
Kid Friendly: ****
Adult Friendly: *****
Features: *****
Estimated Load Time (28.8): 25 secs.
Overall: *****

▼ JC MACAW
URL—users1.vastnet.net/~jcmacaw/index.html
by Sophia, 5 years old (our Macaw mascot . . . as dictated to Parry)

This is the site of JC Macaw. JC is a distant cousin of mine, and we hope to get together at our next family reunion. I liked the family photos. You'd think they'd put some family photos up at our site, but n-o-o-o-o . . . I have to surf the Web to see other Macaws.

I'm a little concerned that that OmniPoint bird will get his own website first. Every pet seems to have their own website but me . . . Well, anyway, it's nice to be able to visit my relatives online. One of my friends, Sarah (she's 6 years old), got a letter from her grandma with the website of her grandma's bed & breakfast in Maine. Her grandma had put up pictures of her pets (see . . . everyone has a site but me) at the site. When Sarah's class wanted to get online for the first time, Sarah told her teacher about her grandma's website and the whole class got to see her grandma's house and pets. (Don't get me started again . . .)

▼ "THE SOCKS WHITE HOUSE TOUR FOR KIDS"
URL—www.whitehouse.gov/WH/kids/html/pretour2.html
by Sophia, 5 years (our Macaw mascot . . . as dictated to Parry)

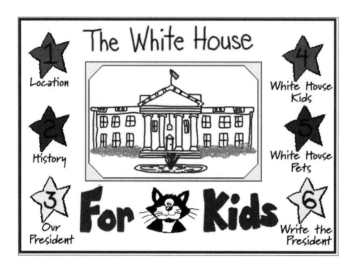

No one ever gives me any respect. What do I find while surfing the Web? A cat has its own site, and a site of The White House yet! Is there no end to this humiliation? Even if it is for children . . . I like children. I like children more than that ol' cat does, I bet!

I'd be happy to give the tour of the White House. I know that President Washington never lived in the White House, and that it was the biggest house in the United States until the Civil War. (I did take the tour, you know!) There's lots more I learned too . . . about a special desk built from an old ship that President Clinton is using in the Oval Office and the history of the White House.

A cat! Even if it is President and Mrs. Clinton's cat, it is only a cat after all. Can it even talk? No! How can a cat who can't even talk give a tour of the White House? I could fill in if President Clinton is too busy to take a call "Hello . . . President Yeltsin . . ." can Socks?

And Socks is only black and white. Black and white isn't anywhere as pretty as blue and gold. I could give a tour of the Blue Room, and the Green Room and still match. What room does Socks match, I ask you? None! I didn't see any black and white room in the tour. Just think about how much prettier the site would be with me leading the tour!

And the maps to the White House showing it from a global view all the way down to a street map view . . . I could do that from the air. Can Socks? Absolutely not!

I need a better agent . . . I should have known when Murphy Brown did a whole show on Socks that it had a better agent than I did . . . I'll have to call that OmniPoint bird and see who's representing him. Anyone have an "in" at the White House? I could do better than that ol' cat any day. Just give me a chance!

▼ MSN's Disney Daily Blast
URL—www.disneyblast.com
by Taylor, 18 years

This colorful and entertaining site was a trip out of reality into cartoon land. Aptly named . . . it's a blast for people of all ages. (It comes free with MSN membership. Otherwise, you have to subscribe at a monthly charge of $4.95, directly at the site.)

The site opens with a funny daily comic that is supposed to provide the reader with a laugh-a-day. (I not only laughed out loud, but I called others over to view the screen!) Coming soon attractions paraded across the screen in bright colors, and Mickey Mouse shone his bright, smiling face to me, as I waited for other hosts to be contacted. Alice in Wonderland was the character of the week. This interactive site kept me involved in voting for next week's character and other contests.

Although I really liked the site, there were three things I didn't like. One was the Hercules quiz. When you got the answer right, you were a "herk." When you got them wrong, you were a "jerk." I don't think it's good for kids who miss a question of the quiz to be called a "jerk" by their online site. In addition, and to my confusion, advertisements danced in a little segregated box in the bottom right hand corner of the screen, which I mistook for content links. (Although the ad links led me to games, like "Make-A-Monster" and to a heart-warming story on Walt Disney himself, I wished that they were more clearly marked. I found myself disappointed following links to a Winnie the Pooh page, only to find out that it was an advertisement for a Winnie the Pooh product.)

Lastly, it took a long time for the site graphics to load. Once they're loaded, though, the site is fast to navigate. I suggest loading them while your children aren't waiting anxiously to surf the site.

But these three things are relatively minor, given the wonders for children of all ages found at the site. This site was great for families who play online together, because it's so interactive and has something for everyone!

▼ FASHION INTERNET—FASHION MAG. ON-LINE
URL—www.finy.com
by Taylor, 18 years old

I thought that this site was current, colorful, and upbeat. It was full of international charm and fashion tips, actual runway snap shots, fall trends and informative articles on all the top models.

The superb color scheme kept me interested in the screen at all times and the interviews with several of the 'most wanted' designers were cool to read. Runway reports, upcoming models, and designers to look for, accompanied the beauty tips given by models.

Vibrant pictures of dancing fruit and vegetables caught my attention and kindly informed me of recipes, including carrots, garlic and oats, that are the mere solution to having model-perfect skin. Some features to pick from on the web page, including fashion, entertainment, designers, models, and beauty tips, were fun and entertaining to explore. (I even read a long passage written by a fellow teenage girl about her family and her favorite pair of Levis' 501 jeans.)

This site was a definite winner, in my opinion. It offers a lot to males and females between the ages of 15 and 30, who enjoy fashion talk and close-ups with the stars!

▼ PETERSONS—THE EDUCATION AND CAREER CENTER
URL—www.petersons.com
by Taylor, 18 years old

This site is every parent's, (and teenager's), prayer to the behind-the-scenes information regarding colleges, universities, elementary education, studies abroad, summer pro-

low, and provides extensive descriptions of each institution and the application process.

As a teenager starting to look at schools next year, I personally conducted searches on colleges and universities according to the availability of my future major, name, location and religious affiliation.

I also checked out the category called summer programs and it offered information on tons of summer activities, like camping, abroad studies, summer college courses and international experiences.

The thorough descriptions in all these areas gave me personal insight to each school, and the tours around the virtual campuses were great. This site definitely gave me some great ideas for next year!

▼ THE FROZEN TUNDRA
URL—www.rossfleege.com/tundra
by Tim, 18 years old

The Green Bay Packers may use the old fashioned approach in their famous offense, but the team's website, The Frozen Tundra, is state of the art to say the least. Designed to give the diehard Packer fans enough to do until each Sunday's game, the site covers the team better than any newsletter could ever do. GreenBay fans can look at the team's history and even look to the future all on this page, which happens to include over 40 of its own pages and a page of links to all the other major Packer home pages.

The home pages serve as a table of contents to the other pages, while also presenting a cover story of the week, and Vince Lombardi quote of the week and the most recent game's score and a summary. The other pages are divided into groups, the first being a list of current statistics such as: team roster, draft pics, team schedule, TV and radio listings, Green Bay's weather forecast, training camp guide, off-season news and notes and practice reports. A second list shows the final standings and final scores of the previous season. The third list, is the history of the team, which is highlighted by the Packers victories in Super Bowl I, II and XXXI. The fourth and final list is the most broad, and tends to be fan information. This includes a guestbook, Packer Chat, a bulletin board, an NFL Pool, and scores from around the league. Also among these pages are free .gif files of Packer players, free cursors, wallpaper, screen savers, and a nationwide list of bars that show Packer games!

CHAPTER 26

Parry's Picks

A Bird's Eye View—

▼ What's Parry's Picks?

▼ For Newbies

▼ For Younger Kids

▼ For Slightly Older Kids

▼ Older Kids

▼ Teens

▼ What's Parry's Picks?

There are some tips we can suggest to get you connected fast. In addition, in the course of surfing the Web and online services and talking to families around the United States and several other English-speaking countries around the world, our team has developed certain favorite products and services. We've debated whether I should suggest these tips and recommend any of these products and services outright.

While we were still debating it, I watched Rosie O'Donnell's television show and noticed that she recommends products she uses and likes. She even gets Chinese food delivered for her audience from her favorite Chinese restaurant. Well . . . if she can do it, so can I. (Would you prefer pot stickers or sesame noodles? . . . sorry, I got carried way with the comparison.) Here goes.

I've made some suggestions for newbies, to get you up and surfing as fast and painlessly as possible. I've also included recommendations for children's sites and online areas broken into four age groups:

Younger Kids—ages 3 to 8
Slightly older kids —ages 9 to 11
Older kids—ages 12 to 14
Teens —ages 15 to 18

▼ For Newbies

▼ GETTING CONNECTED

The fastest and easiest way to get online is to use an online service , like America Online, Compuserve, Prodigy or Microsoft Network (MSN). That way, you don't have to configure a web browser right away. Online services are designed to be easy to use.

I prefer America Online, since it has far more content and, at least for now, the most child content. It gives you more choices and, I think, is the most user-friendly of all the online services.

If you want to use an ISP, I would choose MSN, instead. You'll get Disney's Daily Blast for no additional cost and more local access number choices than any standard ISP.

Some good sites that will help you understand family websurfing fast are *Family PC*'s site (www.familypc.com), and Family.com (www.family.com). There's one parent' site devoted to newbies you should visit as well, Folksonline (www.folksonline.com). Also try some of the other parenting sites, like ParentsPlace (www.parentsplace.com), Parent Soup (www.parentsoup.com), Family Internet (www.familyinternet.com) and ParentTime (www.parenttime.com) to see which one you like the most.

Consider joining a parenting list serv, or sign up for an e-zine (an e-mail newsletter or electronic magazine) at one of the parenting sites. Net-mom has a newsletter (www.netmom.com) and you can sign up to receive it from the site, and many of the parenting sites I recommend have their own list servs too.

▼ For Younger Kids

▼ GETTING CONNECTED WITH YOUNGER KIDS

AOL is a great place to start, especially because of their Kids Only forum. (Several of our younger kids reviewed their favorite Kids Only areas.) MSN is a good place to get started too, if you want Disney's Daily Blast.

▼ PRODUCTS FOR YOUNGER KIDS

Microsoft Plus! for Kids, is a program that makes Windows 95 safer and more fun for kids ages three through twelve. The program costs $24.95 and is available at most computer retailers.

Microsoft Plus! for Kids protects in two different ways with its "Protect It!" feature. First, it allows parents to set limits on what each family member can access on the computer's hard drive. This will prevent children from deleting or opening files that parents do not want them to have access to. The part I like best about this feature is that the startup Windows 95 screen is customized for each child, so when the child signs on to the computer, she will only see programs in the Start menu that she is permitted to access. (It saves lots of arguments and the forbidden fruit cravings most kids have.)

Second, it makes it a little easier to use the PICS technology and the Recreational Software Advisory Council (RSACi) ratings (as well as the other rating services supported by Microsoft's Internet Explorer). You have to use Microsoft's Internet Explorer to be able to use this function, however.

Microsoft Plus! for Kids also makes using Windows 95 more fun for kids. It allows kids to choose their own customized desktop from among ten kid-oriented desktop themes, such as "Messy Room" or "Underwater". Its other features include "Paint It!," which has drawing and painting tools; and "Picture Picker," which contains over 1,000 clip art images for kids.

Our favorite feature and the one our kid reviewers loved the most (I did too!) is "Talk It!" When your child types in a word, the computer says it. (You need a sound card, though.) It's terrific fun when your children are learning to type, read and spell. Given my lack of decent typing skills, we laughed often at the results of my typos.

Microsoft Plus! for Kids is well worth the purchase price.

KeyWack 1.3 by Paul Duffy E+P Ware 1993 is a great shareware product for very young kids. (Shareware means it's free, or almost free, with a small registration fee if you like and use the product of $15-$25 per program. It's totally on the honor system.) It is available for Macintosh only, and you can find out how to purchase it by e-mailing epware@world.std.com.

It starts out using a white screen that responds to any key. Bright, huge multicolored geometric shapes appear every time your child hits a key. If you use sound, it also plays a musical note with each key you hit and even intermingles animal sounds—moo, quack, nay etc. Once the overlapping shapes cover the majority of the white screen it clears and starts again.

According to my sister, the pediatrician, it's very easy to use once your child is old enough to bang on objects, so 4-month-olds could do it while parents hold them and 6–7-month olds who on their own could do it propped by a pillow in front of the keyboard. (Whether you want them using a computer that young is another matter . . .) My sister advises that you use a second keyboard for this game if you want to save yours from graham cracker hands and toy hammers that "accidentally" seem to gravitate toward the keys.

I suggest that, instead, you use the kid's keyboard we found, My First Keyboard.

▼ KIDS-SIZE PRODUCTS I LIKE

There are two special kids-size products we tested and like a lot.

My First Keyboard is designed just for kids, and is peanut butter and kids' hammer proof. It's designed for ages between 1-1/2 and 5, and manufactured by KidTech. (It's also made in the U.S.)

One feature we liked allows parents to type in tandem with their kids, since their adult keyboard can be attached along with the child's keyboard. It makes it easier to family-surf online. (Like a student driver and two steering wheels.)

The suggested retail price is $59.95 and you can contact KidTech at 1-800-681-4056 to find a local retailer or to order it directly. KidTech can also be reached at their website www.kidtech.com.

The second product is **Microsoft's EasyBall**, a childsize trackball device you can use instead of a mouse. (It's featured on our back cover photo of Allyssa and Sophia.)

EasyBall is designed for kids from 2 to 6 and has a handgrip about the size of a tennis ball.

It's much easier for kids to control than a typical mouse. It also comes with a fun selection of cursors which you can use, so kids aren't stuck with the arrow and hour glass cursors we grown-ups use.

They've also developed a game that is distributed with the EasyBall, called Pointerland, to help kids learn how to use a mouse-type product. (It comes with a free copy of Microsoft's Explorapedia too.) The suggested retail for the product is $54.95. EasyBall is easily located at most computer retailers.

▼ PLACES TO GO ON AOL WITH YOUNGER KIDS

Start with AOL's "Kids Only." Use parental controls to block e-mail. Spend some time showing them what's available in the "Kids Only" area, and go online with them, especially before they can read and write well enough to manage on their own.

The favorite Internet sites we discovered for younger kids are:

Nickelodeon	www.nick.com
KidsCom	www.kidscom.com
Disney	www.disney.com
Children's Television Workshop	www.ctw.org
Disney's Daily Blast	www.dailyblast.com (unless you use MSN, there's a monthly charge)

▼ For Slightly Older Kids

▼ PLACES TO GO ON AOL WITH SLIGHTLY OLDER KIDS

Stick with AOL's "Kids Only," but allow them e-mail (assuming you're going to keep an eye on the messages they're getting). Make sure you screen outgoing information, at least until you're sure they've understood the importance of keeping personal information secret online.

▼ ON THE WEB FOR SLIGHTLY OLDER KIDS

Parental control software becomes more important as the kids get a little older. Use whichever parental control software meets your needs best, referring to my chart for help. Most of them screen outgoing information. I recommend using Surf Watch (it's the easiest to setup) or Cyber Patrol (if you can get someone to help you install it). You'll get the added protection of being able to monitor how much time your children spend playing games on the computer as well. (This is a good feature for parents who work outside of the home.)

Yahooligans! is a good place for them to start any web search. It screens the sites listed, to make sure that they are kid-friendly. I would block other search engines, unless you're with your children when they are conducting searches. (Surf Watch's new version can block all search engines, allowing your kids only on to Yahooligans!) Once Net Shepherd and AltaVista come out with their search engine, I'd use that too.

These sites are very popular with this age group.

Nickelodeon	www.nick.com
KidsCom	www.kidscom.com
Disney	www.disney.com
Disney's Daily Blast	www.dailyblast.com
Fox for Kids	www.foxkids.com
Headbone Zone	www.headbone.com
Kellogg's	www.kelloggs.com
Children's Television Workshop	www.ctw.org

▼ Older Kids

▼ GETTING CONNECTED WITH OLDER KIDS

They're ready for the full online service content. I'd use AOL and separate parental control software if you're concerned that your kids might give out personal information online, especially in chatrooms. Since AOL has over 55,000 different message board areas and forums, I'd spend some time with them trying to find a few favorite places, so they know where to start.

Some interesting sites for older kids include:

Kid Link	www.kidlink.org
National Geographic	www.nationalgeographic.com
Kidscom	www.kidscom.com
World Kids Network	www.worldkids.net
KidPub	www.kidpub.org
Headbone Zone	www.headbone.com
Nickelodeon	www.nick.com
World Surfari	www.supersurf.com
Sports Illustrated for Kids	go to www.pathfinder.com and search for the site, the address is very long and complicated
Time for Kids	go to www.pathfinder.com and search for the site

▼ Teens

▼ GETTING CONNECTED WITH TEENS

It's more of a toss-up when the kids get older—between AOL and an ISP. (I still like using MSN instead of a standard ISP.) As the kids surf the Web more, and do more research, being able to access Gopher and newsgroups becomes more important and speed becomes the most important factor. (Although, AOL has FTP access, and recently added Gopher and newsgroups, speed is still a problem.) If you can afford it, I'd have both AOL and an ISP (or MSN).

Now the really hard part . . . do you rely on trust or parental control software to make sure your children stay out of trouble and away from the offensive sites (however you, as a family, define "offensive")? I personally think that educating our children, helping them understand our values and maintaining good communication is enough, but other parents disagree. Based upon our testing, we recommend two products, Surf Watch and Cyber Patrol. Surf Watch has the most reviewed and blocked sites, currently, and is the easiest to setup. Cyber Patrol has the most features, which gives you a greater choice about what to block and filter, but is harder to setup. You have to decide which of these two fits your needs best. In my opinion, there is no such thing as "best overall."

As more and more sites get rated, PICS technology will give us all more options.

Some sites teens told us they enjoy:

MIT Postcard Site	postcards.www.media.mit.edu/postcards
Internet Gaming Zone	www.zone.com
An Income of Her Own	www.aioho.com
J. Crew	www.jcrew.com
Fashion Internet	www.finy.com
ESPN	www.espnet.sportszone.com
Petersons	www.petersons.com
Princeton Review	www.review.com

CHAPTER 27

Afterword

A Bird's Eye View—

▼ The Bottomline . . . On Balance

▼ The Bottomline . . . On Balance

We need to make sure our kids are cybersmart and cybersafe. We, as parents, don't need to be worried about cybermonsters hiding under our virtual beds or the boogiemen online anymore. You now know what the risks are, and how to limit them. It's a learning curve for all of us. But, hopefully, a fun and rewarding one.

I hope that this book will inspire you. (I demand a lot of my readers . . . being inspired is only the beginning . . . hopefully, you'll name your children after me and send me home baked cookies . . .) Surfing the Web together is one of the best ways to enjoy yourselves as a family, and learn something at the same time.

This book is only a map. Hopefully, by the time you've been online for awhile you won't need it anymore. I suspect before long . . . you'll be teaching me!

Amen.

Appendix

FAQs

A Bird's Eye View—

▼ How Do Bots, Spiders and Crawlers Work?

▼ How Do You Register a Site with a Search Engine?

▼ Who's on the Net?

▼ What's the Commercialism Controversy all About?

▼ How Do You Register a Domain Name?

▼ What's a "Hit" and Why are They So Important

▼ Some Basic How To's

▼ How Fast are the High Speed Modem Lines?

▼ What is Java?

▼ How Do Bots, Spiders and Crawlers Work?

Spiders and web crawlers are programs which scour the web for sites. They usually select the first 25-50 words in your site, unless you've designated keywords and a description. (This happened to us when we first set up our site.) If you'd rather not have your site described as "Hello . . . welcome to our site. This site was last updated on May 14, 1997. This week we have many new features for our visitors . . . " or something like that, you can use hidden code that the crawlers and spiders can read, but your web site visitors can't. (That's called "META" text.)

▼ How Do You Register a Site with a Search Engine?

Registration with a search engine is quick, painless, and generally free. It is done by visiting each of the search engine sites. Each search engine contains an option to submit a site for registration. The user submits their Web site address, e-mail address, and a short description of the content of the site along with keywords. Keywords are the words that someone might search under, that you want to identify your site. If you have a site for children's toys, the keywords might include the company's name, "kids," "children," "toys," "games," "computer games," and the name of any particular toys you're featuring. Keywords for other sites might include topics included at the site, geographical locations, or names. The keywords are generally included in the META text.

Within a few weeks (sometimes as early as a few days), the site is registered with the search engine, and anyone searching for your domain name or a keyword contained within your site will retrieve your Web site as one of the selections. The spiders and crawlers search and may update the listings to reflect changes

Previously you had to register the site with each of the search engines individually. Now there's a great new online Web service called Submit It that registers your site on several different search engines at one time. Access their website, and you provide the information on one form, and the software tailors it to each search engine's particular demands. Then, with the click of a few keys, the appropriate information is sent to each individual search engine, substantially streamlining the registration process. Submit It can be located at www.submit-it.com. (See how important an easily remembered domain name can be?)

▼ Who's on the Net?

Statistics on Internet growth and use abound. But, no matter which statistic you accept, everyone agrees that the Internet is exploding with new uses and users. Find/SVP, an Internet research group, reports that 90% of Internet users use it at least once a week, and 28% of them believe the Internet is an indispensible part of their lives.

And those who aren't on the Internet yet are talking about getting on the Internet. Homenet, in its 1997 Carnegie-Mellon study, reports that more than 55 million U.S. adults who are not using the Internet want to learn more about the Internet or plan to start using it over the next year. If you're not already online, you're probably part of that 55 million.

To help understand how quickly things are moving, in 1984 there were only 1,000 host computers linked to the Internet. Five years later, in 1989, the number had increased a hundredfold, to 100,000. By 1994, there were about 1 million host computers on the Internet. There are now more than 5 million!

The development of the Web has been primarily responsible for the explosion of growth on the Internet and the fact that so many consumers can use and enjoy it today. In 1993, the watershed year for the Web, the annual traffic grew at an annual rate of 341,634%!

▼ What's the Commercialism Controversy all About?

Even though Mosaic (and later Netscape Navigator) provided the missing piece of the puzzle, allowing the Web to be open to all types of information and users, Tim Berners-Lee was reportedly unhappy with the browser. He foresaw the Web being taken over by commercial and trivial information, rather than remaining a serious medium.

Tim Berners-Lee was right; some of the earliest websites were filled with StarTrek facts and fantasies and the commercialism exploded. Now, although there are still a lot of fun sites, commercial sites dominate the Web. Before the Web explosion in 1993, out of the 130 initial webservers, only two were commercial sites. Only three years later, by the end of 1996, 90% of websites were commercial sites. Now with more than one million websites, worldwide, the Web has become every person's and every business's medium, and is no longer for academics only.

▼ How Do You Register a Domain Name?

Domain names are administered by InterNIC Registration Services, through Network Solutions, Inc., in Herndon, Va. InterNIC is funded by a cooperative agreement from the National Science Foundation to provide registration services for the Net. Domain names are generally supplied on a first-come-first-served basis.

Once an individual or entity registers a domain name with InterNIC, InterNIC will not allow any other user to register the same name. (However, derivations in the name may be sufficient to allow similar names to be registered. Some website operators have begun promoting websites using famous names, but with a "typo.") Thousands of domain name requests are handled each week by InterNIC. As a result of this huge demand, easy to remember first level commercial domain names, those with "something."com, are almost all taken.

When you register a domain name you have to designate an applicable zone. If you are registering an international site you may also have to designate a country code.

There are many companies, including your ISP (internet service provider, remember?) which will help you register a domain name for a fee. You can even check the current domain name availability online.

You should note, though, that given the significant lag time in registration of domain names, the name that you find is available today may not still be available when your application is processed, but it's fun to check it out anyway. To access InterNIC's site to check on a domain name's availability, type the URL http://rs.internic.net/cgi-bin.whois into your web browser's header and then click "send."

If you decide you want to register a domain name, and don't want to pay a premium for another company to register it for you, you can go right to the Inter-NIC site itself, with the application template available online. To get to the Inter-NIC site, type in its URL, http://rs.internic.net/cgi-bin/itts/domain, and fill out the form. You can complete the entire application and submit it directly to Inter-NIC, all online.

▼ IF YOUR NAME IS MARY SONY, CAN YOU REGISTER A DOMAIN
NAME USING YOUR LAST NAME—SONY.COM?

No, you can't. In the early days of the Web, squatters (as they are now called) registered a lot of famous names. InterNIC never asked whether the person registering kraft.com or some other famous tradename had the legal right to use that name. They used to leave the policing of intellectual property rights to the courts. Many people believe that this allowed the domain name black market to flourish.

Now, InterNIC will suspend the use of a domain name by someone, if another entity is able to prove a valid tradename or servicemark registration covering the domain. This is helping to cut down on the pirating of domain names that represent registered trademarks or servicemarks.

Some famous Net stories include the registration of mcdonalds.com (with the owner, who works for the Net magazine, *Wired*, reachable at Ronald@ mcdonalds. com), coke.com and hertz.com and how *some* people, quick to understand the implications of open registration and preemptive registration, profited by selling the names to the companies to which such trade names are registered. The market price for very famous and prized domain names varied based on the demand, but currently a recognized domain name may command about $5,000 - $10,000 for a quick and easy transfer to the registered tradename or servicemark owner. Some high profile domain names, such as "business.com" have sold for six figures.

But you could use a subdomain. There are two levels of domain names: a top level name and a sub-domain name. A top level domain name identifies only your domain name, while a sub-domain name identifies your site as a sub-site of another site. For example, a sub-domain name would be the "your name" in "http://www.<hosting company's name>.com/your name," while "http://www.your name.com" would be a top level name. You could use "<hosting company>.com/sony" as your personal website, and Sony would probably not object, assuming you're not selling electronic appliances from your site.

▼ What's a "Hit" and Why are They So Important?

"Hits" are the number of times a web site has been visited. Hits or visitors to the site is generally how a webmaster gains a reputation as a great webmaster. A great site that no one visits can't be really great. Simple ones, which give you what you want, draw lots of visitors and lots of attention, which is the name of the game on the Web. (This is especially true since so many sites depend on advertising revenue.)

Since the demand for hits is so important to most webmasters, many have discovered unscrupulous ways in which to increase their hit statistics. A few webmasters have been known to plant a few references to sexual topics in the hidden META text code or typed in the same color as the background of the site (so that it's invisible to the naked eye, but can be "seen" by a web spider) to increase their hits, since people searching the engines for sexual topics will be directed to the sites by the search engines.

Although this may increase their hits in the short term, it's likely to result in many angry and misled visitors who are looking for information that they may think is far more stimulating than the latest Supreme Court case analysis. This is just a reminder that you need to keep a sense of humor on the Net.

▼ Some Basic How To's

If you want to send a copy of an e-mail you received to someone else ...

You forward it. Click on "forward" and type in the address of the recipient (from scratch or using your addressbook).

If you want to send a file with the e-mail ...

You attach it. Click on "attach" and a screen will pop up displaying your computer drives and files. (This is why it's very important to name your files and remember where you keep them.)

Copy, Cut and Paste:

Copying, cutting and pasting are shortcuts for those of you who don't want to spend the time downloading an entire file just to get that one quote or picture.

Copying and Cutting Text:

Copying and cutting involve the same basic actions. Remember, however, if you copy something, it stays on the screen. If you cut, it's just like using scissors, it's gone, but don't worry, you can click "paste" and whatever you cut reappears. First, position your mouse near the text you want to copy or cut. Drag the mouse while holding down the left mouse button (remember to let go of the button once you've got everything you need). This will highlight the text. Next, you can either place the pointer within the selected area and click on the right mouse button—which will give you a pull down menu from which to chose cut or copy—or, you can go to the "Edit" menu and select either option from the pull down menu there.

Pasting:

Once cut or copied, the text is in computer limbo until you "paste" it. So, if you've copied a quote from a site (being careful not to infringe on anyone's copyright or trademark protected information—see Chapter 11, *The Bad Stuff Goes Both Ways . . . Protecting Others and Yourself from Your Kids and Their Friends*, if you want a thumbnail explanation of copyright law) and you want to insert it into another document, just open the document, put the cursor where you want to insert the text and by right-clicking or using the edit menu, "paste" the image directly into your document. You can paste the same thing over and over until you cut or copy something else, replacing whatever was in the clipboard before.

Saving:

Unlike bookmarking (adding a site and its address to a list so you can access it later), saving actually copies the "document" you are viewing to whatever media you tell it. You can then access it offline. You have a lot of choices so let's go through them one by one.

"Save As":

There are two different ways to save a file, and many more places to put that file. We'll use Netscape as an example again (but the process is essentially the same no matter what web browser you are using). First, point the cursor on your "File" menu, and scroll down until "save as" is highlighted. When you double click on "save as," you'll get a box (geeks call it a "dialogue box") with several choices. You can save it as an html file (usually what an Internet document is to begin with) or as a word processing file (like Word Perfect or Word).

Where do you save it:

The caption outside of the top window of the dialogue box reads "Save in" and in the box adjacent to it, there will be a folder icon (picture) next to that folder's name. If you simply select save at that point, the document will be saved under whatever default folder appeared in the Save In box. You CAN change this!

Next to the box containing the folder icon and its name is an arrow. If you click on that arrow, you will see a "pull-down" menu. This is essentially a map of your computer. You will see listings for "desktop" and each of your drives (ex: hard drive, floppy drives, disk drives). If you double click on any one of these, you change the "destination" for your saved file. At this point, it is a matter of choice, and you can double-click your way to any folder on your computer.

Or, you will see another picture of a folder next to the Save in window, and if you click on that it will take you to the next level "up" in the hierarchy. (This gets confusing if you're not sure where you are in the hierarchy to begin with and might be more trouble then its worth for beginners. Ask your kids to help you.)

Printing:

What, there's more? Yes, but don't worry, this is the easy part.

You can print anything you see on your screen, whether you are on-line or off, or working with graphics or text. Printing is easy (use this as your inspiring mantra and work from there if you've stumbled on other functions).

Most of the web browsers operate the same way. Netscape, for example, has a button in the middle of the tool bar on the top of the screen that looks like a printer (sort of). By pressing this button, whatever appears on your screen will be printed. Or, you can use the "File" menu and scroll down to "print." Same thing, different method.

Unless you are running an ancient printer, you will be able to print out any pictures or graphics. This can be a big help to your kids. After all, no report would be complete without pictures. Go on, print that picture. Just remember that pictures on the Web (like those in books or magazines) are often copyrighted and may require special permission to print and use.

Saving Images:

If you want to copy an image, position cursor or pointer on the image and "right-click" on the image (That means clicking the right button on your mouse, assuming you haven't reconfigured the buttons on your mouse.) This action brings up a pull down menu. Chose the "save as" option and repeat the steps above to save the image so you can use it later on.

Downloading:

Downloading is easy. There are two ways to download. The first way is to click on any button on the screen that says "download." The second way is to save whatever you want to download to file, by clicking on the little floppy disk icon (on the top icon tool bar), or by opening the "file" dropdown menu (from the text tool bar) and clicking "save as." Remember to save it under a directory you'll recognize, something original like "download." Then name it so you'll remember what it is.

As much as you might want to practice downloading, the best way to copy something from a website may be to copy and paste it. (Look under *cut, copy and paste* for a quick lesson.) If you want to copy an image (graphic or photo), the easiest way is to click on it with your right mouse button. (Read *Saving Images*, above.)

▼ How Fast are the High Speed Modem Lines?

When you are choosing an ISP, you will be asking them what high speed lines they have. Just as a point of reference, a T-1 processes 1.544 million bps (bits per second), roughly 50 times the speed of a 28.8 modem, while a T-3 processes 45 million bps (30 times faster than a T-1 and 1500 times faster than a 28.8 modem).

As technology improves, other communication technology is used to speed access to the Internet. The new technology is aimed at bypassing the POTS limitations (remember, POTS are Plain Old Telephone lines). ISDN lines convert the POT analog transmissions to digital transmissions at 128 kbps (128,000 bps), approximately 4 times the speed of a 28.8 modem. They can be installed by calling your local telephone company. You'll need an ISDN modem, though, to access it. (Actually, they're not called modems, but who cares?)

The new cable modems blow all the other types of high speed access away, unless you have your own T-3 line.

▼ What is Java?

Java is essentially a mini-application coded into a document available on the Web. (Although it has many other applications, I'm limiting this answer to Java's use on the Web.) It allows interactivity, motion, sound and the use of other multi-media on a standard website. When your Java-savvy browser (both Netscape and Explorer 3.0 and higher) scans the site, it loads the application (called an "applet") onto your computer, which then runs the application. The applet is able to be used by all types of computers, and was designed to be uniformly readable by MACs and PCs. (It's called a cross-platform application.)

Designed by Sun Microsystems' "Green Team," a group of software application and operating system designers formed to design consumer electronic applications (for personal information devices, like Sharp's Wizard), Java was an abyssmal failure. Although they managed to design a system that was cross-platform, it was too "buggy" for the consumer electronics market, and the project was abandoned. Later, luckily for webbers, it was adapted to be used on the Web, and has and will change the direction of the Web, single-handedly.

Technophobes usually nod off at this point, so I'll keep this part brief. Java has added sound to the formerly silent Web. It has added Technicolor to the formerly black and white Web. It has added dynamic motion to the static text and graphic page. And, most importantly, it has added interactivity to the former one-way street of a website. It has given the Web life. As innovative webbers test the various methods where applets and Java script can be used, it will make changes none of us can even imagine, and in an exponential fashion. And this may be an understatement, by far.

Originally called "Oak" rather than "Java," the application's name was changed when the name "Oak" was discovered to have already been taken. While meeting at a local coffeeshop for breakfast, the Green Team coined the name "Java," and the rest is history. (Others claim it was "just another virtual application" and deny the coffee shop theory.) In retrospect, Java is a very appropriate name since it is clearly addictive and allows you to do more than you would have been able to do otherwise. (Hot Java is the web browser the Green Team designed to allow Java to be read on the Web.)

▼   WHY ISN'T EVERYONE USING JAVA, IF IT'S SO HOT?

The biggest problem associated with the growth of Java is the inability of many web browsers to read Java applets and Java script. A non-Java savvy browser will just ignore any Java applet, as though it were not there. Therefore, you have to design the website two ways - one for those capable of reading Java and another for those who can't.

Only a web browser capable of reading Java will allow the webber to explore the benefits of Java. Luckily, Netscape reads Java. Netscape is the web browser used by an estimated 70% of the ISP webbers, and can be enabled to read Java. Unfortunately, the real growth in Web usage comes from the online service members and many online services, such as AOL, Compuserve and Counsel Connect use proprietary web browsers or earlier forms of Netscape which may not be able to read Java. This, however, is hopefully changing as they update their browsers and allow their members to use the browser of their choice.

Java also can't be read by computers using certain operating systems, such as Windows 3.1. Since converting to Windows 95 or NT requires more memory and faster machines, many webbers using older equipment may not be able to reap the benefits of Java until they upgrade. Therefore, either because of the web browser available to them , or because of their operating systems, a significant portion of the webbers cannot read Java, and are missing out on all the benefits of a Java coded site.

Designing for the Web has always been a dilemma. Webmasters are always seeking the next frontier...a way to bring the latest in website technology and innovation to their visitors. But, given the shortcomings of browsers and equipment used by the majority of the webbers on a worldwide basis, a smart Webmaster designs for the lowest common denominator of the Web. Too many complicated graphics will slow down the loading of your site to those with 14.4 modems and slower and having to load application reading software to allow video clips and sound clips to be shared from your site can be a serious detriment to building traffic at your site. As equipment is improved, high speed access lines made more available throughout the world, and the web browsers made more universally friendly to new innovative techniques, this will change. Until then, however, it may not make economic sense for a Webmaster to use the newest bells and whistles for only a small minority of the visitors to the site.

There are lots of websites which contain information about Java and give sample applets. I recommend Sun Microsystem's Javasoft's official java information site (www.javasoft.com/ nav/whatis/) and

SunWorld's Online Cover Story: The Evolution of Java (www.sun.com/sun-worldonline/swol-07-1995/swol-07-java.html).

Glossary Terms (for non-geeks)

 *A Bird's Eye View—*

▼ Buzz Words . . . To Impress Your Kids

▼ Buzz Words ... To Impress Your Kids

Applet: A small Java program that is imbedded in whatever file you're viewing.

Bandwidth: The rate at which information can travel through the wire into your computer. Usually measured in bits-per-second. A full page of English text is about 16,000 bits. A fast modem can move about 15,000 bits in one second.

Baud Rate: How many bits can be sent or received per second.

Bps (Bits-Per-Second): A measurement of how fast data is moved from one place to another. A 28.8 modem can move 28,800 bits per second.

Blocking Software: Special program that allows parents to "block" access to certain sites and information on the Internet.

Bookmark: A URL saved in your browser.

Bookmarking: The process of saving a URL in your browser that allows it to be recalled instantly in the future.

Browser: A program, such as Netscape Navigator or Microsoft's Internet Explorer, that enables you to surf the Web and read graphics, videos and hear sounds.

BBS (Bulletin Board System): A computerized "meeting" and announcement system that allows people to carry on discussions, upload and download files, and make announcements without the people being connected to the computer at the same time.

Byte: A set of bits that represent a single character. Generally there are eight or 10 bits to a byte, depending on how the measurement is being made.

Cache: A device or place on your hard/drive, usually RAM, used to temporarily store data. It is a time saving feature that can be especially helpful on the Web, allowing the cache file in your computer to store sites that you have recently visited, so that you can get back to them quickly.

CD-ROM (Compact Disk - Read Only Memory): Optical disks that can only be read (i.e., the data cannot be changed or deleted). New technology allows a read/write option, if you have the equipment. (That's called "burning a disk.")

Chatroom: A virtual room where users can "talk" with each other in real time by typing.

Client: The computer browser that "asks" for information. One computer can be a client and a host at the same time (see Host).

Cookies: A piece of information sent by a web server to a web browser that the browser software saves and uses to send back information to the server in the future.

CPU(Central Processing Unit): The main internal component of a computer where executions of instructions are carried out and calculations are performed. It's included in the tower or main box of your computer.

Cyberspace: Coined by author William Gibson in his novel *Neuromancer*, the word Cyberspace is currently used to describe the whole range of information resources available through computer networks.

Daemons: Small programs that perform specific tasks. For example, a program that "wakes up" to deliver a message upon arrival.

Disk Drive: The device that holds a disk, retrieves information from it, and stores information on it.

Domain: The last part of an Internet address — tells the type of general category.

DOT: The period character. For brevity people say "dot".

Download: To copy a file from a multi-user system (Ex: WWW or AOL) to your computer.

Emoticons: Computer speak for "emotion icons" describing tone, body language or feelings (e.g. :->).

E-mail (Electronic Mail): Messages, usually text, sent from one person to another via computer.

Ethernet: A very common method of connecting computers into a network.

FAQs (Frequently Asked Questions): Documents that list and answer the most common questions on a particular subject.

File: A collection of information stored on a computer as a unit.

FTP (File Transfer Protocol): A way to copy or transfer files from one FTP site on the Internet to another. Files may contain documents or programs.

Flaming: Directing insulting or derogatory comments at someone through e-mail, newsgroups or chat rooms.

Floppy Disk: A disk made of plastic that stores computer data. The most common types of floppy disks are 3-1⁄2" and come in three types: high density (1.4 MB capacity), double-sided (800K), and single sided (400K).

Gateway: In general, any mechanism that provides access to another system, e.g. AOL might be called a gateway to the Internet.

Gopher: A method of making menus of material available over the Internet. Although Gopher spread rapidly across the globe in only a couple of years, it has been largely supplanted by the WWW (World Wide Web).

Homepage: Usually the first page of a World Wide Web site. From there you interactively explore that site.

Host: Any computer on a network that sends information to other computers on the network. It is quite common to have one host machine provide several services, such as WWW and Usenet. (See Client)

Hyperlink: The images or words on the Web that are linked to another URL and give you access to new information with the click of a mouse. Textual hyperlinks are distinguished by their different color font.

Hypertext: The text that is a link to other documents.

HTML (Hypertext Markup Language): The coding language used to create all Web pages.

HTTP (Hypertext Transfer Protocol): The protocol (set of instructions) for moving Hypertext files across the Internet. HTTP is the most important protocol used in the World Wide Web (WWW).

Internet (with a capital "I"): The vast collection of inter-connected networks that all use the TCP/IP protocols and that evolved from ARPANET in the late 60's and early 70's.

internet (Lower case): Any time you connect two or more networks together, you have an internet.

IRC (Internet Relay Chat): A huge multi-user live chat facility.

ISDN (Integrated Services Digital Network): A way to move more data over digital phone lines. It can provide speeds of up to 128,000 bits-per-second over regular phone lines.

ISP (INTERNET SERVICE PROVIDER): Any commercial institution that provides access to the Internet for a fee.

Java: A programming language that allows files to be used by all kinds of computer platforms. Java runs through applets. (See *What is Java?* in the FAQs).

Keyword: On the Web, they are the words that you input into search engines to find information on a particular topic. On AOL, they are a single-word "shortcut" to get to a particular area.

Kilobyte: 1,024 bytes.

Link: Allows a viewer to click on a highlighted item on a WWW page and immediately link to whatever the HTML programmer wants them to see (see *Hyperlink*).

Login: The name used to gain access to a computer system (not a password); or the act of entering into a computer system (e.g. login to AOL).

Macintosh: A line of computers manufactured by Apple Computer that run on a different OS than PCs.

Megahertz: 1,000 hertz. Often used to measure CPU speed (ex: 133MHz).

Megabyte: Approximately one million bytes (or one thousand kilobytes).

Modem: Abbreviation for modulator-demodulator. A modem is the device that enables a computer or terminal to communicate over a telephone line to another computer or computer network.

Newbie: Somebody new to the Net.

Netiquette: The etiquette of the Internet. (See *Ms. Parry's Guide to Netiquette.*)

Netizen: A "citizen" if the Internet.

Network: Any time you connect two or more computers together so that they can share resources.

Newsgroups: The name for discussion groups on Usenet.

OS or Operating System: The program that boots up your computer and tracks and controls files, disks, memory, etc.

PC: Personal computers, using an IBM-compatible operating system.

PICS (Platform for Internet Content Selection): PICS is the technology that allows web browsers to read ratings of websites. PICS is not a rating system itself.

Plug-In: A small "program" that adds a feature to a bigger, more complicated program. Plug-ins usually cannot be used by themselves.

Processor: A chip that takes data, performs calculations and returns the results.

Program: A set of instructions that can be executed to perform one or more tasks.

Protocol: The technology rules the web browser uses to locate and retrieve files.

Posting: A single message entered into a network communications system; or the process of entering that message.

Rating Services: Services that rate websites. The "official" rating service is RSACi. Most use a PICS standard for labeling.

RAM (Random Access Memory): The memory that is used to keep programs open and run them.

RSACi: Recreational Software Advisory Council's Internet rating entity.

Search Engine: A software program that allows a user to search databases by entering keywords. A search engine or vehicle quickly finds any item pertaining to those keywords.

Server: A computer that provides a specific kind of service to client software running on other computers.

Snail Mail: Using traditional methods, such as the United States Postal Service, to send a letter.

Spamming: Inappropriate use of a mailing list by sending the same unsolicited message to a large number of people. (The term has been attributed to a famous Monty Python skit which featured the word "spam" repeated over and over, presumably referring to Hormel's Spam™ meat product.)

URL (Uniform Resource Locator): The address that tells the browser how to locate a Web page.

Web Page: A special file on the Web that uses hyperlinks to access text, images, animation, and sound, using a browser.

Website: A group of interlinked Web pages.

WWW (World Wide Web): The multimedia portion of the Internet, consisting of documents viewed using a browser, using HTTP.

Directories (of companies, products and websites referenced)

A Bird's Eye View—

▼ Directory of ISPs, Online Services and Products

▼ Directory of Websites

▼ Directory of Credits, Copyrights and Trademarks

▼ Directory of ISPs, Online Services and Products

America Online (AOL)
address: 22000 AOL Way
Dulles, VA 20166
telephone:
(800) 827-6364 (to order software)
(800) 827-3338 (technical support)
website: www.aol.com

AT&T (WorldNet Service)
address: 55 Corporate Drive
Bridgewater, NJ 08807
telephone: (800) WORLDNET
website: www.att.com/worldnet

Bess (N2H2, Inc.)
address: 1301 5th Avenue
Suite 1501
Seattle, WA 98101
telephone:
(800) 971-2622 (sales)
(206) 971-1400 (technical support, Mon.-
    Fri., 8am-6pm, PST)
email: techsupport@n2h2.com (technical
    support)
website: www.n2h2.com

CompuServe
address: World Headquarters
5000 Arlington Center Boulevard
P.O. Box 20212
Columbus, OH 43220
telephone:

(800) 848-8990 (customer service)
(800) 944-9871 (technical support)
(800) 998-9622 (Mac technical support)
e-mail: 70006.101@compuserve.com
website: www.compuserve.com

Cyber Patrol (Microsystems Software, Inc.)
address: 600 Worcestor Road
Framingham, MA 01701
telephone:
(800) 828-2608 (to order software)
(508) 416-1000 (technical support, Mon.-
    Fri., 8:15am-5:45pm, EST)
(508) 416-1050(technical support, Mon.-
    Fri., 5:45pm-11:45pm, EST)
email: cybersup@microsys.com (technical
    support)
website: www.cyberpatrol.com

CYBERsitter (Solid Oak Software, Inc.)
address: P.O. Box 6826
Santa Barbara, CA 93160
telephone:
(800) 388-2761 or (805) 967-9853   (to
    order software)
(805) 884-8204 (technical support, 9am-
    5pm, PST)
email: support@solidoak.com (technical
    support)
website: www.solidoak.com

Juno
telephone: (800) 654-JUNO
website: www.juno.com

MCI (MCI Internet)
address: P.O. Box 73881
Chicago, IL 60673
telephone: (800) 950-5555
website: www.mci2000.com

Microsoft:

Easy Ball
address: One Microsoft Way
Redmond, WA 98052
telephone:
(800) 360-7561 (sales)
(206) 635-7040 (technical support, Mon.-
    Fri., 6am-6pm, PST)
website: www.microsoft.com

Internet Explorer
address: One Microsoft Way
Redmond, WA 98052
telephone:
(800) 360-7561 (sales)
(425) 635-7123 (technical support)
website: www.microsoft.com

Plus for Kids
address: One Microsoft Way
Redmond, WA 98052
telephone:
(800) 360-7561 (sales)
(425) 635-7140 (technical support)
website: www.microsoft.com/kids

Microsoft Network
address: One Microsoft Way
Redmond, WA 98052
telephone:
(800) 386-5550 (general information)
(813) 557-0613 (customer service)
(206) 635-7019 (technical support)
website: www.msn.com

Mindspring
address: 1430 W. Peachtree St., NW
Suite 400
Atlanta, GA 30309
telephone: (800) 719-4332
website: www.mindspring.com

Net Nanny
address: 525 Seymour Street
Suite 108
Vancouver, BC
CANADA V6B 3H7
telephone:
(800) 340-7177 (to order software)
(604) 662-8522 (technical support, Mon.-
    Fri. 8am-5pm, PST)
email: NNsupport@netnanny.com
    (technical support)
website: www.netnanny.com

Net Shepherd
address: 250, 815 8th Avenue SW
Calgary, Alberta
CANADA T2P 3P2
telephone: (403) 205-6677
email: info@netshepherd.com
website: www.netshepherd.com

Netcom
address: Two North Second St.
Plaza A
San Jose, CA 95113
telephone: (800) NETCOM1
website: www.netcom.com

Netscape
telephone:
(415) 937-3777 (sales)
(800) 639-0939 (technical support)
email: personal@netscape.com
website: home.netscape.com

Prodigy
address: 445 Hamilton Avenue
White Plains, NY 10601
telephone: (800) PRODIGY (customer
    service & technical support)
website: www.prodigy.com

Sprint (Sprint Internet Passport)
address: 8140 Ward Parkway
Kansas City, MO 64114
telephone: (800) 747-9428
website: www.sprint.com/fornet

Surf Watch (Spyglass, Inc.)
address: 175 S. San Antonio Road
Suite 102
Los Altos, CA 94022
telephone:
(888) 6-SPYGLASS or (408) 430-1370
    (sales)
(888) 6-SPYGLASS (technical support,
    Mon.-Fri. 7:30am-5:30pm, PST)
e-mail: surfwatch_support@surfwatch.com
    (technical support)
website: www.surfwatch.com

WebTV (Sony Electronics Inc.)
address: 1 Sony Drive
Park Ridge, NJ 07656
telephone:(888) 772-SONY (sales)
website: www.webtv.net/pc/wtvnet.html

▼ Directory of Websites

I have divided up the directory of websites we mentioned in the book into nine categories: Search Sites; Computers and Accessories; Computer Programs; Internet Services and Access; Internet Safety; Parents' Sites; Kids' Sites; Shopping; and Entertainment Reviews/Ticket Purchases.

▼ Search Sites

▼ SEARCH ENGINES

AltaVista	www.altavista.com
Deja News	www.dejanews.com
Excite	www.excite.com
Infoseek	www.infoseek.com
Lycos	www.lycos.com
Multi engine search	www.all4one.com
Yahoo!	www.yahoo.com

▼ FINDING PEOPLES' AND BUSINESS' PHONE NUMBERS AND ADDRESSES:

Business Yellow Pages	www.bigbook.com
Companies that are online	www.companiesonline.com
Directory assistance	www.555-1212.com
Directory of 800 Numbers	att.net/dir800
Directory Organization —companies, e-mail, etc.	www.dir.orge-mail, etc.

▼ E-MAIL ADDRESSES, PHONE & ADDRESS, COMMUNITIES, HOME PAGES, INTERNET PHONES, U.S.

Government Pages	www.whowhere.com
E-mail directory search	www.bigfoot.com

Financial calculators, help directory	www.moneyadvisor.com
Finding people	www.1800ussearch.com
Finding people and addresses	www.switchboard.com
Finding telephone area or country codes	www.inconnect.com/~americom/aclookup.html
411—Internet white pages, find an e-mail address	www.four11.com
Looking up people and businesses	www.databaseamerica.com/
National Corporate Records Directory	www.ljextra.com/courtguides/main5.html
National Telephone Book—White Page	www.yahoo.com/search/peopleNYNEX
Nationwide Yellow Pages	www.niyp.com/newvisit.html
Yellow Pages	www.yellownet.com
Yellow Pages on-line	www.ypo.com
Yellow Pages, White Pages, Government and international listings	www.infospace.com
Zip code look-up	www.usps.gov/ncsc

▼ Computers and Accessories

Apple Computer	www2.apple.com
Microsoft's EasyBall	www.microsoft.com

▼ Computer Programs

▼ FILTERING/BLOCKING

BESS	www.n2h2.com
Cyber Patrol	www.cyberpatrol.com
CYBERsitter	www.solidoak.com
Microsoft Plus! for Kids	www.microsoft.com/kids
Neosoft (Product Review)	www.neosoft.com/parental-control
Net Nanny	www.netnanny.com
Net Shepherd	www.netshepherd.com
Surf Watch	www.surfwatch.com

▼ Miscellaneous:

McAfee—virus protection	www.mcafee.com
Pretty Good Privacy (encryption program)	www.pgp.com

▼ Internet Services and Access

▼ Online services

America Online (AOL)	www.aol.com
CompuServe	www.compuserve.com
Microsoft Network	www.msn.com
Prodigy	www.prodigy.com

▼ Internet service providers

AT&T WorldNet Service	www.att.com/worldnet
MCI Internet	www.mci2000.com
Mindspring	www.mindspring.com
Netcom	www.netcom.com
Sprint Internet Passport	www.sprint.com/fornet
C|Net	www.cnet.com/Content/Reviews/Compare/ISP/sample.htm

▼ Web browsers

Microsoft Internet Explorer	www.microsoft.com
Netscape Navigator	home.netscape.com

▼ Miscellaneous

Comcast's @Home website for local content	www.InYourTown.com
InterNic (name availability)	rs.internic.net/cgi-bin/whois
InterNic (domain registration)	rs.internic.net/cgi-bin/itts/domain

Java	www.javasoft.com
Juno (free e-mail account)	www.juno.com
Submit It	www.submit-it.com
WebTV	www.webtv.com

▼ Internet Safety

Avery KidsSite	www.avery.com/kids
Bill Bickel	www.concentric.net/~Bbickel
CARU	www.bbb.org/advertising/caruguid.html#making
cookie test—FTC	www.ftc.gov/WWW/bcp/privacy2/
	comments1/junk/cookies.htm#request
Direct Marketing Ass'n's booklet "Get CyberSavvy"	www.the-dma.org/pan/intro.html
Enough Is Enough	www.enough.org
National Center for Missing and Exploited Children	www.missingkids.org
Parents' Guide to the Internet	www.familyguidebook.com
RSACi	www.rsac.org
Safe Surf	www.safesurf.com

▼ Parents' Sites

▼ GENERAL

CTW-Sesame Street Parents	www.ctw.org/parents
Disney's Family.com	www.family.com
Family PC magazine	www.familypc.com
Folks Online	www.folksonline.com
Home and Family	www.homeandfamily.com

Home PC magazine	www.homepc.com
Jean Armour Polly/Net-mom	www.netmom.com
KinderCam	www.kindercam.com
Mom and Pop Get Wired	www.mompop.com
MultimediaMom	www.multimediamom.org
Outdoor Online	www.outdoor-online.com
Parenthood Web	www.parenthood.com
Parent Soup	www.parentsoup.com
Parenting magazine	www.parenttime.com
Parenting on the Web	www.geocities.com/heartland/9530
ParentsPlace	www.parentsplace.com
Steve and Ruth Bennett's Family SurfBoard	www.familysurf.com
Try Parenting—Q&A	www.parenting-qa.com

▼ SPECIAL NEEDS

Convomania	mania.apple.com
The Disability Connection	www2.apple.com/disability/welcome.html
Disability Information and Resources	www.eskimo.com/~jlubin/disabled.html
Dragonfly Toy Company	www.dftoys.com
Family Village	www.familyvillage.wisc.edu
Internet for Deaf Cyber Kids	dww.deafworldweb.org/kids/internet.html
The Mining Company	www.homeparents.miningco.com
Our Kids	www.rdz.stjohns.edu/library/support/our-kids
Parents Helping Parents	www.php.com
WOW Online	www.wowusa.com

▼ ADOPTION AND FOSTER PARENTING

Adoption.com	www.adoption.com
Adoptive Families of America	www.adoptivefam.org
Adoptive Parents Committee	www.wp.com/apc/home.htm
Foster Parent Community	www.fosterparents.com
National Adoption Information Clearinghouse	www.calib.com/naic

▼ Single parenting and step-parenting

Daddys Home	www.daddyshome.com/index.html
Divorce Central Parenting Center	www.divorcecentral.com/parent
Single Parent Resource	rampages.onramp.net/~bevhamil/ singleparentresourcece_478.html
Stepfamily Foundation	www.stepfamily.org
Steve Kennedy's Parenting Links	www.apc.net/steveknndy/parent2.htm

▼ Parenting twins (and higher multiples)

National Organization of Mothers of Twins Clubs, Inc.	www.nomotc.org
Twins Magazine	www.twinsmagazine.com
Twinz Unlimited	www.twinz.com

▼ Grandparenting

Grands R Us	www.eclypse.com/GrandsRuS

▼ Kids' Sites

▼ Colleges and college-search related

Cornell University	www.cornell.edu
FinAid	www.finaid.com
Petersons	www.petersons.com
Princeton Review	www.review.com
Stanley Kaplan	www.kaplan.com
Universities.com	www.universities.com

▼ Study related

Internet Public Library	www.ipl.org
Kids Connect (ALA)	www.apa.org/ICONN/kidsconn.html

Kids Connect (ALA)	www.ala.org/ICONN/kidsconn.htm
Multnomah County Library	www.multnomah.lib.or.us/lib/kids
The Study Web	www.studyweb.com

▼   GAMES

Games Kids Play	www.corpcomm.net/~gnieboer/ gamehome.htm
Internet Gaming Zone	www.zone.com
Video Game Spot	www.videogamespot.com

▼   HOBBIES

AOL's "Sports"	keyword "sports"
Arts of Avalon	www.poseyent.com/index1.htm
The Bolshoi Theater, Ballet, and Opera	www.alincom.com/bolshoi/index.htm
Capezio Cafe	www.capezio.com/cafe/cafe.html
The Dinosaur Society	www.dinosociety.org/homepage.html
ESPNET-Sportszone	espnet.sportszone.com
Fashion Internet	www.finy.com
Green Bay Packers/The Frozen Tundra	www.rossfleege.com/tundra
JC Macaw	users1.vastnet.net/~jcmacaw/index.html
The Metropolitan Museum of Art	www.metmuseum.org/htmlfile/ education/kid.html
Moviesounds.com	www.moviesounds.com
Pollstar	www.pollstar.com/homenf.htm
Star Wars Page at Texas A&M	www.aero25.tamu.edu/~swpage/index2.html

▼   NATURE/SCIENCE

| Discovery Online | www.discovery.com |
| National Geographic | www.nationalgeographic.com |

▼ Penpal sites

Cyber Sisters	www.worldkids.net/clubs/CSIS/csis.htm
GIRL	www.worldkids.net/girl/learn.htm
Guys	www.worldkids.net/clubs/guys

▼ General

ABC Online	www.abc.com
	keyword "abc" on AOL
AOL's "Kids Only"	keyword "kids"
Children's Express	www.ce.org
Children's Television Workshop	www.ctw.org
Disney.com	www.disney.com
Disney's Daily Blast	www.disneyblast.com
Family Internet	www.familyinternet.com
Fox	www.fox.com
Fox for kids	www.foxkids.com
Global Show-n-Tell Museum	www.telenaut.com/gst
Headbone Zone	www.headbone.com
Just for Kids	www.eagle.ca/~matink/kids.html
Kellogg's	www.kelloggs.com
Kid Web	www.teleport.com/~rhubarbs/kidweb
KidLink	www.kidlink.org
KidPub	www.kidpub.org
Kids of the Web	www.hooked.net/~leroyc/kidsweb/index.html
Kids.com	www.aha-kids.com
Kidscom	www.kidscom.com
KidsSpace	www.kids-space.org
Kidzine on AOL	keyword "kidzine" or "kids"
Lisa's Home Page	www.geocities.com/Heartland/8580
MIT postcard site	postcards.www.media.mit.edu/postcards
Nickelodeon	www.nick.com
Prodigy's kids' area	kids.prodigy.net

Sports Illustrated for Kids	www.pathfinder.com (and search)
The Family Channel	www.familychannel.com
Time for Kids	www.pathfinder.com (and search)
World Kids Network	www.worldkids.net
World Surfari	www.supersurf.com

▼ MISCELLANEOUS

An Income of her Own	www.aioho.com
The Socks White House Tour for Kids	www.whitehouse.gov/WH/kids/html/ pretour2.html
The White House	www.whitehouse.gov

▼ Shopping

J. Crew	www.jcrew.com
Spiegel's	www.spiegel.com

▼ Entertainment Reviews/Ticket Purchases

Movielink	www.777film.com
NetTicks	www.telecharge.com
Playbill	www.playbill.com
Screen It	www.screenit.com

▼ Directory of Credits, Copyrights and Trademarks

We have not identified specific marks within the text of the book with ® or other identifying designations in order to make reading easier.

All logos, trademarks, tradenames, servicemarks and copyrights, and screenshots and specifically identified materials used in this book remain the property of, and are used with the kind permission of, the following:

American Computer Resources, Inc.(for The Study Web)
Apple Computer, Inc.
Bill Bickel
Call For Action
The Children's Advertising Review Unit
CompuServe Incorporated
The Direct Marketing Association
Divorce Central Parenting Center
Global Show-n-Tell
Headbone Zone
Internet Public Library
J. Crew
Al Kandziorski
Steve Kennedy
Kidlink
Kids of the Web
The KidsCom Company
KidsSpace
Master Lock Company
Microsoft Corporation
Microsystems Software, Inc. (for Cyber Patrol)
Mom and Pop Get Wired!
N2H2 Inc.(for Bess)
Net Nanny, Ltd.
Net Shepherd Inc.
Our-Kids

Outdoor Online, Inc.

Parenting on the Web

ParentsPlace

Jean Armour Polly (Net-mom)

Prodigy, Inc.

Single Parent Resource Center

Solid Oak Software, Inc.(for CYBERsitter)

Spyglass, Inc. (for Surf Watch)

The Walt Disney Company

The White House

AltaVista logo reproduced with the permission of Digital Equipment Corporation.

All uses of the AOL and Kids Only logos and any screen shots. Copyright 1996-97 America Online, Inc. All Rights Reserved.

Copyright 1996 Netscape Communications Corp. Used with permission. All Rights Reserved. No electronic file or page containing Netscape's copyrighted material may be reprinted or copied without the express written permission of Netscape.

Netscape Communications Corporation has not authorized, sponsored, or endorsed, or approved this publication and is not responsible for its content. Netscape and the Netscape Communications Corporate Logos, are trademarks and trade names of Netscape Communications Corporation. All other product names and/or logos are trademarks of their respective owners.

All screen shots of Yahoo! and Yahooligans! include text and artwork Copyright 1996 by Yahoo! Inc. All rights reserved. Yahoo!, Yahooligans!, and the Yahoo! and Yahooligans! logos are trademarks of Yahoo! Inc.

In addition, at the time this book went to press, AOL announced its acquisition of CompuServe. We have been informed, however, that CompuServe will continue to operate as a separate brand name entity.

My Model Internet Use Policy

A Bird's Eye View—

▼ My Agreement About Using
the Internet

▼ My Agreement About Using the Internet

I want to use our computer and the Internet. I know that there are certain rules about what I should do online. I agree to follow these rules and my parents agree to help me follow these rules:

1. I will not give my name, address, telephone number, school or my parents' name, address, or telephone number, to anyone I meet on the computer.
2. I understand that some people online pretend to be someone else. Sometimes they pretend to be kids, when they're really grown ups. I will tell my parents about people I meet online. I will also tell my parents before I answer any e-mails I get from or send e-mails to new people I meet online.
3. I will not buy or order anything online without asking my parents or give out any credit card information.
4. I will not fill out any form online that asks me for any information about myself or my family without asking my parents first.
5. I will not get into arguments or fights online. If someone tries to start an argument or fight with me, I won't answer them and will tell my parents.
6. If I see something I do not like or that I know my parents don't want me to see, I will click on the "back" button or logoff.
7. If I see people doing things or saying things to other kids online I know they're not supposed to do or say, I'll tell my parents.
8. I won't keep online secrets from my parents.
9. If someone sends me any pictures, or any e-mails using bad language, I will tell my parents.
10. If someone asks me to do something I am not supposed to do, I will tell my parents.
11. I will not call anyone I met online on the telephone unless my parents say it's okay.
12. I will never meet anyone I met online, in person, unless my parents say it's okay.
13. I will never send anything to anyone I met online, unless my parents say it's okay.
14. If anyone I met online sends me anything, I will tell my parents.
15. I will not use something I found online and pretend it's mine.
16. I won't say bad things about people online, and will practice good Netiquette.
17. I won't use bad language online.

18. I know that my parents want to make sure I'm safe online, and I will listen to them when they ask me not to do something.
19. I will help teach my parents more about computers and the Internet.
20. I will practice safe computing, and check for viruses whenever I borrow a disk from someone or download something from the Internet.

_____

I promise to follow these rules.

_____

I promise to help my child follow these rules. (Signed by the parents)

Index